Women in American History

Series Editors

Mari Jo Buhle
Jacquelyn D. Hall
Anne Firor Scott

Books in the series
Women in American History

Women Doctors in Gilded-Age Washington: Race, Gender, and Professionalization
Gloria Moldow

Friends and Sisters: Letters between Lucy Stone and Antoinette Brown Blackwell, 1846–93
Edited by Carol Lasser and Marlene Deahl Merrill

Reform, Labor, and Feminism: Margaret Dreier Robins and the Women's Trade Union League
Elizabeth Anne Payne

Private Matters: American Attitudes toward Childbearing and Infant Nurture in the Urban North, 1800–1860
Sylvia D. Hoffert

Civil Wars: Women and the Crisis of Southern Nationalism
George C. Rable

I Came a Stranger: The Story of a Hull-House Girl
Hilda Satt Polacheck
Edited by Dena J. Polacheck Epstein

I Came a Stranger

I Came a Stranger

The Story of a Hull-House Girl

By Hilda Satt Polacheck

Edited by Dena J. Polacheck Epstein

With an Introduction by Lynn Y. Weiner

UNIVERSITY OF ILLINOIS PRESS

Urbana and Chicago

Illini Books edition, 1991

Manufactured in the United States of America
P 5 4 3

This book is printed on acid-free paper.

Library of Congress Cataloging-in-Publication Data

Polacheck, Hilda Satt, 1882–1967.
I came a stranger : the story of a Hull-House girl / by Hilda Satt Polacheck ; edited by Dena J. Polacheck Epstein ; with an introduction by Lynn Y. Weiner.
p. cm. — (Women in American history)
Bibliography: p.
Includes index.
ISBN 0-252-06218-3 (alk. paper)
1. Polacheck, Hilda Satt, 1882–1967. 2. Jews—Illinois—Chicago—Biography. 3. Chicago (Ill.)—Biography. 4. Hull-House (Chicago, Ill.)—Biography. 5. Women—United States—History—20th century. 6. Social reformers—United States—Biography. 7. Women social reformers—United States—Biography. I. Epstein, Dena J. Polacheck, 1916– . II. Title. III. Series.
F548.9.J5P65 1989
977.3'110049185—dc19
[B] 88-34656
CIP

Contents

Preface

The manuscript for *I Came a Stranger* had to be reconstructed from the loose sheets and revisions found among Hilda Satt Polacheck's papers, a complete version being assembled from seven incomplete ones, which differed in minor details and in the order of chapters. The best version of each chapter was used, preserving Hilda's style, syntax, and chronology but eliminating most of the repetition and standardizing punctuation and spelling. As in many autobiographies, some incidents are described that could not have happened precisely as narrated, and some are out of chronological sequence. These matters are fully discussed and clarified in the Afterword or in the endnotes. For the interested reader, full documentation is provided in the endnotes.

I am most grateful for the assistance of a number of Chicago libraries and librarians in providing obscure or unusual items. Mary Ann Bamberger, university archivist, University of Illinois at Chicago, went out of her way to locate documents and pictures relating to Hull-House, while Mary Ann Johnson, director of the Jane Addams' Hull-House Museum, encouraged and helped in many ways. Daniel Meyer, archivist of the University of Chicago, assisted in locating documents relating to Hilda's short student career, as did the late Jean Block. Elsie Orlinsky, of the Chicago Jewish Archives, did her best to locate documents that apparently have not survived.

The Inter-Library Loan staff at the University of Chicago Libraries was of great help in borrowing files of the *Milwaukee Leader* and the *Wisconsin Jewish Chronicle*. The collections of the Joseph Regenstein Library, University of Chicago, the Chicago Historical Society Library, the Newberry Library, the Library of Congress, and the Asher Library, Spertus College of Judaica, were all consulted. Their combined resources made it possible to document the manuscript, demonstrating its overall accuracy. To the staffs there go my most grateful thanks. A special thank you is due Maria Calderisi Bryce, of the National Library of Canada, for her efforts in searching the ship registers for the Port of Quebec.

—Dena J. Polacheck Epstein

Introduction

Lynn Y. Weiner

This is the story of Hilda Satt Polacheck, a Jewish woman who came to Chicago from Poland as a child in 1892. Her memoir joins the growing collection of oral histories, autobiographies, and fiction that documents and reconstructs the social history of the United States in the late nineteenth and early twentieth centuries.[1] The richly detailed narrative both corrects and confirms scholarly interpretations of immigration, family dynamics, work, and progressive reform during these years.

When Hilda first attempted to publish her autobiography in the 1950s, she was told there was no interest in the life of an "obscure woman." Who then cared about the memories of a Jewish immigrant, by turn a working girl, a suburban housewife, a widow? Today, however, there *is* interest in her words. Many of Hilda's experiences were commonplace and many were extraordinary, yet her memories of them recall fading aspects of America's past.

Because of the circumstances of her family's settlement in Chicago and her interest in progressive causes, Hilda crossed paths with many of the leading political and cultural personalities of her day. She lived through what historians term the Progressive Era—a time from the turn of the century through the 1920s during which many Americans attempted to reform a variety of social ills and to expand the concepts of democracy and social justice. Through Hilda's narrative we can therefore view the settlement house, woman suffrage, and peace movements from the perspective of a participant; we can walk with public health pioneer Dr. Alice Hamilton as she "gathers dust" for a study of tuberculosis; we can listen to the famous anarchist Emma Goldman memorialize the fallen martyrs of the Haymarket affair; and we can watch as Theodore Roosevelt ignores a bullet wound to the chest to campaign dramatically for election.

By far, the most formative influence on Hilda Satt's life was Jane Addams, the progressive reformer who, with Ellen Gates Starr in 1889, founded Hull-House—arguably the most influential social settlement house in the nation. Hilda dedicated her book to Addams, whom she credited with making her an "American." Her commentary on Addams and the inner workings of Hull-House is the fullest we have by an immigrant woman from the neighborhood; her viewpoint therefore provides an invaluable document of social and urban history.

Born Hinda Satt in 1882 in Wloclawek, Poland, a town of some 50,000 on the Vistula River, Hilda was the eighth of twelve children of Dena Satt, a housewife, and Louis Satt, a tombstone carver. Unlike many Jews who immigrated, the Satts were relatively prosperous. In the beginning of the autobiography, which vividly summons up the rhythms of Jewish life in nineteenth-century Europe, the language reflects a Yiddish cadence and the bittersweet blend of pathos and humor that typifies the writings of Jewish immigrants at the turn of the century.

Hilda is a skilled storyteller. Her talent for writing first emerged in an English composition class at Hull-House, and she went on to develop her style with small articles for magazines and newspapers and in work for the Illinois Writers' Project during the New Deal. Many of her best stories are found in the first third of the autobiography. The tale of a kindly servant's misguided gift of a Christmas tree speaks of the relationship between religious groups in Poland; the humorous narrative of her introduction to bananas—her mother would not let the children eat them because they looked like yellow sausages—serves as a metaphor for the immigrant's first encounters with a new land.

For Jews, life in the Russian empire had, by Hilda's childhood, become increasingly onerous. After the 1881 assassination of Czar Alexander II, the Russian government began systematically to exclude Jews from education, employment, and landownership but not from compulsory military service. Pogroms destroyed Jewish lives and homes and cast a pall over hopes for a future in Europe. Polish Jews feared the expansion of this oppression to their own communities. From 1880 through 1900 some 600,000 Jews left the czar's regime; by 1924 another million and a half had joined them.[2]

In 1892 the Satts left Europe for America, "the land of milk and honey." In a pattern typical of immigration in the 1890s, Louis Satt came first, earning the money to bring over the rest of his family a year later. Confirming other accounts of immigration, the Satts suffered many losses when they left their native land. In Wloclawek they enjoyed relatively high status, but upon immigration they became outsiders.[3] The children attended the Jewish Training School on Chicago's West Side, where they took the first steps toward Americanization by learning English from sympathetic and patient teachers and by having their names changed. Hinda became Hilda; her sister Gutcha was given the name Rose for the color of her cheeks.

As the Satt children assimilated, they drifted from old-world ways—a common experience in immigrant families. In an article she wrote for the magazine *The Butterfly* in 1909, Hilda describes how immigrant children came to reject parental religion and traditions and how ignorance of English was seen as intellectual poverty.[4] Her brothers subverted their mother's effort to enroll them in Hebrew school, slipping out the back door after going in the front. Of Hilda's own religious education we know little, although respect for her mother's piety is evident in that she tried not to write on the Sabbath. Still, her drive for education pulled her away from the orthodox Jewish tradition, which held that a woman's role was strictly to support the home rather than achieve in the realm of learning or leadership. In this regard Hilda was like many other immigrant Jewish women who found schooling in the New World to be a path away from more traditional gender roles.[5]

The immigrant neighborhood into which the Satts moved comes alive in these pages. Hilda beautifully describes the sights, sounds, and smells of turn-of-the-century working-class Chicago, savoring her perceptions of this world of her youth, from the mundane to the astounding. Because of her skill as a writer, we too can appreciate the popular reception of social and cultural change.

Hilda's relatively idyllic life changed profoundly when her father died in 1894 and the family suddenly faced poverty. Through the narrative we can appreciate the impact of a parent's death on the family in the era before social welfare legislation emerged, which would provide at least minimal assistance to many Americans faced with the unexpected loss of a provider. We can also appreciate the complexity of the interactions between different ethnic and religious populations, as we learn of how not only relatives but gentile neighbors came to the assistance of the Satts.

One common practice of poor families in the late nineteenth century was child labor, which affected nearly one out of five children from ten to fifteen years of age. The Satt sisters became part of this group. Rose left school to go to work in a knitting factory, and at the age of thirteen Hilda joined her there. Their wages were necessary for the support of the family.[6] As a "working girl," Hilda became one of that generation of young, single women who found new necessities and widened opportunities for labor in the late nineteenth century. Her employment possibilities were limited, however, with industrial sewing work being the trade frequently chosen by urban Jewish immigrants and their daughters.[7] For ten years she endured what she termed the "monotony of work" in industry. Her descriptions of factory life evoke the abysmal nature of industrial conditions in the years before government regulations—including long hours, unsafe machinery, and the lack of adequate sanitary facilities. Hilda's leisure time before she became active at Hull-House was absorbed with reading popular romantic fiction and viewing vaudeville shows and such melodramas as *Bertha the Sewing Machine Girl*. Her experience was typical of hundreds of thousands of working women at the turn of the century.

Hilda first visited Hull-House, which stood just four blocks from the Satt family's first residence on Halsted Street, for a Christmas party, probably in 1895. An Irish playmate took her there, after convincing her that Jewish children would not be killed if they appeared at a Christmas celebration.[8] It was an occasion that Hilda believed made her a "staunch American," for she realized that differing nationalities and beliefs could be tolerated rather than feared. By the time she became an active participant in Hull-House life, the settlement was entering its busiest years; in 1908 there were thirteen buildings housing a multitude of services and activities. From about 1900 to 1910 Hilda spent many evenings at Hull-House, attending classes and club meetings, reading literature, exercising in the gymnasium, performing plays, socializing with other young men and women, and helping out in the Labor Museum. She worked as a receptionist and "toter"—a guide to visitors—during the period when up to 2,000 people a day entered its halls, and to her delight she was also accepted as an instructor in English. By 1910 Hilda had come a long way from the "greenhorn" who had timidly entered the settlement's reception room to have Jane Addams literally take her by the hand.

Social scientists have suggested that settlement houses and social welfare institutions have been motivated by an interest in "social control"—the discipline of the poor and the imposition of middle-class values on working-class culture. The historian Michael Katz, for example, has suggested that for Jane Addams the educational functions of Hull-House ideally accommodated industrial workers to their work by relieving mental drudgery and socializing them to be content with their lot in life, at which point inner controls made external social controls obsolete.[9] But Hilda's autobiography qualifies this interpretation. Her experiences made her venturesome rather than accommodating, and she developed a life-long interest in progressive causes. In Hilda's opinion the influence of Jane Addams and the larger community of Hull-House residents served to broaden her cultural and political interests.

factory conditions. Hilda was at some level aware of the links between these efforts to achieve social change and the personal services of the settlement.[18]

The Hull-House years ended for Hilda in 1912 when she married William Polacheck and moved with him to Milwaukee. Typical of her generation, Hilda left the ranks of wage-earning women to devote her energies to her family and to voluntary political and community activities. The United States Census recorded in 1920 that only 9 percent of all white married women worked for wages;[19] generally, married women sought employment only if driven by dire economic need.

Hilda lived in Milwaukee between 1912 and 1930. In her autobiography she not only recalls the lively cultural and political activities of that city, but she opens a window on such larger issues as pacifism during World War I and the movement for woman suffrage, which ended with the passage of the Nineteenth Amendment in 1920. Both movements exemplify the way in which middle-class married women volunteered their efforts for political causes in the early decades of the century.

Jane Addams had helped to found the Women's International League for Peace and Freedom as the Woman's Peace party in 1915, and in the 1920s she traveled widely on behalf of that organization. The league was based on the premise that women—in part because of their experience as mothers—could better appreciate the value of life than men. Thousands of Americans were involved in this movement for disarmament and peace, and Hilda was among them. In 1921 she helped to organize the Wisconsin chapter of the league, inviting Addams to speak at an initial meeting. With Addams she attended an international congress of the league in Washington, D.C., in 1924. The peace movement would remain an important part of Hilda's life into the 1960s.[20]

Hilda often cited her mother's comment, "Women will never vote and there will always be a czar," challenging both statements. During her Hull-House years she stood on street corners passing out leaflets for woman suffrage rallies. The Hull-House suffragists, she commented, were "rather polite" in their demeanor and considered it best to remain "ladylike" so as not to offend the men who had the power to enfranchise them. But in Milwaukee, Hilda joined the National Woman's party, the most militant of the suffrage groups, and noted, "I am quite sure that Miss Addams did not approve of this new organization."

The National Woman's party, founded by Alice Paul as the Congressional Union for Woman Suffrage in 1913, was known for its colorful and militant tactics. When the party sent a "Prison Special" train across the country to arouse public opinion by having women speak who had been jailed for suffrage activities, Hilda housed one of the travelers in her home. When woman suffrage became law on 26 August 1920, it was Hilda to whom the local newspapers turned for information about the amendment. Later in the 1920s when labor and radical feminists split over the issue of equal rights versus protective labor legislation, Hilda resigned from her position as a local officer of the Woman's party, consistent with her labor sympathies.[21]

In December 1927 William Polacheck died. Hilda soon returned to Chicago, where to support her family she worked as a hotel manager. In 1937 she joined the Illinois Writers' Project of the Works Progress Administration. She describes well the culture and politics of that New Deal program, including the humiliation of becoming "certified" as a pauper every eighteen months and the rancorous yearly debates in Congress over funding.

While Hilda's autobiography teems with descriptions of external events in her life—observations of community, politics, and world affairs—we hear relatively little of her American family life before her marriage. The death of her mother in 1913 merits only a sentence, although it is clear that there was some estrangement between mother and daughter. The irony of Hilda teaching English to immigrants while her mother failed to master the language is passed over, as is her evident rejection of the orthodox religion of her ancestors. Similarly, she gives only perfunctory attention to her siblings. Of her own family she is more forthcoming; she tells some anecdotes about her children, recalls her courtship, and expresses pain and sorrow at her husband's death. Her disinclination to reveal more of the emotional and personal aspects of her life was shared by many other women writing autobiographical accounts, including Jane Addams and Florence Kelley, who had been active at Hull-House before Hilda's time there.[22]

Other Jewish immigrant women have also written memoirs, but often theirs is a story of rebellion not only against religious expectations but also against gender roles. Anzia Yezierska, who was nearly the same age as Hilda, rejected old-world values as well as new-world conventions of family life, surrendering the custody of her one daughter to the girl's father in order to live independently. Yezierska wrote often of conflict between parents of the Old World and children of the New and of the tension involved in "Americanization." Other autobiographers similarly cited this tension and their own rejection of its dialectic.[23] In Hilda's work the tension is implicit rather than explicit.

She too documents the drive for education and the desire, as Yezierska said, "to be people—not 'hands'—not slaves of the belly!"[24] The sweatshop girls of Yezierska's fiction worked twelve hours a day and attended school at night; Hilda remembers working long hours in miserable conditions and then attending school or Hull-House functions. But unlike Yezierska, satisfaction for Hilda—as for the majority of women—was found in family life as well as in the public sphere.

Implicit in Hilda's story is her acceptance of conventional roles for married women. When she asked if Jane Addams was disappointed in her lack of writing productivity, Addams responded that "one baby is worth a dozen books" and that Hilda would write again after her children were grown. For years the focus of her life was her family, but Hilda's definition of mothering and domestic life was a broad one. She was always active in community and political affairs and exemplified the Progressive tenet that the larger family of the world was a proper concern for women as well as men. As a mother, Hilda directed her energies into a different but not necessarily narrower arena. Although she left the public world of work for domestic concerns, she maintained her interests and activism in wider social and political issues.

Hilda's life was shaped by what the historian Sheila Rothman has termed the "ideology of educated motherhood." Rothman suggests that the settlement houses attempted to train immigrants not only to be good citizens but also to serve as forces for progressive change—in short, to share the reform impulses of their mentors. Hilda Satt Polacheck shared the dreams and desires of the Progressives in part because of her exposure to the ideologies of the Hull-House community.[25]

The autobiography ends with the funeral of Jane Addams in May 1935, which is, in a way, regrettable since Hilda lived for another thirty-two years. She worked for the Federal Emergency Administration of Public Works in the late 1930s, selecting tenants for the Jane Addams Housing Project, and was associated with the Federal Writers' Project into the early 1940s. During World War II, Hilda ran a sewing room for Russian war relief. She subsequently was supported by her children and traveled around the country visiting them and her sixteen grandchildren. In the 1950s she wrote this autobiography but failed to find a publisher. Hilda remained interested in politics for the rest of her life, attending conferences of the Women's International League for Peace and Freedom as late as the mid-1960s. In 1967, at the age of eighty-five, she died.[26]

How are we to read this memoir? Hilda's often witty and engaging narrative is flawed by her carelessness with dates and by what appears to be her revisionism of personal and historical events. Both problems are addressed by Dena Polacheck Epstein in the Afterword and in the endnotes, which use primary sources and her mother's correspondence to verify, question, and augment the historical accuracy of these memories. Nevertheless, the value of this first-person account is unquestionable. This is a fascinating story by a gifted writer living during a time of great social change. If not every event occurred exactly as it is recorded here, that is within the tradition of other memoirs, including Jane Addams's own *Twenty Years at Hull-House*.

I Came a Stranger is, on the one hand, the most complete chronicle we have by a "Hull-House girl." Through Hilda's eyes we can look behind the red brick walls of Hull-House and come to understand the remarkable range of activity within. On the other hand, this is also the story of a generation of immigrants who struggled with poverty and with efforts to become "American," the story of choices commonly made by women living in the first decades of the twentieth century. It both supplements the published works on Hull-House and Jane Addams and complements oral histories and fictional accounts of immigrant life in America. Above all, Hilda Satt Polacheck has bequeathed a document abundant in social history, humor, and human drama. For an "obscure woman," her life was rich indeed.

I Came a Stranger

Hilda Satt Polacheck

In Humble Gratitude

to the Memory of

JANE ADDAMS

to whom

I Came a Stranger

PART I

A Polish Childhood, 1882–92

Memories of Poland 1

The place where life began has some meaning for each of us. We may look back to the place with fond memories or indifference or hatred, but we do look back. Pages of history have been written even about the lowly potato, as to where it originated and how it had been brought from one part of the world to another. And so, though I consider myself a small potato, I wish to record that I was born in Wloclawek, a beautiful city on the Vistula River in Poland.[1]

Some indelible impressions had stamped themselves on my mind by the time I reached my seventh year.[2] It was then that my family left Poland and came to America.

I was the eighth of twelve children. Four of them I was destined never to know. They and my maternal grandmother had died within one month during a cholera epidemic, before I was born. During my lifetime, I remember a brother who died at the age of two and a sister at the age of sixteen. They both died of smallpox.

I have been told that there was great consternation in the family when I was born. There were no boys in the family at the time, and I was the fourth daughter to arrive. While daughters were tolerated, it was important to have sons in the family, so that they would recite the Kaddish (the mourners' prayer) for their parents after their death. The recital of the Kaddish by a daughter was not acceptable.

There was great rejoicing, therefore, when eighteen months after my birth a son was born. I have heard many stories of that notable event. The feast, when the boy was circumcised, has been described so many times that it has become a legend in the annals of the family history.

There were no geese in Wloclawek good enough for the auspicious occasion. They had to be brought from Warsaw. The livers from these geese were the largest ever seen in Poland. And after they had been chopped with onions and hard-boiled eggs, the mounds of chopped liver formed small islands in goose fat.

The fish that were transformed into gefilte fish were caught to order. They had to be delivered live. There never had been such tasty gefilte fish since the world began. Rachel, our cook, had stayed up all night to prepare and slowly simmer the prized catch.

Special wines and schnapps were ordered from Warsaw. And the feasting and drinking went on for two days.

How my mother gloried in telling that story!

To add to the great joy of my parents, two more sons were born during the following two years. I have not heard any details of the feasts prepared for their entry into the world.

The most vivid impressions in my mind are the big house in which we lived and the Vistula River with its white, sandy beach. This beach was but a short distance from the house and became our playground. The house had large rooms with high ceilings. When I was put to bed at night, I would lie there and wonder whether I would ever grow tall enough to touch the ceiling.

In the living room, a heater of yellow and blue tile was built into the wall. There was a space on each side of that heater where we children would hide while playing hide-and-seek. In the kitchen, the stove was also made of tile and built into the wall. I do not recall whether there were any other heating units, but I do know that we were kept warm during the long, cold winters.

Back of the kitchen was my father's shop. He was a tombstone carver. I remember that shop very vividly. It was filled with tombstones of all shapes and sizes. There were marble and granite and sandstone markers. Rich people could have a marble or granite tombstone. Poor people had to be satisfied with sandstone. Where was it said that death is the great equalizer?

My father had been sent to school where he had learned languages and mathematics.[3] But he had never gone to an art school. The art of carving he had learned from his father, who had learned it from his father; the craft had been handed down from generation to generation.

I believe that my father was the only Jewish tombstone carver in Wloclawek. And since people died fairly regularly, and since their families felt a deep responsibility to mark every grave of a departed relative, Father was kept busy and earned considerable sums of money. In short, we were not poor.

How well I remember my father bending over a tombstone, with a chisel in one hand and a wooden mallet in the other. He was always meticulous about his work and took great pride in it.

On rainy or cold days I was permitted to play in the shop. Father was always patient when answering my endless questions. Why were different designs carved on different tombstones? What did the words mean? Why were some stones small and some large?

Father explained that a married woman's tombstone always had carved at the top a pair of candlesticks with candles. This was a symbol that it had been her special privilege to usher in the Sabbath, by lighting the candles. A broken tree on a tombstone meant that a young person had died and that life had been broken and that there would be no further growth. There were many other symbols, depicting the life of the deceased.[4]

I recall a ghost story that was told in the family in connection with my father's shop. The windows of the shop had shutters with half-moons cut into them. One night Father had put his mallet on a tombstone and then had put his hat on the mallet. For some mysterious reason someone had looked through the half-moon of the shutter and saw what appeared to be a man's head on the tombstone. A horrendous scream pierced the quiet night air. My father dashed out to see who was being murdered. He found a neighbor pointing hysterically to Father's shop. When he regained his voice, he said: "There is a ghost sitting on the tombstone!"

Father looked through the half-moon and recognized his hat. He sent the neighbor home with the admonition to stop looking into other people's shops.

In back of Father's shop was a small garden where we were taught to plant flowers.[5] The first realization that green leaves would come up from the black earth after a small brown seed had been planted was an exciting event.

Next door to our big house and small garden was a small house and a big garden. In this small house lived a little old woman and her two goats. I recall how she would bend over her flower beds and pull out every intruding weed. I do not remember anyone ever coming to see this old woman. But I was a daily visitor. She always greeted me with a cheery *"Djin dobri"* [good morning] when I brought the peelings from fruit or vegetables for her goats. She would come out from her small cottage and pick some flowers for me in payment for my contribution. I have often thought of how simply we solved our garbage problem in Wloclawek.

The Vistula River is a very happy memory. I remember people promenading on the cement walk every afternoon, while an orchestra played for their enjoyment. There were small tables and chairs scattered about where they could sit and buy tea and small cakes. The beach of this river was a playground, not only for my family, but for all the children in the neighborhood. My fondest recollection is Mariana, the rosy-cheeked peasant girl who watched over us while we played in the sand. She came from a small village where her parents tried to eke out a living for their numerous children from the small plot of ground they called a farm. But there were always too many mouths to feed. So Mariana was sent to the city to work. I do not recall any time that she was not with us. She had become a member of the family. She was always dressed in gay costumes consisting of a red skirt and white blouse, profusely embroidered in cross-stitch. During the long winters on the farm the only recreation was embroidering, so her blouses were a joy to look at. On her neck she wore many strings of beads and on her left shoulder there was a cluster of ribbon loops. From each loop there was a streamer of ribbon, and when these red, yellow, blue, green, pink, and lavender ribbons would blow about in the breeze, they looked like a flying rainbow that had suddenly dropped from the sky. On her head she wore a bright red babushka.

It was on this beach that I first became aware of religious differences and animosities that existed between Jews and Gentiles. While sitting on Mariana's lap one afternoon, I noticed a thin black cord among the many strings of beads. My curiosity was aroused, and while she was busy making a mouse out of a handkerchief for me, I pulled the cord. I found a small black square of cloth at the end of the cord. There was the face of a beautiful woman on it.

"Why do you wear this?" I asked, holding the square of cloth in my hand.

I will never forget how red her face became as she quickly jerked the cloth out of my hand and hid it in her bosom.

"You must never touch this again," she said very sternly.

"Why not?" I asked.

"If your mother knew that you touched this, I would be discharged," she whispered.

"I will not tell her," I said. "Tell me why you wear it and who the pretty lady is."

Mariana was twisting the handkerchief into various shapes, but she would not say a word. I persisted in my questions as only a pesky child can persist and she soon weakened. She told me that the black square had been given to her when she was confirmed and that it had the power to keep away all evil spirits, as long as she wore it. She kept reminding me that I was not to tell my mother what she had told me. I wanted to know whether this sacred charm could keep evil spirits from me, too. She said that Jews were not allowed to wear charms with the face of the Virgin Mary on them. She suddenly decided it was time to go home. I think she was eager to end that question period.

I began to notice that everything connected with the Christian religion was prohibited in our house. I began to see Christmas trees in the windows of our neighbors. I was told that Jews do not have

Christmas trees. I remember the first Christmas when I was not allowed to leave the house. I overheard my father saying that a pogrom had been planned on this Christmas Eve after church services. Young hoodlums had been seen running about the streets and had been heard shouting "Christ killers" in front of Jewish homes. This incident made a deep impression on me. I had not heard of Christ having been killed. I was wondering when it had happened. And what was there about goyim that set them apart from Jews? I knew Mariana was not Jewish, but she seemed to love us, and we loved her. The men who came to our house to sell Mother eggs and fruit were not Jewish, yet they seemed very friendly. And why was it that the word "pogrom" was always connected with Gentiles?

I soon found out. Before long I began to fear anyone who was not Jewish. The fear became a superstition; the superstition became hysteria. It was bad luck to pass a church. So when I approached one, I would cross the street. It was bad luck to touch a crucifix. And never, under any circumstances, was I to speak the word "Jesus." From conversation I heard around the house, I soon decided that pogroms were started by overzealous, ignorant priests and the people they were able to influence.[6] It became natural that what was sacred to the Catholic church must bring bad luck to the Jews.

Christmas was a day to be feared by Jews in Poland. While many of our gentile neighbors seemed friendly during the year, when Christmas approached tensions became strained. I soon heard that gentile people had been taught in their churches that the Jews had killed Christ. So the birthday of Christ was celebrated by murdering Jews, burning their synagogues and destroying their homes. Christmas had indeed become a day to be feared by the Jews. I had not escaped being infected with this fear.

In addition to religious intolerance, I can recall national hatreds. The part of Poland where we lived was under Russian domination at that time. Some of our relatives lived in the part of Poland that had been acquired by Germany. As far back as I can remember, the Poles hated the Russians and the Germans. The Germans looked down on the Poles and the Russians. There was a mutual hatred among the people of the three countries. But there was always a double dose of this hatred for the Jews.

I remember the first time I saw lighted candles in the windows of all houses on the block. I asked Mother why all those candles had been lighted. I was told that a member of the royal family was having a birthday. That evening I heard my father muttering under his breath, for fear the walls would hear him, that many people had spent their last few kopecks on candles when they should have bought bread for their children. Mother quickly silenced him. If he had been overheard and reported to the authorities, he would have been arrested.

Stories of compulsory military service began creeping into my mind. I gathered that my father hated the Russian military system, which compelled every boy to serve in the army. I dimly recall my father being opposed to all military systems. He prayed three times a day for peace. And still there was no peace.

The story of how my father escaped military service was another in my mother's great fund of stories. When he was called for his physical examination he was found to be too short. He was only five feet tall. But the following year, the height had been reduced to five feet, and he was called back. This time, he had shrunk to four feet eleven inches. My grandmother insisted her prayers had caused him to shrink. But I suspect that my grandfather had bribed the officer who did the measuring.

The Russian army had devised an ingenious method of feeding and housing any extra soldiers that were sent to the city. They were billeted to private families.

Two such soldiers were sent to our house on the Sabbath. My mother never tired of telling that story. The traditional dish of the Sabbath was *cholent*. This was a casserole of meat, potatoes, lima beans, and a coarse barley. The dish was prepared on Friday and sent to the public bakery, where it baked very slowly, all night, until noon the next day. Mariana would then bring it home in time for the noon dinner.

The family and the two soldiers, as our enforced guests, were seated around the big family table when the large casserole was placed in front of Mother. As a polite and gracious hostess, she served our guests first. One of the soldiers shoved a forkful of the *cholent* into his mouth, then spat it out and threw the plate with the food on the floor, shouting: "This is only fit for pigs!"

The other soldier went through the same performance. Then they both started demanding proper food.

My father very quietly told them that he would get them the food they wanted, if they would just wait a little while. He put on his coat and hat and left. He went straight to the barracks and told the commanding officer, whom he knew, what had happened. The officer came back to the house with Father and tasted the food. He then asked for a plateful, which he finished, smacking his lips. He took the two soldiers away. Several days later my father told us with great satisfaction that the soldiers spent the next thirty days in the brig, where they did not have to eat *cholent*.

In spite of the persecutions and discriminations and national hatreds, there were many happy times in our home. The Sabbath and all the holidays were not merely days of rest. These days brought a certain solemnity and peace into the home that cannot be recaptured.

The celebration of the Sabbath really started on Thursday, when Mother would start out on her marketing chore. Mariana always went with her and carried a huge basket, which became heavier every time they stopped at a stall. The basket would hold live hens and live fish, which often made a feeble effort to get out. Fruits, vegetables, butter, eggs . . . , in short, whatever was needed for the Sabbath, went into that basket.

Thursday night was a busy time in our household. Chickens that had been slaughtered in the traditional way by a *shochet* had to be drawn and carefully examined to make sure that no blemishes were on any of the organs. If the slightest pimple was detected, the organs had to be taken to the rabbi to determine whether the hen was really kosher. His findings were never questioned; if he decided the hen was not kosher, it was discarded.

All meats and poultry had to be soaked in cold water for half an hour. The meat then was salted and placed on a specially made board where it remained for an hour. This was done so that every drop of blood would be drained from the meat. The salt then was rinsed off.

This preparation of the meat calls to mind an incident that made a deep impression on me at the time. I was playing a game, similar to the American game of jacks, with a little gentile girl, when, in the most matter-of-fact manner possible, she asked me if my mother had already secured her supply of blood from a gentile boy with which to prepare some Passover dish. I rose from the ground and asked her what she meant. She said that her mother had told her that all Jews need blood from a male Gentile at Passover time.

I flew into a justified rage and told her that we never used blood for anything and that I would never play with her again. I rushed into the house crying hysterically and told Mother what had happened. Mother comforted me and said that was part of the *galut* (exile) that every Jew had to bear. The important thing was that I knew that what had been said was a falsehood. That was all that mattered.

Food cooking and baking in the kitchen on Friday added a zest to living. There was a huge copper kettle of gefilte fish simmering. Another shiny copper kettle contained the golden chicken soup. Mother was cutting hair-thin golden noodles with lightning speed, which would be boiled and allowed to float about in the soup. Braided loaves of white bread, topped with poppy seed, were baking in the large oven. When these were taken out, permeating the air with mouth-watering odors, pans of kuchen would be put into the oven. Then the aroma of cinnamon and raisins would fill the kitchen and spread throughout the house.

To this day, when I bake kuchen my thoughts go back to that kitchen in Wloclawek and to Rachel, the faithful cook who did most of the cooking and baking.

Rachel was a widow when she came to work for us. She had no children or near relatives. She had been left an orphan when she was six years of age and had been shunted from one distant relative to another. Then the townspeople where she lived collected a small dowry for her and married her to the town idiot. After three years of marriage, her husband was killed in a pogrom. And she still said that God had been good to her by giving her a home where there was piety, charity, and love; where all she had to do was cook for twelve people and keep the dishes washed and the pots shining. Her own great joy in life was to watch us eat what she had cooked or baked.

The actual ritual of celebrating the Sabbath remains a memory that cannot be erased. About an hour before sundown, every Friday, Father would lay down his chisel and mallet, cover them lovingly, and come into the house. A bundle of clean underwear and a large towel were always waiting for him; he would take these and go to the public bath. When he returned, cleansed from the week's toil, he dressed in his Sabbath clothes and went to the synagogue. The children were all bathed in a homemade tub and dressed in clean, starched Sabbath clothes. Mother always wore a white dress on Friday night.

The house had been scrubbed until it shone. The table was set with fine linen and the best dishes and silver. At the head of the table were two loaves of braided bread, covered with an embroidered doily. I recall asking Mother why she always put two loaves on the table when most of the time we ate only one.

"On the Sabbath two loaves are put on the table," she said, "to remind us that when the Jews were in the wilderness, God supplied them with a double portion of manna for the Sabbath."

In the center of the table were two shiny brass candlesticks with white candles. When the last ray of light left the sky, Mother would put a white lace shawl on her head and pronounce the blessing of the candles, which ushered in the Sabbath. After that the only work permitted in the house was the serving of food and the washing of dishes.

When Father returned from the synagogue, the family gathered around the table and respectfully listened to the kiddush, the blessing of the wine, which God in his wisdom permits us to drink. The glass of wine, which Father barely tasted, was passed around and each member of the family took a sip. The meal was then served.

First the tasty gefilte fish was brought in. With it was served a glass jar of beautiful red horseradish. Slices of bread were given to us, over which we each intoned the *motzah* (blessing).

Then the golden noodle soup was served. There was magic about that soup, otherwise how can one remember the taste after a span of sixty-five years? The chicken was always brown and tender and juicy.

The Sabbath day, as I recall it, was a day of quiet meditation. The only cooking that was permitted on that day was boiling water for tea. If the tea kettle came in contact with the coals, it had to be lifted off the fire by a Gentile.

The outstanding feature of the Sabbath, as I remember it, was Father's nap. It had been firmly stamped on our minds that we must do nothing that would disturb Father's nap on the Sabbath. We were told that it was a great sin to disturb Father on the Sabbath. So we walked about on tiptoe and whispered.

This Sabbath nap must have been a well-established custom, as folk tales were circulated about it. This folk story comes from the famous Chelm, the city of fools. It tells the story of two sons who came home one Sabbath afternoon and found their house on fire. Since it was a sin to spread an alarm, as it would wake their father, they stood in front of the house and whispered to each other: "Fire! Fire! Fire!"

The Havdalah was a pleasant ceremony. As soon as the first star appeared in the sky, Mother would prepare the table. A bottle of some kind of alcoholic liquor, a bottle of sweet wine, a spice urn, a lighted candle, and a special dish were set out. Father would pour a little of the liquor into the dish and ignite it with the candle. He would then touch the flame, inhale the aroma from the spice urn, and recite a prayer. Then he would pour each of us a tiny glass of wine, and we would all drink to the passing of the Sabbath. The meaning of the ceremony, as recited by my father, stands out very clearly:

"The Havdalah marks the end of the Sabbath. We must again awaken all our senses for the work of the coming week. We thank God for having given us five senses, so we can do the work that has to be done in the world. We must be able to taste, smell, touch, hear, and see. So we drink the wine to taste. We smell the spices in this urn, we ignite the spirits and touch the fire with our fingers, we recite the prayer so that all may hear, and we watch for the first star in the sky, so that all can see."

The Jewish holidays as celebrated in Poland did not merely mean a day of rest. They were consecrated days. Into the preparation of some of them went weeks of work. And they all had meaning and a very definite influence on all of us.

Beginning with the New Year, which was a joyous holiday, we lived in great anticipation for each holiday to come along. The meal on New Year's Eve was started with a piece of apple dipped in honey, so that the year would be sweet and full of harmony. The food served on this holiday, as I remember it, was pretty much the same as that served on the Sabbath. The only variation I can recall was that sometimes we would have duck instead of chicken. And that duck, as prepared by Rachel, is a fond memory: there was just a suggestion of the taste of garlic that sort of lingers on. The pudding, made of apples, raisins, and nuts, flavored with cinnamon and wine, served on this holiday, is another pleasant memory.

The Day of Atonement, which came ten days later, brought with it a feeling of awe, almost fear. We were told that on this day every Jew was either entered into the Book of Life or was destined to die during the year. And that all the sins that we had committed during the year would be forgiven, with proper prayer and fasting and repentance.

The meal the day before this holy day had to be eaten before dark. The fasting started as the last rays of light left the sky. In addition to the regular candles, on this night there was a tall candle in the center of the table that would burn for twenty-four hours. The light of that candle furnished the only light in the house during that night.

In my childish imagination I had somehow connected this tall candle with life itself. If the candle would keep burning, till the wick was all burned, I would live during the coming year. So I kept watching that candle until I fell asleep. The next day, while my parents were in the synagogue, I would sneak into the house at intervals to make sure that the candle was still burning.

When the first star appeared in the sky, and my parents came home from the synagogue where they had prayed and fasted all day, I would breathe a sigh of relief. I felt that the family was safe for another year.

Sukkoth was the happiest holiday of the year. We then celebrated harvest time. My father had a collapsible sukkah which was put up in the backyard, just outside the kitchen window. This sukkah had three sides and was hooked to the house so that the wall of the house served as the fourth wall. The top was made of strips of wood so that the sky could be seen. The top would be covered with branches of trees and all kinds of fruit would be hung from these strips.

Only male members of the family ate in the sukkah during that week.[7] I do not know why this discrimination existed. I do know that I resented it at the time.

The food was handed to my father and brothers through the kitchen window, while Mother and the girls ate in the dining room. Sukkoth lasted a week and ended with Simchas Torah. That was the most fun. The children were taken to the synagogue for that celebration and were given paper flags. Each flag had a shiny red apple on the top, and in this apple was fastened a small candle. This holiday commemorated the day when God gave the Torah to Moses on Mount Sinai. Such an event really called for a celebration, with much eating and drinking of good wine. There were bowls of candy and fruit and cookies, and we could eat as much as we wanted on this day of days.

Passover, which comes in the spring of the year, was really housecleaning time, though it commemorated the most important event in the life of the Jewish people: the emancipation from slavery. The cleaning and scrubbing that preceded that holiday started two weeks before Passover. Not an inch of space in the house was left unscrubbed. Windows were polished. Clean curtains were hung on every window.

The cooking utensils and all the dishes and silver that had been used during the year were packed in boxes and barrels and were carted to the woodshed. Special dishes and utensils were brought in from the shed for that one week. All those dishes had to be washed and all the copper pots had to be polished and arranged in the scrubbed cupboards.

On the day before Passover, by noon, all bread was banished from the house with this prayer: "All manner of leaven that is in my possession, which I have seen and which I have not seen, which I have removed and which I have not removed, shall be null and accounted as the dust of the earth." The only starch permitted in the house during that week was potato flour. Matzos took the place of bread. The matzos crushed into a meal took the place of flour. And what heavenly pancakes Rachel used to make out of this meal and eggs.

The Seder table had a special setting. We had a silver tray that was used only for the Seder. On this was arranged a dish of *charoseth,* a mixture of ground nuts, chopped apple, and wine. Some bitter herb, which was shaved horseradish, was on the opposite side of the tray. Then there was a plate of parsley, a baked egg, and a lamb shankbone. In the center of the tray were three matzos covered with a heavily embroidered cloth. This tray was set in front of Father's place, as it played an important role in the ceremony. There was a wine goblet at each place; small ones for the children, large ones for the grown-ups. There were always two extra places set at the table on this night. One was for the mythical Elijah and the other for the real guest who might be a stranger in the city and would be found by Father in the synagogue during the service. I do not recall any Passover when my father did not bring someone home for the Seder.

When Father came home from the synagogue, he would take off his coat and put on a white robe with a collar of silver braid and a white skull cap. Instead of sitting on a chair, on this night he reclined on a small sofa which had been put at the head of the table. We would gather around the table and the long service in Hebrew would begin. I am sorry to say that I did not understand a word of that service, as read by my father. But I had been told what it meant by my mother, so I could follow in a sort of hazy way. I know that before we drank the wine, we recited a prayer: "Blessed art thou, O Lord our God, King of the universe, who created the fruit of the vine to gladden the heart of man."

I recall that there were *kashes* (questions) to be asked on this night. "Wherefore is this night distinguished from all other nights?" This question was usually asked by the youngest male member of the family who was able to speak. I do not recall a girl ever asking this question, which has been asked in Jewish homes since the days of the Exodus.

But even girls knew why we ate matzos. We were told that when the Jews left Egypt, there was no time to take adequate provisions. They had left in haste, and so the only food they took with them was flour. While wandering in the wilderness, the only thing they could do was to mix the flour with water and make unleavened cakes. To this day, matzos are made out of flour and water; not even salt is added for Passover use. The bitter herbs are eaten to remind us of the days when the lives of the Jews were bitter.

The drinking of the wine and the eating continued until very late, as the story of the Passover was a long one. Most of the children fell asleep at the table and were carried off to bed. But the memories of those celebrations linger on.

Then there were the never-to-be-forgotten impressions of my grandmother. She had come to visit us in Wloclawek from Kutno, and while gathering some wood in the yard, she fell and broke a leg. Mother called the doctor and the leg was put into a cast with yards and yards of bandages. Grandmother groaned and complained and finally made up her mind that my mother had all those bandages put on because she wanted to kill her.

"After all," she confided to a visitor, "a daughter-in-law is not a daughter and she wants to get rid of me."

Father was in Warsaw at the time, where he had gone to buy

tombstones, and when Mother heard what Grandmother had said, she took a knife and cut off all the bandages.

When Father returned, he was furious with Mother and called the doctor to replace the bandages. Father listened to Grandmother's accusations for several days, then he, too, cut off the bandages. The break in her leg never healed and she spent the rest of her life on crutches.

I had heard many stories of my grandmother's piety. Her one regret in life was that none of her seven sons became a rabbi. They were all destined to carve tombstones. But she consoled herself with the thought that the commemoration of the dead was a noble cause, and she supposed that God had set them apart to do that work.

In spite of her devout piety, Grandmother was the innocent cause of our having the only Christmas tree ever to enter a Jewish home in Wloclawek. To her, a Christmas tree was an evil omen and she would shudder when she saw one.

Grandmother was laid up with her broken leg during Christmas. The maid, who did the cleaning, had come to work for us that summer. She had never worked in a Jewish home and did not know that Christmas trees were taboo. She had been very kind to Grandmother; she stopped any work she was doing to bring Grandmother her glass of tea with a lump of sugar. She was forever slapping the giant pillows to make Grandmother comfortable. And she was the only person in the house that Grandmother honored with the task of bringing and removing the bedpan. So when Christmas arrived, Grandmother decided to give our maid a substantial sum of money as a gift.

The generous girl had noticed that no move had been made to get a Christmas tree. So she went to the market and bought the tallest tree she could find and as many ornaments as her money would allow. She brought her purchases home while Mother was away and proceeded to decorate the tree with frosted ginger cookies, gilded walnuts, gaily wrapped candies, and small candle holders with candles of all the colors of the rainbow. When the tree was lighted and glittering with the shiny ornaments, she called the children and proudly presented her gift to the family.

When Mother came home and saw the tree in an honored place in the living room, she groaned with horror; at the same time, she did not want to offend the girl who had gone to all the trouble of decorating the tree, to say nothing of having paid for it all. I have always thought that Mother did a very good bit of acting at the time.

"Where did you get the money to pay for all this?" Mother asked.

"Baba gave it to me as a Christmas present," she said.

Poor Mother was in a spot. She could not tell the kind, generous girl that her gift was not welcome. She solved her problem by telling the girl that because she had been so thoughtful, she could go home for the Christmas week, with full pay, and that Mother would pay her transportation. She told my sister to help the girl pack so that she could get a train in an hour. The overjoyed girl kissed my mother's hands and departed.

As soon as she had left, the poor tree was removed to the woodshed, where the mice, no doubt, had a merry Christmas.

PART II

The Voyage to America: A New Life Begins, 1892–95

The Voyage to America 2

On one of his business trips to Warsaw, Father heard stories of a great world's fair that would be held in a city called Chicago, in America. This was 1891; the fair would be held in 1893. He had decided several years before that someday he would migrate to America. This would be a good time to go to this new world.

I have a dim recollection of Father saying that he could no longer live under the Russian yoke.[1] And never would he subject his sons to Russian military service. There was only one escape: going to America. Father thought it would be practical for him to go to America by himself, get himself established, then send for the family. The idea had become quite an obsession with him, since that trip to Warsaw. Even the fact that Mother was pregnant at the time did not deter him.

I have a faint suspicion that Mother was not in complete accord with Father at the time. She wanted him to wait until after the child was born. I have a feeling that she did not want him to go to America. I heard her tell a relative that her six children were buried in the sacred soil of the Jewish cemetery and that she would never be able to visit their graves. Her roots had been sunk deep in the soil of Poland and it was not easy to pull them up.

Father sold the shop and the house before he left. There were many plans to be made. The Russian government at that time did not allow families with boys to leave the country. But ways could be found. Some people left saying they were going to visit relatives in Germany and once over the border it was easy.

Then there was the usual method of bribing the border patrol. The government paid so little to its workers that one could hardly blame them for accepting bribes.

Nor could anyone be blamed for not wanting to serve in the army. The corrupt government officials cared very little for the welfare of the people. And the people had no loyalty or love of country.

But Father was determined and the day soon arrived when he was to leave. I recall the friends and relatives who came to say good-bye to Father. But the most vivid memory is of Grandmother. Her tragic face haunts me. Seven sons had been born to her. Six had died. Father was the only one left and now she was losing him. She sat there in her best blue silk dress with a cap made of the same silk, edged with narrow lace ruffles. In later years, when I saw pictures of Martha Washington, I thought of Grandmother's cap. I do not remember ever seeing Grandmother's hair. She always wore a cap. There she sat with her crutches, holding my father's strong hand in her wrinkled one, while the tears rolled down her wrinkled cheeks.

Father left for America. Three months later my youngest brother was born. As I recall it, it was not a happy time. We all missed Father. Many duties that he would have assumed fell to my oldest sister, who was then about twenty years old, and she was not too happy about the whole affair. I have a feeling that my new brother did not get the welcome into the world that had been accorded the other boys.

Father must have left enough money as the meals were regular. The only change in our lives that I could notice was that Mother was beginning to sell things. And then one day the steamship tickets arrived and the selling was stepped up.

The partings with favorite toys were tragic events. They were eased somewhat by the promise that I could take my doll and that Father would buy us American toys. While most of our possessions were sold or given away, there were certain things with which Mother would not part. She insisted on taking all the feather beds and pillows. Had she not stripped all those feathers with her own fingers? The bulky pillows and covers were packed in burlap bags and then put into huge hampers. Glassware and silver and brass and copper kettles were packed in large wooden cases. Our clothes were carefully packed in trunks.

Then there were huge hampers of food. Mother packed many hampers with food. She was not going to permit any of us to eat anything that was not kosher.

On the day we left, all these trunks, boxes, hampers, and bags were loaded onto a wagon.[2] A carriage had been hired for us and we all crowded in.

Our beloved Mariana and Rachel, the cook, had come to say good-bye. They were standing in front of the house that had been home to me ever since I was born. They were both crying. The carriage started moving and slowly the beloved city and the clear winding Vistula River were left behind. Mother was holding the baby and crying. I clutched my doll, but I confess that I was filled with a feeling of adventure.

We were driven to the German border; it was getting dark when we arrived. The wagon with all our belongings was waiting for us. We were stopped by a man in a uniform and asked where we were going. Mother produced some papers and said we were going to visit some relatives in Germany. She then handed him a bulky envelope. He carefully looked at the contents and waved the driver to go ahead. I recall thinking that this was a pretty big load for a short visit, but I had been told to keep quiet, and I obeyed.

It was many years later that I found out that the man in the uniform had been bribed, and I then knew what was in the envelope.

We arrived at the railroad station at Thoren [Torun], I think, and took a train for Berlin. Then we changed trains and went to Hamburg. There we boarded a ship that took us to Hull, England. Then we went by train to Liverpool, and here at last was the big ship that was to take us to America!

Mother presented her steamship tickets to the purser and asked him when we would reach New York. The purser looked at the tickets, then at mother and the six children, and sighed.

"What is wrong?" asked Mother in alarm. "Are the tickets all right?"

"Your tickets," said the purser with a touch of sympathy, "are not for New York. This ship is going to Montreal, Canada."

"Are the tickets for another ship," asked Mother.

"Oh, the tickets are for this ship," said the purser.

"But what can we do now?" Mother was becoming hysterical.

"Get on the boat," the purser said kindly. "Montreal is not too far from New York. You can go there by train."

Mother soon realized that there was no turning back. Our "bridges had been burned behind us." So, weeping and trusting in God, we embarked on the great adventure.

There were many comedies and tragedies at this port of embarkation. My oldest sister never tired of telling of the young woman who was joining her husband in America. She had a three-month-old infant with her, and when the baby cried for any length of time, she would scream hysterically: "What do you want of me? Why don't you go to your father?" This poor frightened creature had everybody's sympathy, but she also furnished a good bit of fun. When it was her turn to present her steamship ticket, she pulled a huge bundle of papers from her bosom and laid them before the bewildered purser.

She had brought her engagement contract and her wedding certificate. She had brought her mother's engagement and wedding and divorce papers. She had brought all sorts of useless receipts. But there was no steamship ticket. When she was told there was no steamship ticket, she began to tear her hair and scream. She called on her dead ancestors to help her. But as there was no answer from the Heavenly Host, she turned to my sister for help. My sister looked through the heap of useless papers and still there was no steamship ticket.

"Why did you bring all those papers?" my sister asked.

"How was I to know what they are?" she said. "I can't read."

I have often wondered what became of the helpless, bewildered woman and her baby.

I remember very little of that historic voyage. I became very ill as soon as the ship sailed. The ship's doctor was not at all sure that I would ever reach America. I was kept on deck, on an improvised bed, day and night. Mother and my sister took turns watching over me. The only food I was given was a few drops of rum every hour.

There is one event, however, that I do remember vividly. Every day a group of people gathered on the deck, not far from my improvised bed, and sang lovely songs. A kind-faced middle-aged man led the singing. He would ask everybody on deck to join the singers. That singing is the only pleasant memory I have of that voyage.

A few years later, I went to Hull-House to hear Handel's *Messiah* for the first time. Imagine my delight and surprise when the man who directed the singers on the boat came out to direct the large chorus assembled on the stage of the Hull-House Theatre. It seemed as if destiny started leading me to Hull-House while I was on the boat that brought me to America.

The man was Peter Christian Lutkin, to whom I want to pay this tribute:[3] His music on that ship found its way into the heart of a very sick little girl and furnished the only spark of pleasure for her during a long and painful voyage.

The voyage was much longer than anticipated. We ran into icebergs and the ship had to change course. The food that Mother had brought had been eaten. The small children were permitted to eat the ship's food, but Mother and my oldest sister lived on potatoes boiled in the jackets and hard-boiled eggs for three days. They were able to get these two foods from the ship's kitchen. They were boiled in a small teakettle which Mother had brought with her.

At last the long voyage was over. Before our eager eyes lay the Promised Land.

Transplanted 3

The ship docked at Montreal on a bright morning in June.[1] By this time I had recovered from my illness, but I was still a little unsteady on my feet. The whole family was a sorry, bedraggled-looking group. The voyage had taken longer than it was supposed to, so that our food supply had run out. We had not been bathed during the entire trip. In addition to being hungry and dirty, there was no friendly face to greet us. We were taken to a sort of detention camp, with many other immigrants, men, women, and children who were herded into one enormous room and told to wait.

After several hours a large cart was rolled into the room and the man in charge gave each of us some dry bread and some vile coffee. This was our first meal in the Promised Land! Although Father had sent a considerable amount of money for the trip, Mother was too generous on the boat.[2] She had paid well for every little attention or service. After all, she thought, we would not need any money in New York; we would be cared for when we got there by our numerous relatives. She gathered us into a little group and told us that she had one dollar left. Did we want to buy some food or send a telegram to Father? My oldest sister, who was twenty years old at the time and had been at school, told Mother that we could send telegrams collect, so we all voted for food. It was decided that my sister would venture forth in search of a shop. I insisted that I wanted to go with her, and my mother was too tired and worn out to object, so I trotted along. Mother implored us not to go too far lest we not find our way back to camp.

We left the camp, I clutching my sister's skirt. I am sure we were fearful of getting lost, but we went on. We had walked a short distance when we saw a man with a cart on which were displayed some bright yellow things that we had never seen before and some shiny red apples. Being of an adventuresome nature, my sister decided to try the yellow things. She held up seven fingers and pointed to the bananas, for that's what they were called, the man told us. The man put the newly found treasures into a bag, my sister gave him the dollar, he gave her some change, and we ran off excitedly with our purchase.

When Mother saw what we had bought she was afraid the things were not kosher; they looked like sausages, and she would not allow us to eat them. After that eventful shopping expedition, we had eighty-five cents and we were still hungry.

The room in the detention camp was hot. There was no ventilation. I have always had a keen sense of smell, and I recall to this day the odor from the many unwashed bodies. The drinking water was warm and had a fishy taste; although we were very thirsty, we could not swallow that water. There we sat.

At noon we were given some bread and tea. The benches were just boards nailed together and soon became very uncomfortable. When night crept upon us we looked around; no one said anything about beds. Mother managed to pull a few small blankets from a basket and spread them out on the floor, and the younger children were put to sleep on the floor. I tried to sleep, sitting next to my mother with my head in her lap. I awoke just as the sun was rising, and I believe it was the first time I saw a sunrise. But I was hungry, thirsty, dirty, and weary, and the magic of the colors in the sky made no impression on me.

When the children awoke, Mother took all of us into the washroom, carrying one of her wonderful baskets. She pulled out some clean, soft towels and wash cloths and washed our faces, necks, ears, and as much of our bodies as she could reach without removing our clothes. A clean face, wiped on a clean towel, does make a difference. We all felt a little more hopeful. Again, dry bread and coffee were served.

My sister was now determined to find a telegraph office, even though she could speak no English. Armed with the address of the camp, she assured us that she would find her way back, and she started off on her mission.

She walked down the street for several blocks and came to a school. As it was still early in the morning, the children were playing in the school yard. My sister stopped to look at the clean, happy children. Her eyes almost popped out of her head! Could it be? Yes, right in that circle of children was a little girl who had been a neighbor in Wloclawek! Her family had left Poland the year before and had probably gotten as far as Montreal and stayed there. My sister rushed into the school yard and broke her way into the circle.

"Are you Rose Woldenberg?"[3] my sister asked, clutching the girl's arm.

"Yes," the little girl answered, "and you are a Satt."

"Where do you live?" my sister asked excitedly.

"Just two blocks from here," the child answered.

"You must take me to your mother," my sister said, clinging to the child.

"The bell will ring any minute," said the child, "and I must go to school."

"Then take me to your teacher," my sister said. "You can tell her that I must see your mother."

The little girl took my sister into the school, and she explained to the teacher what had happened to us. The teacher listened sympathetically and told Rose to take my sister to see her mother. The two girls ran all the way to the Woldenberg house.

Mrs. Woldenberg summoned her husband from the store, and they all came to the detention camp. They gathered up our baskets, suitcases, bundles, and children and took us to their home.

A telegram was sent to Father. Then each of us was given a warm bath and head wash. We were served a delicious breakfast of fresh eggs, homemade bread and butter, honey, and rich, sweet milk. I have eaten many exotic foods since then, but nothing had the magic taste of the food we ate that day in the home of these good friends. To this day I feel the warm glow of friendship that these kind people showed us on that far-off day—the voluntary sympathy that one human being feels for the other. The kindness of these friends gave us a new lease on life that day. "God's in his Heaven, all's right with the world."

I have since learned that it was a common practice of the steamship agents in America to cheat and exploit the poor immigrants who bought tickets for their relatives.[4] The steamship ticket business was flourishing at the time, when thousands of people were leaving Poland, Russia, Germany, Ireland, and other countries in Europe in search of a better life. There probably was no law regulating the sale of this transportation, and the people were at the mercy of the dishonest agents.

My father lost no time in sending the money for our transportation to Chicago. In three hours the money arrived by telegram. Father insisted that we leave at once. Mr. Woldenberg made all the arrangements to have our baggage sent to the railroad station. Mrs. Woldenberg filled our baskets with a fresh supply of food for the trip. Bidding our good, kind friends good-bye, we left on the last lap of that eventful journey.

We arrived in Chicago a few minutes after midnight, on June 16, 1892.[5]

It was raining as we stepped off the train. The station was dark and gloomy. But it became light and sunny when we caught sight of

Father. He was standing near a lamppost. I could see his eyes shining. He had hired a wagon to transport us to our new home. The bags, boxes, hampers, suitcases, and children were loaded onto a wagon for the last time. We were covered with some sort of tarpaulin to keep off the rain. As the horse clattered over the brick pavements of the station yard, Father opened a brown paper bag and gave each of us a banana.

South Halsted Street 4

My first home in Chicago was on South Halsted Street, four blocks south of Hull-House.[1] I did not realize that my future as an American would be measured by that distance.

I remember the first morning after the arrival of the family. I jumped out of bed and ran to the window. The sight that greeted me brought on such hysterical weeping that my father and mother came running out of their room to see what was wrong.

"Where is the river?" I cried.

Father put me on his lap and explained that Chicago had a lake that was so big that the Vistula River would look like a dishpan full of water.

"But where is it?" I cried. "I want to see it."

"Now, stop your crying. We will see it someday," said my father.

But the summer passed and I did not get to see Lake Michigan. The only part of Chicago that I saw that summer was the block on South Halsted Street, where we lived, and a few of the side streets.

Father went to work very early every morning. On the Sabbath, the day of rest, we were not allowed to ride on streetcars; we were told it was too far to walk to the lake. The lake was only a mile from our home, but it may as well have been in Poland, as far as we children were concerned. We were left to our own devices. No one seemed to have time to show us the lake.

The only play space was the street in front of the house. The small yard in back of the house had been rented to a junk man and was used to store junk.

Halsted Street is thirty-two miles long. It runs from the extreme north end of Chicago to the extreme south. Hull-House is located at 800 South Halsted.

The home to which Father brought the family was a six-room flat, the upstairs of a two-story wooden house. The first floor was a steamship ticket agency. It was typical of the houses that had been built after the Chicago Fire, just twenty-one years before we arrived. Compared with some of the homes of children that I played with, our home was luxurious. We had a toilet with running water in a narrow hall just outside of the kitchen. One of my playmates, a little girl, lived in three rooms in back of a basement grocery store with her two sisters, five brothers, a father, and a mother.[2]

Most of the houses had privies in the yards. In many cases the owner of the front house would build a shanty in the rear to bring in additional income. Very little attention was paid as to how near the privy was to the shanty. On hot days the people living in these shanties had to keep their windows closed to keep out the stench.

The sidewalks were wooden planks, which became slimy and slippery after a rain. The streets were paved with wooden blocks, and after a heavy rainfall the blocks would become loose and float about in the street.[3] During the drying process the stench was nauseating. There were many places where the blocks did not return to their mooring and the smelly water would remain for days. If this happened at an intersection, it was impossible to cross the street . . . and there was no Sir Walter Raleigh to spread a coat.

I have a feeling that some of the young people were politically minded in those days and put some of the blame for these conditions on the shoulders of the city fathers. I remember a sign that some pranksters put up at one such intersection after it had been raining for a week:

The Mayor and the Aldermen
are invited
to swim here

There was not a tree or a blade of grass anywhere in the neighborhood. Here I played my first American game, which was called "run sheep run." I do not recall any of the rules of the game, but I do know that we ran out into the street while playing it. But the streets were fairly safe for play. We did not hesitate to run into the street as there was very little traffic. An occasional horse and wagon would clump down the street, but the horse was nearly always old and tired and would drag along at such a slow pace that we could easily get out of the way.

The wagons were filled with either fruits and vegetables or junk. Potatoes were sold for five cents a peck, apples were ten cents a peck, and bananas were five cents a dozen.

The peddlers had their distinctive calls. After several weeks, Mother could tell by the call if her peddler was in front of the house. Most of the day the air was filled with these calls:

"Any rags, any bottles, any junk today?"<br>"Ripe bananas, five cents a dozen."
"Shiny red apples, come out and see."

Even if the prices were low, the women would still complain that they were too high. It seemed to be a custom never to pay what was asked. The haggling was always good-natured. The peddlers seemed to expect it and perhaps would have been disappointed if a woman paid the price asked. Often a compromise would be reached by the peddler giving an extra banana or a few extra apples or potatoes to consummate the sale.

It was on this street that I learned my first English words. I was very eager to learn English. At that time it was my only goal in life. The sooner I could speak English, the sooner I would not be regarded as a greenhorn. So I decided to listen to what people would say and to try to remember and to repeat the words. It was only a week after my arrival that I heard a man and a woman quarreling; but they talked so fast that I only caught the last words. As the man left the store I heard the woman shout after him: "Go to hell!" I repeated the precious words to myself a dozen times and then rushed into the house to tell Mother that now I could speak English. No one paid any attention to me. No one in the family knew what the words meant.

The ground floors of all the houses on the block were shops and stores.[4] There were saloons where people would buy a big pail of beer for five cents. Women and children were not supposed to go through the front door of the saloon, but it was proper to go through the side door. Then there were so-called cigar stores where all sorts of tobacco were sold. Most men bought little bags of tobacco and small books of tissue paper and rolled their own cigarettes. Chewing tobacco and snuff were also sold in these stores. In front of each cigar store stood a wooden Indian, painted in many bright colors.

The barbershops were designated by a red-and-white striped pole, and every drugstore had large glass globes filled with colored water.

The grocery stores were filled with large burlap bags containing rice, beans, coffee, barley, and other staples. Everything had to be weighed by the grocer. I remember when there were no paper bags. The grocer would roll a sheet of brown paper into a cornucopia and fill it with whatever was bought. Eggs were shipped in boxes and baskets and many would be cracked on arrival at the grocery store. All cracked eggs were sold a penny cheaper. The only canned foods that I can remember were salmon and peas. When I was sent to the store for a can of salmon, the grocer had to open the can, as can openers were scarce. I would then have to walk home very slowly in order not to spill the liquid in which the salmon was packed.

The windows of the bakery shops were filled with large loaves of rye bread and with rolls covered with poppy seed. There were kosher butcher shops, Chinese laundries, and ice-cream parlors, where I was introduced to my first ice-cream soda. Then there were stores where bridal gowns were exhibited. I would stare starry-eyed at these stiff figures dressed in lace and satin with long net veils hanging down the back. There were stores where steamship tickets were sold, and every time I saw people come out of one of those stores I wondered whether they had been sold tickets to Montreal.

All the people who owned these stores lived in back of them. I did not know of any storekeeper who did not live in the back of the store.

Although it was twenty-one years since the Great Chicago Fire, I recall children singing songs about that historic event. One of these songs still lingers in my memory. It was sung to the tune of "A Hot Time in the Old Town Tonight," and these are the words:[5]

> One moonlight night, when families were in bed,
> Mrs. O'Leary took a lantern to the shed,
> The cow kicked it over, winked her eye and said
> There'll be a hot time in the old town tonight.

The Chicago Fire started on De Koven Street, just two blocks from where I lived.[6] But I do not recall anyone showing any interest in the historic place. After hearing the children sing the song on the street, I asked a playmate where this fire had started. She took me to the spot and there I saw a dilapidated two-story house that had been built on the lot where the famous O'Leary house had been. The paint was peeling and some of the windows were broken. But there was an elegant bronze plaque nailed to the house, which proclaimed to the whole world that "the great fire of 1871 started here."

It was on South Halsted Street, during that first summer in Chicago, that I first heard the words "earning a living." I recall asking my father why he carved tombstones. He told me that graves of departed relatives had to be marked. But I did not connect the carving of these tombstones with the food I ate, or the clothes I wore, or the toys that I enjoyed.

The upper flat of the two-story wooden house which was our first home in Chicago was large and roomy. It was divided into six rooms and every piece of furniture that Father had bought before our arrival was brand new. He had boasted that we were to start a new life in a new country with all new furniture.

As I look back on that first year in Chicago, I feel that it was a good year. While the surroundings were not what they had been in Poland, the family life was a happy one. Father earned enough money for good food and none of the children were asked to work.

The furnishings of that first home did not impress me too much. The furniture in Poland had been nicer. But the one thing that did excite me was the kitchen stove. It was made of shiny black iron and was trimmed with much nickel plating. I could see my face in the shiny metal and I often wondered if the mirror would break from the heat.

The stove was constantly being fed coal from a large wooden box, which was always filled. And many were the pots of chicken soup and gefilte fish that were cooked on that stove.

The job of keeping that stove shiny was relegated to my oldest sister. And how she rubbed to keep it shiny. Every Thursday was the day of the ritual. And how enraged she became when Mother would drop some food on it the day it was polished. She did not seem to mind if food was spattered the next day.

I also remember a red plush sofa on which we were not allowed to sit. This sofa was for company only. There was an elegant rug on the floor of the living room on which we were not supposed to step. Thick lace curtains were hung on the windows of this hallowed room, which somehow did not seem to belong to the rest of the house. In the fall of the year an imposing parlor stove was brought into this room. This heater was also ornamented with nickel plating. The red coals would gleam through the isinglass openings and give a warm glow to the room. On rare occasions we children were allowed in the room.

I do not recall any pictures on the walls of this living room. My father had an aversion to having people photographed, and he may have had the same aversion to all pictures.[7] As I think back, I have a feeling that this might have had something to do with false idols. There were no photographs of any member of the family displayed in the house. The only picture I can remember is a calendar hanging in the kitchen, which would change from year to year.

The only decoration in the living room was a cabinet that fitted into a corner of the room. On this cabinet were displayed the family treasures. I remember a beautiful music box that played Brahms's "Lullaby." This box had the place of honor on the center shelf. There was also a beautiful hand-carved snuff box that had belonged to a revered member of the family. There were many cups and saucers with garish unnatural flowers painted on them.

The wallpaper in this room had enormous bunches of purple grapes with birds flying between the bunches. From the ceiling was suspended a huge lamp. This kerosene lamp was my mother's pride and joy. How lovingly she used to clean the ornamented chimney! The shade was made of red glass decorated with green leaves. The lamp was lighted only when we entertained company.

The dining room was used for all our meals and in it we spent many happy times. Here the walls were one mass of huge red roses with bees buzzing through the petals. The rug in this room was spattered with huge flowers. I never had seen this particular flower grow in any garden, and I now feel that the design was the figment of some designer's imagination. In the center of the room was a large round table with twelve chairs around it. The lamp in this room was even larger than the one in the living room. The shade was of green glass and there were many strings of beads fastened all around it. A huge silk tassel in the center completed this magic lamp.

There was a carved sideboard in this room on which were displayed the lovely pieces of glass and china that my mother had brought from Poland. There was a handsome wine decanter and twelve wine glasses on a beautiful glass tray that I used to admire.

Twenty-eight years after we came to Chicago, I attended an exhibit of glassware and china that had been taken from the palace of the czar of Russia, and there I saw a duplicate of Mother's decanter and wine glasses.

My Father 5

The stories of Father's first year in Chicago were repeated to everyone who came to the house. He arrived in Chicago on a Friday morning and went straight to the home of a *landsmann,* whose address he had brought from Poland. Father was given a warm welcome, and, as it happened, the people he had come to see had a spare room. He rented it and moved in. In the evening he went to the synagogue and met more men from Poland.[1] He spoke to no one about a job, as not only would he not work on the Sabbath, but he would not even talk about work.

Early Sunday morning he went to see the rabbi and asked him where he could find a Jewish tombstone carver. To his amazement he found out that as far as the rabbi knew there was no Jewish tombstone carver in the neighborhood, nor did he know of any in the city. But he did know of a large concern where not only were the inscriptions carved on the tombstones but the stones were shaped and polished out of huge blocks of marble and granite.

The next morning Father found his way to the shop of F. B. Bagley & Co.[2] I think that was the name of the firm.

To all Jews the marking of the grave of a departed relative was a religious responsibility. And since thousands of Jews were coming to Chicago from Europe, tombstones were needed with Hebrew inscriptions. There were many German and Polish people who ordered tombstones and wanted their mother tongue carved on the stones. When Father applied for a job and told the man who interviewed him that he could read and write Hebrew, Yiddish, Polish, German, and Russian, he was welcomed with open arms. It had been especially difficult to get Hebrew inscriptions for the tombstones.

At a time in the history of America when ten dollars a week was considered good pay, my father asked for ten dollars a day. And he got it! He worked that week and the people were more and more pleased with his work. But on Friday, as the sun was setting, he laid down his mallet and chisel and said he would be back on Monday.

The foreman, who spoke German, told Father this was not done in America. A worker had to work a full week or not at all. So Father told him that it would have to be "not at all." He wrapped up his tools and left.

I am sure that he would rather have starved and let the family starve before he would desecrate the Sabbath.

On Monday afternoon he received a telegram asking him to return to work. I have often wondered if he was the first man in Chicago to demand and get a five-day week.

During that year Father saved enough money to pay the passage to America for Mother and the six children, furnish a six-room flat with new furniture, and set up his own shop. He was in business for himself when the family arrived.

I remember that shop very clearly. It was a wooden shanty with a dirt floor. It had no heat or artificial light, so that Father worked only in the daytime when the weather permitted. There really was no need to work during the winter as no one would have a tombstone set when the ground was frozen. And it was too difficult to get to the cemetery when the only transportation was a horse and wagon. But he earned enough during the summer to keep us well provided during the winter.

Next door to Father's shop was the Jewish Training School.[3] This was not a public school. It had been established in 1891, the year that Father arrived in Chicago.[4] The school was supported by wealthy German Jews who had come to America years before and had established themselves in the commerce and industry of the city.

The first principal was Professor George Bamberger, a wise and understanding educator.[5] The school embodied many of the ideas of Francis Parker and was really on a par with some of the best private schools. The school paid special attention to the children of immigrants. Many of the children had gone to school in Europe and needed only special help in learning English. These children had the special facilities of ungraded classes,[6] and as soon as they could speak the language, they were transferred to the class where they belonged.

The Jewish Training School stressed arts and crafts.[7] In addition to reading, writing, arithmetic, and geography, there were classes in both vocal and instrumental music. There was a department of painting, drawing, and clay modeling. There were sewing classes for the girls and manual training for both girls and boys. Gymnastics were taught in a real gymnasium. In many public schools in Chicago today, the children are still given gymnastics in the aisles of the classroom.

As soon as the school had opened, Father went to call on the principal. The two men became friends, and Father made up his mind that this was the school we would attend when we arrived. The great day came in September when Father took my sister, my oldest brother, and me to be enrolled in the Jewish Training School. My oldest sister had finished school in Poland and my other brothers were too young to go to school.

The first step toward our Americanization was the changing of our given names. Because my sister had rosy cheeks, she was named Rose. The clerk who did the registering probably found it too difficult to pronounce Gutcha, which was my sister's name. My brother's name was Welvel, so they named him Willie. My name was Hinda, but the registrar thought Hilda would be better, so I became Hilda.

We had been to school a few days when my brother decided to go home by himself; he had been told to wait for my sister and me. When he reached Halsted Street, he turned south instead of north and was soon lost.

My sister and I ran all the way home for lunch and told Mother that Willie had disappeared. It was a Friday when Mother was busy cooking the Sabbath meals. So my sister was dispatched to Father's shop to tell him what had happened.

Father did not exactly know what to do, so he went to the school and asked the school secretary. She told Father not to worry and telephoned the police. At that time my brother had not yet been picked up by the police, but they said that as soon as a boy of that description was found, they would telephone the school.

The school was almost ready to close when the telephone call came. My brother had wandered off miles from the house. Father had to take a streetcar to the police station to get him. When Father got there, Willie was seated in a big armchair with a big red apple in one hand and several candy sticks in the other. The policemen were entertaining him with tricks. He was having a wonderful time and did not want to go home.

By this time the sun was setting, and that was the first time that Father rode on a streetcar on the Sabbath. I think he would have walked, no matter how great the distance, but it was too far for a little boy to walk.

As soon as I learned the alphabet, I tried to pronounce the name of the street where the school was located. The street was called "Judd Street." I pronounced it "Yude Street." "Yude" was the German word for "Jew," and I somehow got the impression that only Jews were permitted on the street and in the school. Although the school was nonsectarian and many of the teachers were not Jewish, I did not know of any non-Jewish children in the school.

My first teacher, in the first grade, is a special warm and grateful memory. She was Anna Bryan Torrance, a warm and understanding human being. Her patience and sympathy with the children who could not speak English was boundless. I am sure that it was due to her faultless training that almost none of the children in her room retained any foreign accent. I remember being called to her desk for the first time. I noticed that she was writing with a golden pen point. Before she put it down, she carefully wiped it with a pen wiper. At one time I had visualized that only the czar could have a golden pen. Then I thought I would rather that she had it. When I went to the sewing class for the first time, I was asked what I would like to make. Without a moment's hesitation I said a pen wiper for my teacher so that she could wipe her golden pen point with it.

One incident stands out very clearly in my memory. While I was learning to read, I was called on one day to read out loud in the classroom. I was doing very well, till I came to the word "Jesus." I stopped short as if I had suddenly been paralyzed. Mrs. Torrance urged me to go on, but I just sat there staring at her.

"The word is 'Jesus,'" she prompted me.

"I know what it is," I said, "but I can't say it."

"Why not?" Mrs. Torrance asked.

"My mother said I must never say that word," I said.

Some of the other children backed me up. They, too, had been told not to pronounce the word. I was allowed to finish the story, but every time I came to the word "Jesus," I just passed over it. The fear and superstition inculcated in me in Poland was still with me.

Mrs. Torrance was about fifty years of age when I came to the Jewish Training School. She had come from Salem, Illinois, to teach in this school in the slums of Chicago. The school was a half block from Jefferson Street, which was then the outdoor market. I will have more to say of this market in due time.

It is difficult to say why Mrs. Torrance ever came to this school to teach children who knew very little or no English. Perhaps she was attracted by the stories of the great influx of people from all over Europe and wanted to know something of the lives of these people. But there never was a person more suited for the job. She not only taught us English and arithmetic and geography, but she made us love what we were doing. She gave a part of herself to the children every day of the week. She kept a box of combs and when a girl came to school without combing her hair, she would give her a comb and tell her to go to the washroom and comb her hair. One day I saw her scrub those combs with soap and water.

Every child in that room felt as if he or she was Mrs. Torrance's special charge but never a special pet. I have rarely come across a person who could be so impartial to a group of children. She loved us all, whether we learned quickly or slowly. The only partiality she ever showed was when she announced that she would award a book to the child who had the highest marks for a period of six months. I won that book.

The last time I saw Mrs. Torrance I was fourteen years of age, but I often wished that I could have known more about her. She was a woman with great spirit and an unbounded love for immigrant children.

As I look back to the time that I attended the Jewish Training School, I realize that the school was primarily organized for poor children, but not all the children in the school were poor. I suppose that many kindhearted people got a great deal of satisfaction from their pet charity. The important thing is that at no time did I feel that I was the object of anyone's charity.

I have often wondered if the Jewish Training School was not set up as an example for the public schools to follow. I have recently come across what Francis W. Parker said about the school: "I have looked upon the Jewish Training School from the beginning as one of the nurseries of better teaching and training in the City of Chicago. It has called the attention of the intelligent people to the great value of rational work in the schools, especially the training of the hand and the brain."[8]

In addition to being introduced to an American school that year, other events began crowding in on me and made me realize that I was living in a new world. It was four hundred years since America had been discovered, and for me it was being rediscovered. In school there were special programs about Christopher Columbus, a name I heard for the first time. We were told about the three ships in which the great man had sailed. How the wonderful queen had sold her jewels to make the trip possible. These were wonderful times to kindle one's imagination and I was living in the midst of it all.

At last the great day arrived. October 12, 1892, was a day to be remembered.[9] At dawn we were given glasses of milk and buttered rolls, which we gulped down in a hurry, and rushed to the street where we sat on the edge of the sidewalk all day and watched that historic parade go by. I do not recall whether food was brought to us, or whether we did not eat all day, but I do know that we could not be pried loose from our seats. The great floats went by hour after hour. Each float depicted some phase of the discovery of America. Great shouts went up every time a band approached and a float followed. We had come to America in a truly historic time.

Other great events were to follow. After spending a rich winter in an American school, May 1893 brought the opening of the World's Columbian Exposition. This event was one of the reasons for our coming to America.

Many relatives descended on us at that time. They all came to see the world's fair. Mother improvised beds for us children on chairs so that our guests could have the beds.

And then the greatest of all days arrived. My father decided to take a day off from his work to take us to the fair. We were speechless with excitement. The fair was a world of enchantment to us. The great ferris wheel was shown here for the first time. When you got to the top you could almost touch the sky, we thought. I saw a diver for the first time and wondered how it was possible that he could stay underwater as long as he did—all of five minutes. There was a replica of the snow-covered Alps, showing the great St. Bernard dogs saving the lives of people when they got lost in the snow.

In the exhibit of schools, the Jewish Training School was well represented.[10] And I almost swooned with excitement when I saw my name attached to a small canvas bag that I had made. My sister, who was several years older, had embroidered a delicate white silk cover and pillow for a doll's bed. We were very proud of our work and very proud of our school and even more proud of America, where all these wonderful things were happening.

Greater thrills were still to come. As the light was fading in the sky, millions of lights were suddenly flashed on, all at one time. Having seen nothing but kerosene lamps for illumination, this was like getting a sudden vision of Heaven. Father marveled as much as we did. He told us that all these lights had been turned on with switches.

"Without matches?" I asked.

"Without matches," he said.

"Just like the stars," I said.

"The wonders of America are as wonderful as the stars," he said with great reverence.

He seemed to take a personal pride in the fair, as if he had helped in the planning. As I look back on those days, most people in Chicago felt that way. Chicago was host to the world at that time and we were part of it all.

Father kept telling us that the great fair would never be forgotten by those who were fortunate enough to see it. Not because of the great and startling exhibits, but because it marked the four-hundredth anniversary of the discovery of America.

We went to the fair many times that summer, but that was the only time that Father was with us. He felt he could not spare the time from his work.

Another winter was upon us and Father was home most of the time. Occasionally he would go to see people who had had a death in the family and who, he knew, would want to order a tombstone. By this time he had made many friends. During the winter evenings his friends would come to the house to play chess and to talk. They would spend hours discussing conditions in Chicago. There was much unemployment in Chicago that winter. The people who had been working in the fair lost their jobs when the fair closed. Many had come from foreign countries and wanted to go home but had no money. I'm afraid that it made very little impression on me.

I recall one of my father's chess partners. Whenever he came, Mother always served him food. She knew that he had not been working and that his family was still in Europe. We called him Uncle Mischa, though we knew he was not a real uncle.

Uncle Mischa was a tailor by trade and I heard him say that the "times were hard." He and Father would have long arguments about working conditions in Chicago. I heard Uncle Mischa say that he either worked too hard or not at all. The working day was fourteen hours long at that time, and he thought it ought to be shorter so that the working season would be longer. My father would argue that no matter how hard you worked, it was still better than living in a country where there was compulsory military service. I realize now that no matter how eloquently my father argued, he had never been inside an American factory and perhaps knew very little of this phase of American life.

So the winter passed, and the carefully saved earnings of the previous summer had been used up for food, clothing, coal, rent, and all the other needs of everyday life.

The first Sunday in March was a warm, sunny day and Father started out on his first job of the season. There were two tombstones to be erected and he left early in the morning. It was a long trip from his shop to the cemetery.

In the afternoon an aunt came over with a new baby, which none of the family had seen. There was much merriment in the house and Mother was busy cooking. There was to be a celebration when Father came home.

We heard footsteps on the stairs and Uncle Mischa, who had accompanied Father, came into the room. His face was deathly pale and he told us that Father had become ill while working. Mother insisted that she be taken to him, at once. She was getting her coat when Uncle Mischa told her that Father was dead.[11]

I shall never forget the utter panic that descended on the family. In a very short time, two men carried Father into the house and laid him on his bed. He was still dressed in his boots and working clothes.

I kept wondering how it was possible for a person to be alive in the morning and dead at night.

Mother had decided that I was too young to go to the funeral. But as the friends and relatives were getting into the horse-drawn carriages, Uncle Mischa took my hand and said: "Come, my child, get your coat and hat and come along. It will not hurt you. This will be the last time you will be with your father. You will remember him better if you come."

He lifted me into the carriage and the horses trotted off. It took two hours to get to the cemetery, and during the entire time no one spoke a word.

Father was buried on the spot where he had fallen. There was a legend that if a man dies in the cemetery, he has selected the spot where he wishes to be buried.

I stood among the group of people, clutching Uncle Mischa's hand as Father was lowered into the grave, wrapped in his *talis* (prayer shawl) that he had faithfully worn every day since he was thirteen years old, the day of his Bar Mitzvah. I distinctly remember that the body had been taken from the pine wooden box, and I looked at the beloved face for the last time. He was forty-four years old.

He did not live to really know America. All his hopes and dreams for a good, free life for his family were buried with him. He had applied for citizenship, but he had not lived here long enough to be granted that high privilege.

What was to be our future? What chance had we in a strange country, without funds?

When we returned from the funeral, I heard Mother tell my sister that she had two dollars and there were seven of us to be fed.

I often wonder what kind of life I would have lived if I had not met Jane Addams.

My Mother 6

My oldest sister was the only member of the family old enough to go to work at this time. But she had not learned to speak English as rapidly as the younger children, and she had no training for any kind of work. It had been Father's proud boast that his daughters would not work outside the home. Girls were supposed to help their mother, learn how to be good wives, and get married. And that is just what Mother decided my sister ought to do. She had been engaged for several months, so it was easy to carry out Mother's decision. Sister was married and she and her new husband went to live in a small town near Chicago.

The first step in reorganizing our lives was to move to a cheaper flat. Again Mother was faced with the heartbreaking task of disposing of furniture we had learned to love. There would be no dining room in the smaller flat, so the round table where we had eaten so many happy meals had to be sold. But the kerosene lamp with the beautiful beads was moved and stayed with the family till gas was installed in homes.

We moved into a four-room flat on a side street.[1] There were two houses on a small lot. Each house had two four-room flats. We had the upper flat of the rear house. One outside staircase served the upper flats of both houses. There must have been an inside toilet as I do not recall any privy. The rent was six dollars a month.

Our three neighbors in this new house were Irish Catholics. The woman in the upper flat of the front house and my mother became buddies in no time. They could not speak to each other, as my mother never learned to speak English, but there was a warm friendship between the two women. There were a few things Mother never gave up, even in her reduced circumstances. She continued to bake *chales*, the Sabbath loaves of white bread. As long as we lived in that flat, Mother never failed to bake an extra loaf of bread for Mrs. Teghanny.[2] And Mrs. Teghanny never failed to leave a bag of fruit on our doorstep on Friday, so we could have it for the Sabbath.

The Teghannys had no children and they were unhappy about it. But they started to lavish their affections on us. Mr. Teghanny drove a delivery truck to which were harnessed two fine-looking horses. We had great respect for those horses, when we compared them to the scrawny specimens that pulled the peddler's wagons. Mr. Teghanny's greatest joy was to get out into the middle of the street and play ball with us children. Then he would march all of us to the candy store and tell us to pick out the candy we wanted. What an array of penny candies there was in that showcase! There were long strips of paper with tiny blobs of white, pink, blue, and brown sugar concoctions, called "buttons." There were chocolate mice and roosters, kittens, and bunnies. There were chocolate creams, to which I almost never aspired, as they were a penny apiece and I would not spend my precious penny on just one piece of candy. Lemon drops were five for a penny and they were very popular. There were small peppermint sticks and gumdrops of all colors and flavors. The small flat circles of chocolate covered with tiny white sugar decorations were very elegant. On payday, Mr. Teghanny would always feel good and he would take us to the ice-cream parlor and buy ice-cream sodas for the gang.

I overheard an argument once between Mr. and Mrs. Teghanny. She accused him of spending too much money for "nonsense," as she called it. And he said: "Why should I worry about money? When I die they'll have to bury me for stink."

Mr. Teghanny was short and stocky with red kinky hair that stood up as if to assert itself. His wife was a good bit taller than he, and when she called him a "shrimp" he would answer: "Good goods come in small packages." And she would reply: "So does poison."

But their quarrels were always good-natured. They really adored each other.

Mother faced life with the heroism of the true American pioneer. She, and thousands of those immigrant mothers, earned a niche among the heroic women who helped build America. Here she was, with five small children, unable to speak the language of the country, with no training of any kind to earn a living. The only work she had ever done was to care for her family and her home. She had never known poverty.

She realized that she had to do something to keep us fed, housed, and clothed. This was a time in American history when it was degrading to accept charity. It was said that only loafers and bums could not find jobs. Mother was a living example of the falsity of that position.

The only work open to women in her position was either to scrub floors or do family washing. It never entered anybody's mind that Mother could do that kind of work. She was not strong enough for the work, and I am sure none of her relatives or friends would have allowed her to do it.

Some of the relatives finally solved the problem. Each contributed a small amount of money. They suggested that Mother buy tea, coffee, rice, sugar, and other staples, put them up in pound packages, and peddle them from door to door.[3]

At that time products were not packaged in the attractive boxes that are so popular today. Rice, flour, sugar, salt, barley, dried beans, peas, and many other staples were delivered to small grocery stores and each purchase was weighed and put into a cornucopia of heavy brown paper.

Mother bought a small scale. By this time paper bags had been invented and she spent the evening weighing the merchandise and arranging the bags in a large basket. Who will ever know how many stairs she had to climb to sell her goods, or how often she was rebuffed?

Mother's day would start with cooking breakfast for us and sending us off to school. Then, taking the two boys, who were too young to go to school, with her she would start out on her rounds, carrying the heavy basket. In time she managed to attract a good many people who were willing to buy from her. She added sugar, farina, and a few other staples to her basket. She was always home in time to give us our lunch, and then she would go out again in the afternoon. I shall never forget the weariness of her lovely face at the end of the day. She never told us that she was tired. She did not need to tell us; we saw it on her face.

Passover was approaching about this time, and some friends suggested that Mother try to sell matzos. So she walked miles to get the orders, weeks in advance. The work of delivering the matzos, the endless stairs to climb, was back-breaking work. My sister and I did all we could to help, but I am sure that the work injured her health.

The first Passover after Father's death stands out very clearly. In addition to Mother's work of selling, the house had to be cleaned. Windows had to be polished. Curtains had to be washed and stretched on wooden frames. All this she did after walking all day with a heavy basket on her arm.

The day before Passover Mother did not go out on her rounds. She spent the day cooking whatever she could afford to buy. It never occurred to her that her life had changed, as far as a holiday was concerned. Passover had been observed in Jewish homes since the days of Moses, and she was not going to let the holiday go by without the proper observance.

I did not quite know how the Seder would be conducted without Father. My sister and I waited anxiously to see what would happen. Mother had gone into the bedroom and had closed the door. The table had been set with the linen and dishes that had been brought from

Poland. The beautiful etched bottle of wine was on the table and all of the herbs that are used were in place. Before long Mother came out, dressed in her white dress with her white lace shawl on her head. Her eyes were red and we knew that she had been crying; but we said nothing. After all, even as children we felt she was entitled to her grief. While we stood about watching her movements, she seated herself at the head of the table and motioned us to our places. In a strong, resolute voice she started the immortal story of the emancipation of a people from slavery. "The Lord, our God, delivered us from bondage."

When my sister reached the legal age to work, which was fourteen at that time, she decided, and the decision was hers, that she ought to find some work that would help support the family. She found a job in a knitting factory, where gloves and mittens were knitted. The factory was located about a mile from the house, but she walked to and from work to save the five cents each way. I know she was eager to continue her schooling and I know what the sacrifice meant to her. She was a valiant little soldier. After she had been working in the factory several weeks, she decided to increase her earnings by bringing home some extra work. This work consisted of sewing up the fingertips on the gloves. So after running a machine all day, she walked home carrying a heavy bundle of gloves and mittens to be finished at home.

As soon as the evening meal had been eaten and the dishes cleared away, Mother and my sister would take their places at the table and sew mittens until late into the night. In the morning the brave little girl took her lunch and the bundle of finished mittens and trudged off to work all day at a knitting machine. It was a dreary existence for a young girl.

I could see Mother's health failing from day to day. Not only did she drag herself about every day with her heavy basket, but at night she cooked, baked, sewed, kept our clothes mended, and kept the house clean. And now she was taking on the added burden of helping my sister sew mittens. She often worked late into the night, insisting that my sister go to bed. Many nights I could not sleep and I heard Mother crying to herself. One night I crawled out of bed and looked through the crack in the door. I saw Mother sitting at the table sewing mittens, while the tears were dropping on her work.

> With fingers weary and worn
> With eyelids heavy and red.[4]

I crawled back to bed and cried myself to sleep.[5]

The next morning brought school and the tears were forgotten. The blessed gift of forgetting that only children seem to possess.

Mom takes on her own?: dad's roles

In the Jewish Training School, as a class was promoted, the teacher was not changed. A teacher stayed with her class for the first four years, so that my beloved Mrs. Torrance was still my teacher.

One day when we came to school she told us that her nephew, William Jennings Bryan, had been nominated for the presidency of America.[6] She seemed very happy and so we were all happy with her. As the campaign went on, she told us to ask our fathers to vote for William Jennings Bryan. I raised my hand and asked if my mother could vote for him, since my father had died. She asked me to stay after school that day, and after the children had left, she took me in her arms and told me I had been a brave little girl.

"Why can't my mother vote?" I persisted.

"Women cannot vote," she said stroking my hair.

In February 1898 I began to realize that America was at war.[7] There were many things about the war that I could not understand. I was puzzled by the things that happened every day. I had been told in school that I must not use the word "hell." But now the children came to school wearing huge buttons pinned to their dresses and coats with the words "Remember the Maine; to hell with Spain." What confused me even more was that Mrs. Torrance did not object to the buttons. I recall an assembly where we were told that our country was at war and we must do everything we could to help. I kept thinking, What can I do? It seemed that the only thing I could do was to wear a button with the forbidden word on it. That button bothered me. Why did I have to be profane to be patriotic? One day I asked Mrs. Torrance why she had told us not to use the word "hell" and then allowed us to wear the button with the word on it. I was told that in time of war things were different. I accepted her explanation, but I felt that I was giving up a certain decency on account of the war. Then I tried to justify this by thinking that it was a patriotic duty to hate Spain, and perhaps the only way I could show my hatred was to wear the button.

But the war was still bothering me. One day I asked Mother why we had to have wars. She said that there had been wars since the world began and that there always would be war. Her reasons for the war only confused me more. She said kings, czars, and emperors were all jealous of one another and always wanted to take land from one another, that is why we had wars. But, I argued, there is no king or emperor or czar in America and we still have war. She told me not to worry about it, but I still could not get it out of my head.

One day I said to Mother that maybe someday there would be a president in Germany and Russia, then there would be no more war.

This, she assured me, would never happen.

"The czar of Russia and the emperor of Germany have been chosen by God to rule over their countries," she said.

The day arrived when I began to feel that even mothers could be wrong.

The first moving-picture show appeared on Halsted Street.[8] It was named in honor of the price of admission: a nickel show. My playmates were excited over this new innovation, and I secretly made up my mind to see one of these shows as soon as I could get together the money for the price of admission. I was determined not to ask Mother for the nickel, as I knew we could not squander five cents on a show. Our neighbor now and then asked me to run an errand, for which I would get a penny. I was allowed to keep this penny so I could buy candy. But now I had a better use for the penny. Five errands would give me the much-desired nickel.

The nickel show was my introduction to the theater. I recall that it was not considered "nice" to go to this show. Some people, without knowing anything about it, labeled it as a sort of "den of iniquity." So without telling Mother or anybody else, my best pal and I sort of sneaked into the show.

The place had been a small store. At one end was the screen, which at that time was called a sheet. There were rickety folding chairs set up and an ancient piano was near the screen. Soon the lights were dimmed, and after some "oohing and aahing" on the part of the audience, which was composed of noisy children, the piano began to play and objects began to move across the screen. Was it possible for a horse and wagon to move across a sheet? But here it was, before our very eyes. And then, wonder of wonders—a fire engine raced across.

I came home breathless and told Mother what I had seen. She looked at me dubiously. Now what? she must have thought. She even put her hand to my forehead to see if I had a fever. At last she said that I must be mistaken. Perhaps I had had a bad dream from the night before. I told her just where the show was located and offered to take her to see it. She just looked at me with an unmistakable doubt in her eyes. I was disturbed. Was it possible that my mother did not believe me? I was determined to prove to her that I was right.

My sister and I planned a conspiracy. At the first opportunity we asked Mother to take a walk with us. We steered her to Halsted Street and as we passed the nickel show we pushed her in.

After that eventful episode, I think Mother would have believed anything we told her.

PART III

Growing Up with Hull-House, 1895–1912

I Discover Hull-House 7

Several days before Christmas 1896 one of my Irish playmates suggested that I go with her to a Christmas party at Hull-House.[1] I told her that I never went to Christmas parties.

"Why not?" she asked.

"I do not go anywhere on Christmas Day," I said.

"But this party will not be on Christmas Day. It will be the Sunday before Christmas Day," she said.

I repeated that I could not go and she persisted in wanting to know why. Before I could think, I blurted out the words: "I might get killed."

"Get killed!" She stared at me. "I go to Hull-House Christmas parties every year, and no one was ever killed."

I then asked her if there would be any Jewish children at the party. She assured me that there had been Jewish children at the parties every year and that no one was ever hurt.

The thought began to percolate through my head that things might be different in America. In Poland it had not been safe for Jewish children to be on the streets on Christmas. I struggled with my conscience and finally decided to accompany my friend to the Hull-House Christmas party. This was the second time that I was doing something without telling Mother.[2]

My friend and I arrived at Hull-House and went to the coffee shop where the party was being held. There were many children and their parents seated when we arrived. It was the first time that I had sat in a room where there was a Christmas tree. In fact, there were two trees in the room: one on each side of the high brick fireplace. The trees looked as if they had just been brought in from a heavy snowstorm. The glistening glass icicles and asbestos snow looked very real. The trees were lighted with white candles and on each side stood a man with a pail of water and a mop, ready to put out any accidental fire.

People called to each other across the room. Then I noticed that I could not understand what they were saying. It dawned on me that the people in this room had come from other countries. Yet there was no tension. Everybody seemed to be having a good time. There were children and parents at this party from Russia, Poland, Italy, Germany, Ireland, England, and many other lands, but no one seemed to care where they had come from, or what religion they professed, or what clothes they wore, or what they thought. As I sat there, I am sure I felt myself being freed from a variety of century-old superstitions and inhibitions. There seemed to be nothing to be afraid of.

Then Jane Addams came into the room! It was the first time that I looked into those kind, understanding eyes. There was a gleam of welcome in them that made me feel I was wanted. She told us that she was glad we had come. Her voice was warm and I knew she meant what she said. She was the second person who made me glad that I had come to America. Mrs. Torrance was the first.

The children of the Hull-House Music School then sang some songs, that I later found out were called "Christmas carols."[3] I shall never forget the caressing sweetness of those childish voices. All feelings of religious intolerance and bigotry faded. I could not connect this beautiful party with any hatred or superstition that existed among the people of Poland.

As I look back, I know that I became a staunch American at this party. I was with children who had been brought here from all over the world. The fathers and mothers, like my father and mother, had come in search of a free and happy life. And we were all having a good time at a party, as the guests of an American, Jane Addams.

We were all poor. Some of us were underfed. Some of us had holes in our shoes. But we were not afraid of each other. What greater service can a human being give to her country than to banish fear from the heart of a child? Jane Addams did that for me at that party.

While I felt that I had done nothing wrong or sinful by going to the Christmas party, I still hesitated telling Mother where I had been. I was glad that she did not ask me.

A Funeral 8

I did not go back to Hull-House that winter, as school kept me busy during the day and I was not allowed to go out after dark. Mother was not well and was unable to go about as much as usual on her selling expeditions. The day came when there was no money for coal and we sat shivering with cold. The portions of food became smaller. The only money that came into the house was what my sister earned when my mother was too ill to go out. Mother would not tell any of our relatives that we were in need, so we just stayed cold and a little hungry. The one thing that made life bearable for me at that time was going to school where it was warm.

In the spring, I saw Jane Addams for the second time.

Among my playmates were many children whose fathers worked in clothing factories. Some of them worked fourteen hours a day and still did not earn enough to support the family. At night they would bring home huge bundles of coats, vests, and pants for the family to finish.[1] The wives would do the handwork, sewing buttons, and little children would be put to work pulling the bastings.[2] The clothing industry was still primitive as no machines had been invented to make buttonholes or sew buttons.

Another home industry that was popular at that time was the making of cloth flowers for women's hats.[3] Much of this work was done in the homes near Hull-House. The women would gather around the kitchen table all the children who were old enough to wrap green paper around a wire stem and they would make flowers.

Of these young workers, the one who comes back to me most vividly is Carlotta, a beautiful Italian girl with haunting black eyes set in a pale face. She was about my age, and on rare occasions we would play jacks on the cement doorstep of the house where she lived. I remember how this simple game brought a sparkle into her otherwise sad eyes. She was not on the street as often as some of the other children, and one day I called her to come out and play. She came to the door and told me that she could not come out as she had to help her mother make flowers.

"Make flowers," I said. "You must be fooling; flowers are not made, they grow."

She took me by the hand and pulled me into the kitchen of a small dark flat. There on the table were piles of cloth petals of various colors, green leaves that had been stamped out on a machine, and coils of thin wire. Her mother and four children were sitting around the table making flowers. I left that room forever hating artificial flowers. Every time I saw a woman wearing a hat with flowers, I thought of Carlotta who could not come out to play.

Carlotta told me that her mother and two sisters and a brother worked almost every working hour at making flowers. The father had died of "the consumption," as it was then called. But with all this effort they did not earn enough to have adequate food. The flat, where the family lived, was dark and damp and many times they did not have enough money to buy enough coal to keep the place warm in the winter. And so little Carlotta became ill with the consumption and soon followed her father.

I remember the day when her frail little body was carried from the gloomy flat in a small, white-velvet-covered coffin. The weeping mother was supported by Jane Addams, who had placed a small bouquet of real flowers on the coffin.

It was incidents of this nature that caused Jane Addams to begin her untiring fight for humane child labor laws which have now become an accepted way of life for American children.

Twenty years later I came across a poem written by Florence Wilkinson Evans, a part of which I want to set down in memory of my little friend Carlotta.

> Lizabetta, Marianina, Fiametta, Teresina,
> They have never seen a rosebush nor a dew drop in the sun
> They will dream of the vendetta, Teresina, Fiametta
> Of the Black Hand and a face behind a grating;
> They will dream of cotton petals endless, crimson, suffocating,
> Never of a wild rose thicket or the singing of a cricket,
> But the ambulance will bellow through the wanness of their dreams,
> And their tired lids will flutter with the street's hysteric screams.
>
> Lizabetta, Marianina, Fiametta, Teresina,
> They are winding stems of roses, one by one, one by one.
> Let them have a long, long play time, Lord of toil, when toil is done,
> Fill their baby hands with roses, joyous roses of the sun.[4]

I started to brood over the condition of my family. What could I do to help? One bitter cold day, when the last bucket of coal had been put into the stove, I came to a decision. I would leave school and get a job.[5] That night I confided in my sister and asked her if I could get a job at the knitting factory. She looked at me with great compassion. She wanted me to continue going to school but she knew the few dollars I could earn meant more food, which we all needed, and more coal with which the stove insisted on being fed.

When she came home that evening she told me that she had spoken to the forelady and that I could have a job.

My First Job 9

I went to school and told Mrs. Torrance that I was not coming back to school. I shall never forget that leave-taking. I looked at the beloved—yes, beloved—blackboard where I had learned to write my first English words. The bright pictures on the wall, the cutouts pasted on the windows, the desk, all seemed dear to me that day. My desk, at which I had spent the first happy years in America. I had finished the fifth grade at the time. I was fourteen years old.[1] It looked as if this would be the end of my schooling.

Mother shed many tears when I told her that I was going to work. But she realized that there was nothing else to do and she agreed to the plan. It was God's will, she said, and we had to accept it.

The first day that I left the house with my small bundle of lunch under my arm was a day of inner struggle for a little girl. I had mixed emotions in my heart. I was glad that I could help feed the family, but I could not forget that I would not go to school again. I did not realize at the time that it was possible to study away from school and that there were classes at Hull-House.

Of that eventful day, when I went to work for the first time, many memories keep coming to me. It was still dark when we left the house. We walked down what was then Twelfth Street, now known as Roosevelt Road, over many viaducts and a bridge that spanned the Chicago River and the railroad tracks. It was beginning to get light as we approached the river and I could not help comparing the dirty, slimy water with the clear sparkling water of my dear Vistula.

We arrived at State Street and walked down a flight of stairs to the street below.[2] The factory looked very large and imposing to me. It was a six-story brick building. We got into the elevator, my first elevator ride, and were taken to the fourth floor, I believe. There my name was taken and I presented my working permit. I had become an adult and a worker at the age of fourteen.

I was assigned to a knitting machine and a girl was stationed at my side to teach me the complicated rudiments of knitting. There were about four hundred machines in the room, which covered an entire floor of the building. In front of each machine sat a girl or woman on a high stool. I had no difficulty learning the trade and I was soon able to earn four dollars a week. The work was piecework, and the harder one worked, the more one made. But the pay was so regulated that even the fastest worker could not make over five dollars a week. At that time, however, five dollars would buy food for a family of six. So between my sister's and my pay the family could exist.

We worked from seven thirty in the morning till six in the evening, six days a week.[3] We had a half hour for lunch, which we ate sitting in front of the machine. There were no towels provided for drying hands before eating. Paper towels had not yet been invented. So we brought towels from home.

I had been working there about two weeks when, during the morning, I heard the most agonizing shriek I had ever heard. Soon the power stopped and it became so quiet that our hearts almost stopped beating. Quiet except for the piercing shriek that kept coming from across the room. My sister came up to me and put her arms around me and told me not to be afraid. A girl had caught her hand in the machine. The machine had to be taken apart before the poor girl could be freed. At that time there was no law stipulating that machines had to be equipped with safety devices.

Several months after I started working in the knitting factory, the doors of the toilets were removed so that there was no privacy while performing natural functions. The reason given for this utter lack of consideration was that girls were spending too much time in the toilet. This could not be true, as the girls were eager to make as much money as possible and no one could earn money sitting in the toilet.

Very often a machine would break down, and we had to wait till the repairman came to fix it.[4] Sometimes that would take an hour or more and that time was lost by the worker. That meant less money in the weekly pay envelope. Each machine had about eighty needles, and while running at full speed a needle would jump out of place and break. This was no fault of the worker, but in addition to losing time to change the needle, we had to pay a penny for it.

During the weeks of getting adjusted to work in the factory I did not go to Hull-House. I was usually so tired in the evening that I was glad to just eat supper, help with the dishes, and go to bed. So for several months I had no idea what Hull-House offered in the way of classes and recreation.

One evening, as my sister and I were leaving the factory, we saw a man at the entrance with his arms full of leaflets. As each girl came out of the building she was handed a leaflet. We read it in front of a lamppost. We were being asked to come to a meeting to help organize a union.[5] My sister and I talked about it all the way home. She was reluctant about going. She was always more cautious than I was. I, however, decided to go to the meeting.

This was my introduction to trade unionism. About one hundred girls and a few men were gathered in a small smoky room. A man called the meeting to order and told us of the advantages of an organized union. He urged us to organize a union. When he had finished his formal talk, he asked if anyone had anything to say. There was a dead silence. And then, impulsively, I rose and said that I had a lot to say. The words came tumbling out of my mouth as if they had been stored within me. I asked the girls why we had to pay for broken needles that were broken accidentally. Why was there only one mechanic to keep all those machines in repair? Why did we not object to having the doors removed from the toilets? Were we not entitled to some privacy and a little decency? That was all the meeting needed; a reminder of real grievances. The union was organized that night.

The next morning when I came to work I was called into the forelady's office and given whatever pay I had coming and was told that I was a troublemaker and that I was to get out and never come back.

The bookkeeper had been sent to the meeting and she had reported the part I had played in helping to organize the union. And so ended my four-year career as a knitter.

While walking to work that morning, I thought it would be fine to work in the union. It would take some of the monotony out of the work, for one thing, and it would be good for everybody to have something to say about working conditions. But now my career as a knitter was over and I wondered it there were other unions.

I left the factory, strangely enough, not depressed. I was not sorry for what I had said at the meeting, but I was not impressed with the importance of the trade union movement. I had no idea of the stirring events that were to follow in the days to come. The fact that the first years of my life had been spent in a home where there was no want and where I had never heard of trade unionism or labor troubles of any kind may have had something to do with it.

As I had the whole day before me, I decided to walk downtown. I had heard about the elegant part of State Street, which I had never seen.[6] So far, the only part of State Street that I knew was the sordid, filthy block I had covered each morning and evening. Every house on that block was a house of prostitution. Even early in the morning, as I walked by on my way to work, I saw women and often young girls sitting in the windows or standing in the doorways, beckoning to men who passed by. It was a strange contrast between the two sections of State Street, only one mile apart. One where there was nothing but degradation, and the other where magnificent stores offered all the decencies and even the luxuries of life.

During that one-mile walk all sorts of thoughts kept running through my head. I thought of that speech that the forelady had made to me, telling me that I was ungrateful. What was I supposed to be grateful for? For the privilege of working ten hours a day, six days a week, for four dollars and fifty cents?

Being called a foreign troublemaker stuck in my throat and almost choked me.

I thought of the conversations that Uncle Mischa had had with Father about the conditions of the tailors. You either worked long hours or not at all. And when you did not work, you did not eat.

All of a sudden I was in front of the Marshall Field store. I walked in. To my surprise no one paid any attention to me. No one asked me what I wanted. I wandered about and no one objected. I walked down the aisles, admiring the displays and wondering how many people had the money to buy all those things.

I found myself in front of an elevator and heard the words "Going up." So I went up. When I heard the operator call "Third floor, waiting room," I stepped out and walked to the famous Marshall Field waiting room.[7]

I sank into a luxurious chair and just sat there watching the well-dressed people.

How many times have I thought of that day? Every time I rested between shopping, or when I would meet friends there, that day came back to me. That wonderful room, where people from all over the world met and greeted friends. I have a very warm feeling for that room.

After resting for a while, I decided to find out if there was anything else worth seeing. The thought of looking for a job did not enter my head. For this one day I was a free soul, doing just what I wanted to do. I walked through the book department, looked at the wonderful displays of china and glassware, at silks and satins and velvet.

I left the store and walked down Michigan Avenue and sat on a bench in Grant Park, where I ate my lunch. I looked about me and saw an interesting building down the street. It was the only building on that side of the street. My curiosity was aroused and I walked over. It was the Chicago Art Institute, and it happened to be a free day. I walked in and stood looking at the broad staircase. I wandered from room to room. The pictures looked down from the walls. The statues seemed to greet me. All the sordidness of the world was blotted out. There was only beauty in the world.

As I look back on that day, I wonder how I managed to crowd all the events into one day. I went to the public library next. I was very much impressed with all the marble and inlaid designs. I went up to the fourth floor and found myself in the reference room; there before my eyes was Lake Michigan. It had been about eight years since I had come to Chicago, and this was my first glimpse of the lake. I stood there for a long time, thinking of my father's words. Yes, Lake Michigan was big! I would have to see much more of it. I was almost glad I had been fired from my job.

When I got home that evening and told Mother that I had lost my job, she was understandably disturbed. She was afraid of hunger and cold, not so much for herself as for the rest of us. Food, coal, clothing, and shelter had become her only interests in life.

Being young, I began to rebel against a life that offered only food and warmth and shelter. There were all those books in the public library, and I wanted to read some of them. There were pictures on the walls of the Art Institute and I wanted to look at them. And I wanted to look at Lake Michigan.

After our meager supper had been eaten, I realized that no matter how meager the meal had been, it still had to be bought and paid for.

I assured Mother that I would find another job soon. I would start to look for one first thing in the morning. I was confident that I would find some work.

Growing Up 10

My sister was getting ready to go to work the next morning when I woke up. I was grateful that she had not been discharged, too. I walked to the corner of Halsted and De Koven streets and bought a newspaper.[1] I brought it home and sat down to scan the want ads.

I was amazed at the number of jobs listed. People were wanted to make overalls, neckties, caps, shirtwaists, skirts, dresses, pajamas, kimonos, petticoats, and a host of other things. I began to look at all these commodities that we used every day in a different light. I had just taken things for granted. They were in the stores and we bought them. But now I began to realize that somebody had to make all these things before they could get to the stores, that everything we wore and used in our daily routine of living had a little bit of human effort in it.

Among all those want ads I was sure I would find a job. So I jotted down a few on a piece of paper and started out. That first day I applied at a shirt factory, a cap factory, a necktie factory, and a kimono factory. But everywhere they wanted experienced help only. I found nothing that first day. Nor did I find a job on the second or third day. Things were beginning to look pretty grim.

During those few days that I was home part of the time when I wasn't looking for a job, I watched Mother prepare our frugal meals. For the first time since coming to Chicago I got a nostalgic feeling for Poland. I thought of the well-filled baskets that had been brought from the market and sighed.

I recall that during those days of food scarcity, Mother would cook a wonderful meal of calf's liver, gravy, and mashed potatoes. She would cook this several times a week. I soon discovered that when she bought a few pounds of meat, the butcher would give her a calf's liver free. Does this bring a smile to your face when you stop to think what calf's liver costs today? Well, at that time calf's liver was considered only fit for dogs and cats. But my wise mother had learned in Poland, long before the word "vitamins" was heard, that liver was one of the best foods.

I remember that, at that time, they used to tell jokes in vaudeville theaters about liver. The story was that a little boy was sent to the butcher shop to get ten cents' worth of liver for the cat. "Be sure it's tender," said the boy. "The last time my father said it was too tough."

I was without work for about a week and Mother was beginning to worry about the rent, which was six dollars a month. There really was nothing to worry about. During the time that we lived in this small flat, our landlord, Mr. McCartney, had never come to the house to ask for his rent. He owned considerable property in another part of the city, where he lived. He would come around several times a month and sort of putter around in the yard. When his tenants saw him they would lean out of the windows and call him to come and get his rent. So I was sure we would not be evicted.

Not only did Mr. McCartney not ask for his rent, but he used to bring us gifts of candy and fruit. I will never forget when he came over just before Passover and without saying anything to Mother, he took my three small brothers to the neighborhood department store and bought each of them a complete outfit, consisting of suits, shirts, underwear, caps, hose, and shoes. Then he sent them home, each carrying a package. He did not come into the house, as he told us later he did not want to be thanked. When Mother finally did get the chance to thank him, he said: "Shucks, I got so much pleasure doing it, it was cheap." I wonder if there are any landlords like that in existence today?

Mother had been talking to all of the neighbors, asking them if they knew where I could find a job. One of them finally came in and told us that she had spoken to the foreman in the factory where she worked and he said he was willing to try me. So the next morning she called for me and we set out.

I got the job! But I was told that it was piecework and that I could not expect to earn any money until I had learned how to operate an electric sewing machine. I was assigned to a machine and our good neighbor was given the job of teaching me. She worked on a weekly basis. Her job was to teach all newcomers.

While waiting for my first lesson in the art of making shirtwaists,[2] I overheard my forelady talking to a man: "I don't want any experienced girls. They are too smart and too fresh, and they want good wages. And they turn out less work. Give me the 'greenhorns'—Italian girls, Polish girls, Jewish girls, who can't speak English. Girls who have just come from the Old Country don't know how much they can earn. I make them work hard like the devil. And they work for whatever wages they get."

I soon learned that the conditions described by the forelady prevailed in all factories before trade unions were organized.

The hours were from eight to six, with a half hour for lunch, five and a half days a week. We did not work Saturday afternoon. This was an improvement in working conditions, and I learned very quickly. I was determined to earn as much as possible to make up for lost time.

As I look back on the methods used in the factory at that time, I have a feeling that it was the beginning of the assembly line in industry. No one made a complete shirtwaist. My job consisted of making cuffs. So for ten hours a day I sewed cuffs. The deadly monotony of this work was worse than the actual work.

One day the girl working next to me brought a paperbound book with her, which she read while eating her lunch. I made it my business to find out what she was reading. I do not remember the name of the book, but it was written by Bertha M. Clay.[3] Seeing that I was interested, the girl said that I could have the book when she had finished it. I took it home and sat up half the night reading it. It was all about an elegant lady, dressed in silks and satins and laces, who was having an awful time with her lovers. It seems that many men were in love with her and she had to decide who was worthy of her love. She finally decided and married and "lived happily ever after."

I must confess that the first Bertha M. Clay book brought a sort of glow. For a little while I could forget cuffs. But when I read the second book by the then-popular author, I had the feeling that I had already read it. Then I discovered that the only difference in her books was a change of name and locale.

One evening in 1900, after a particularly boring day at the factory, I decided to walk over to Hull-House three blocks from where I lived.[4] I had not been there since that eventful Christmas party.

This event marked the beginning of a new life for me.

I was lucky. Jane Addams happened to be in the reception room when I came in. She came up to me and asked me whether I would like to join a club or a class or perhaps the gymnasium. For a moment I just stood there looking at her. Her face made me forget cuffs and monotony.

"I really don't know what I want," I said. "I have never been here at night."

"Have you been here before?" she asked.

"Yes, to a Christmas party," I said.

"You come with me," she said, taking my hand. "I think you will like to do this."

She took me up a flight of stairs and then down a flight and we came to the Labor Museum.[5] The museum had been opened a short time before and it was a very special addition to the work at Hull-House and very dear to her heart. As I look back, and this may be wishful thinking, I feel that she sensed what I needed most at that time. She turned me over to Miss Mary Hill, who had charge of the museum.[6] I believe that I became the first student in that endeavor.

Miss Hill started out by taking me on a tour of the museum. Our first stop was in front of four cases that had been set up against a wall. These cases showed the evolution of cotton, wool, silk, and linen. I recall how surprised I was when I discovered that cotton grew out of the ground. I had never thought just how the cotton cloth that I worked with every day was made. I could not tear myself away from the case. Miss Hill started explaining the exhibit.

First, here was the plant; then the various steps of getting the plant ready for spinning it into thread. Then there was the finished piece of cloth in the natural color. Then pieces of cotton cloth that had been dyed. Next in line was a case exhibiting the process of making silk. There were the cocoons in which the silkworm lived. Then the whole process of making the silk thread into fabric. The case on wool fairly made my eyes pop out of my head. I had seen sheep many times, but it never occurred to me that wool came from sheep. So here were photographs of the sheep being sheared. Then how the wool was carded by hand, before combing machines had been invented. There were several methods of spinning the wool, from the most primitive to the most modern. The flax exhibit was a real surprise. I had seen fine linen such as tablecloths and napkins. I had even worn linen dresses. But I did not know that linen was made also of a plant. Here was the flax in the case. Pictures illustrated how the flax was prepared for spinning, how the fibers clung to each other to make it possible to spin it into thread.

When we had finished looking at the cases, Miss Hill asked me whether I would like to learn to weave something that was typically American. Yes, I was ready to learn almost anything. So she brought out a small frame, several balls of heavy cotton cord, and several balls of various colors of wool, and very soon I was weaving a small Navaho-style blanket.

Saturday night was the big night at the museum. It was open to the public and special exhibits were on display. There were two women spinning and one woman weaving. Mrs. Brasnahan [*sic*], I think that was her name, was a plump, good-natured Irish woman, whom I learned to love.[7] She used a spinning wheel with great skill. I was fascinated by her deft hands which gently coaxed the linen thread from the bunch of flax on her spindle. The wheel was operated by a treadle which she gently operated with her foot. The turning of the wheel wound the thread onto a spool.

The other spinner was an Italian, whose name, I believe, was

Mrs. Molinari.[8] Although she did not understand English, we did carry on a friendship in sign language. Mrs. Molinari showed the type of spinning that was done before the spinning wheel was invented. She would pull a thread about a yard long from the bunch of flax that had been arranged on a sort of stick and would have to stop, unhook the thread from a small hook, and wind up the thread by hand. It was a rather slow process, but that was how linen thread was spun for generations, before machinery was invented for spinning.

The woman who did the weaving used the thread that Mrs. Brasnahan and Mrs. Molinari had spun. The thread had been dyed at Hull-House so that we soon learned the entire process of the making of cloth.

Another very popular exhibit was the potter's wheel.[9] A bent little old man was sitting on a stool making the wheel go round by manipulating the bottom part of the wheel with his foot. He would slap a lump of clay on the top of the wheel and with his two hands would shape that lump of clay into a perfectly rounded bowl. The crowds of people who would gather around this little man always gasped at the skill he had in those magic hands.

There were many classes connected with the Labor Museum. Here we could learn how to cook and sew and also learn about millinery and embroidery. My first lessons in cross-stitch embroidery were given to me by Miss Hannig.[10] The first time I met Miss Hannig she was embroidering a strip of green linen with gold-colored thread. I became interested, and she said she was making a bedspread for Miss Addams's bed. Would I like to help? I said I would and she proceeded to give me my first lesson in cross-stitch embroidery. After I had satisfied her, she gave me a strip of the green linen, and so I embroidered one of the strips that made up a beautiful spread. How privileged I feel today to have had a part in the making of that spread. I wonder if it is still in existence?

There was still another function that the Labor Museum filled.[11] Miss Addams found that there was a definite feeling of superiority on the part of children of immigrants toward their parents. As soon as the children learned to speak English, they were prone to look down on those who could not speak the language. I am grateful that I never had that feeling toward my parents, but I often talked to playmates who would disdainfully say: "Aw, she can't talk English."

I recall having an argument with a girl whose mother could speak German, French, Russian, and Polish but had not yet learned to speak English. That girl did not realize that her mother was a linguist. To her, the mother was just a greenhorn.

For such children the Labor Museum was an eye-opener. When

they saw crowds of well-dressed Americans standing around admiring what Italian, Irish, German, and Scandinavian mothers could do, their disdain for their mothers often vanished.

The Labor Museum did not solve all the problems of immigrant parents and their children. There were many problems that were not easy to solve. Children, by going to school and to work, did come in contact with forces in American life and had a better chance of becoming Americanized. But I am sure the Labor Museum reduced the strained feelings on the part of immigrants and their children.

I remember going to the home of a friend whose father was a tailor. This girl had been attending some classes at the Labor Museum and had learned all about the making of cloth. When her father came home from work, she proudly told him what she had learned and that she was glad that her father worked with cloth.

Miss Hill was the first person who invited me to dinner. I had never eaten outside of my home. I hesitated to accept her invitation; she wanted to know why I did not want to come.

"Oh, I want to come," I said, "but I have never eaten anyplace else and maybe I would not know how to act."

"You don't have to act," she said kindly. "Just eat the way you eat at home."

So I agreed to come. On the appointed evening I arrived wearing a clean cotton dress and my hair in perfect order. Miss Hill took me to the coffeehouse and we sat down at a small, black, square table that had no tablecloth. Strange, how this insignificant detail comes back to me. The thought ran through my head that my mother always used a tablecloth when we had company.

Miss Hill asked me if I would like a lamb chop. I was terrified at the thought of eating meat that was not kosher. So I asked her if I could have eggs. She said yes, of course, in fact there was a very nice mushroom omelet on the bill of fare and we would both have it. I ate the omelet, which was very good, but I was tortured with the question of whether the mushrooms were kosher. I had eaten mushrooms many times in soup that Mother prepared, but I had not yet learned the English word "mushrooms."

I soon branched out into other activities. I joined a reading class that was conducted by Miss Clara Landsberg.[12] My fondest recollection of her is that at Christmas that year she presented me with a copy of *Sonnets from the Portuguese* by Elizabeth Barrett Browning.

Miss Landsberg was a fragile, ethereal, gentle woman. I often thought that she did not get enough to eat. She opened new vistas in reading for me. In her class we would be assigned a book, which we were to read during the week and then discuss at the following session of the class. The class met once a week. I not only read the assigned books but every book I could borrow. Dickens, Scott, Thackeray, Louisa May Alcott, Victor Hugo, Alexander Dumas, and many others now became my friends. The daily monotony of making cuffs was eased by thinking of these books and looking forward to evenings at Hull-House.

For ten years I spent most of my evenings at Hull-House. The first three years of that time I saw Jane Addams almost every night. As more and more people found their way to this haven of love and understanding, she began to relegate the work to other people and to seek rest at the home of friends. But her presence was always felt, whether she was there in person or in spirit.[13]

11 The Oasis in the Desert

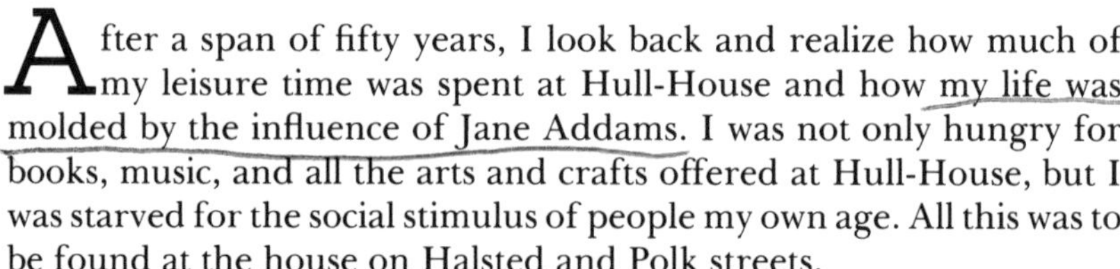

After a span of fifty years, I look back and realize how much of my leisure time was spent at Hull-House and how my life was molded by the influence of Jane Addams. I was not only hungry for books, music, and all the arts and crafts offered at Hull-House, but I was starved for the social stimulus of people my own age. All this was to be found at the house on Halsted and Polk streets.

My family had moved to Bunker Street near Des Plaines Avenue.[1] The street was covered with small two-family houses with cottages in the rear of each house. The only pretentious building in the neighborhood was the Langdon Apartment Building, which was said to have steam heat.[2] This was not its chief claim to fame. The great Clarence Darrow lived there and I saw him almost every day.[3] Our family lived in four small rooms. Half of each week, during the winter, the rooms were filled with wet laundry. Since the clothes were all wrung by hand, it took several days to get the clothes dry. It was no place in which to entertain friends, so while I ate and slept there, I really lived at Hull-House.

There were few activities that I allowed to slip by me. How well I remember the exciting news that a prince was to visit Hull-House. I created a mental picture for myself of a prince. He would wear blue satin knee breeches, a silk shirt with many ruffles, a purple velvet coat with golden buttons, and a big hat with an ostrich plume.

I was at Hull-House when the prince arrived and I dashed out to see him alight from the royal carriage.

I saw a one-horse hack, somewhat spattered with Chicago mud, stop in front of Hull-House and Miss Addams stepped out. She was followed by a short, round-shouldered man with a gray beard. He wore a battered old hat and a Prince Albert coat which was much too large for him. It sort of hung on his shoulders. But he was a prince. He was Prince Peter Kropotkin of Russia, who had come to America to lecture, and while he was in Chicago he stayed at Hull-House as the guest of Jane Addams.[4]

I attended the lecture that he gave the next day. His subject was "Factories, Fields, and Workshops," and I can still remember his vivid description of girls working in match factories. The girls had to carry large pans of sulphur on their heads to supply the match dippers. After a few years of this kind of work, the girls lost all their hair and became bald. Many of the girls died while very young as a result of this work. He was sure that matches could be made of some substance that would not be so destructive to human life.

I had the great privilege of speaking to him during his stay at Hull-House. He was a gentle, kind old man, and I loved him. I told him that I had heard his lecture and that I was deeply touched by what he had said. He said he was glad to see young people interested in the important things of life. Then he leaned forward and kissed me on the forehead.

But I am afraid I fell from grace the next evening. He happened to be passing the room where the dancing class was meeting and he saw me dance. When I saw him, I came out into the vestibule where he was standing and greeted him.

"I am disappointed in you," he said. "How can you give time to anything as frivolous as dancing?"

Another visitor from Russia had an entirely different temperament. Katarina Breshkovsky was in her seventies when she was at Hull-House but she had her moments of lightheartedness.[5] She was in the front ranks of that company of people who had opposed the regime of the czar, and although she was said to be of noble birth, she had been arrested and spent thirty years in a Russian prison. Her spirit was dauntless. I remember her at a ball that was given in her honor, where she lifted her skirt and danced a little Russian folk dance.

Another occasion connected with Russia was a tour of a Russian theatrical company headed by Alla Nazimova and Paul Orleneff.[6] This company was brought to Chicago and sponsored by some wealthy women who were interested in the theater and were eager to see a Russian play. I think that most of the tickets were bought up by these women and a certain number of them were sent to Hull-House. Miss Addams gave me two tickets and I saw *Tsar Feodor* in Russian.[7] I did not understand a word, but the costumes, scenery, and the acting were very impressive.

Then one Sunday afternoon Miss Addams gave a tea for the actors.[8] I remember Nazimova dressed in a thin gray dress holding a single American Beauty rose with a long stem in her hand.

President William McKinley was assassinated in Buffalo, New York, two years after the visit of Prince Peter Kropotkin to Hull-House.[9] A newspaper at that time editorialized that Hull-House was to blame for the assassination, as the prince, who called himself an "anarchist," had been entertained there. I wonder if that editorial writer thought that anarchists were being bred at Hull-House? There were anarchists at the time of the Haymarket incident, before Hull-House came into being. And there were presidents assassinated before the advent of Hull-House. Or did the editorial writer forget about President Lincoln and President Garfield?

Jane Addams was a firm believer in freedom of speech and freedom of the press.[10] And people of all shades of opinion were allowed to speak at Hull-House. I remember her saying: "If anarchists are wrong, it is our duty to show them what is right by precepts and not by silencing them."

Not all events at Hull-House centered around celebrities. I began to see weeping women sitting in the reception room. They were always shabbily dressed, with black shawls tied on their heads. On several occasions I acted as interpreter, if the women were Jewish and could not speak English. On one of these occasions I asked a bewildered woman what she wanted. She told me that a policeman had come to her house and had taken her little boy to the police station and that she did not know what to do. When I told this to Miss Addams, she told me to ask the woman how old the boy was and what he had done. The boy was seven years old,[11] and here the woman began to cry hysterically. He was about to take a bottle of milk from a neighbor's doorstep when the neighbor came out and pulled the boy into the house and called a policeman.

I found out later that the little boy had heard his mother tell his father that she had no money for milk, and he merely wanted to help.

The grief-stricken woman told me that another neighbor had told her that no matter what troubles came, you could always get help at Hull-House. When I told this to Miss Addams, her kind eyes and warm smile assured the woman that she had come to the right place.

The very next evening, while we were eating supper, a neighbor came in and told Mother in Polish that her small grandson had been taken away by a policeman. I left my supper uneaten and took the poor woman to Hull-House. I found out later that the eleven-year-old boy had stolen some coal from a freight car which had been left on a siding. When later he had been asked why he did it, he said that his grandmother was cold and that anyway there was a lot more coal in the train, that he had only taken a little bit.

These groups of bewildered people became a familiar sight to me. They were indeed the "huddled masses yearning to breathe free" that Emma Lazarus spoke of in her poem. While the Statue of Liberty welcomed them to America, it was Jane Addams who took them to her warm and generous heart.

Bad housing of the thousands of immigrants who lived near Hull-House was the concern of Jane Addams. Where there were alleys in back of the houses, these alleys were filled with large wooden boxes where garbage and horse manure were dumped. In most cases these boxes did not have covers and were breeding places for flies and rats. The city gave contracts to private scavengers to collect the garbage. Its responsibility seemed to end there. There was no alley inspection and no one checked up on these collectors.

When Jane Addams called the attention of the health department to the unsanitary conditions, she was told that the city had contracted to have the garbage collected and it could do nothing else. When the time came to renew contracts for garbage collection, Miss Addams, with the backing of some businessmen, put in a bid to collect garbage.[12] Her bid was never considered, but she was appointed garbage inspector for the ward. I have a vision of Jane Addams, honored by the great of the world, acclaimed as the first citizen of Chicago, following a filthy garbage truck down an alley in her long skirt and immaculate white blouse.

The Great Fire of 1871 had left Chicago without homes. The fire had taken place in October, and the people were eager to get some sort of houses for the winter. In their eagerness for shelter, they often overlooked the need for sanitation.

Small wooden houses were erected with the greatest possible speed.[13] If a man owned a lot and could get some lumber, nails, and a hammer, he was permitted to build a home for his family. If he could not afford to buy the plumbing equipment, an outdoor privy was permitted.

In 1872 the real estate dealers were making the most of the situation. They were interested in putting up houses as cheaply as possible and selling or renting them for as much as possible. A house with plumbing was very expensive; so wherever it was possible to avoid plumbing, it was avoided.

The cry was: "Rebuild Chicago! Do it fast! People must have homes for winter."

As long as the houses were occupied by one family, the situation was bearable. But immigrants began to flood Chicago, and people who probably had invested all the money they had in their houses saw a chance to make a little money. So the small houses were converted into two-, three-, and even four-family units. Cottages were built in all the yard spaces and became known as rear houses. During all this feverish rebuilding, again no thought was given to sanitation. The problem of sewage disposal for the increased population seemed to bother no one, until a typhoid fever epidemic appeared.

Hull-House was in the Nineteenth Ward of Chicago. The people of Hull-House were astounded to find that while the ward had 1/36th of the population of the city, it registered 1/6th of the deaths from typhoid fever.[14] Miss Addams and Dr. Alice Hamilton launched an investigation that has become history in the health conditions of Chicago.

At first it was rumored that during heavy rains the defective sewers would back up and the loathsome deposits from the privies would spread through the streets. Many of the pipes supplying drinking water were found to be defective, so the polluted sewage would seep into the drinking water, spreading the germs of typhoid fever.

It was found that 52 percent of the population of the ward had broken the health laws. It is ironic to think that the 48 percent that had obeyed the law suffered just as much as the law evaders. Typhoid fever germs are not respecters of the law.

For some time it was believed that the common housefly was the great carrier of the typhoid fever germs, and so we all bought flypaper and flyswatters to kill flies. But it was a losing fight, since most of the houses had no screens on the windows. I found out later that the fly was not the cause of the epidemic. Dr. Hamilton, in her book *Exploring the Dangerous Trades,* had this to say to vindicate the fly:

> My flies had little or nothing to do with the cases of typhoid fever in the Nineteenth Ward. The cause was simpler but so much more discreditable that the Board of Health had not dared to reveal it. It seems that in our local pumping station, on West Harrison Street, near Halsted, a break had occurred which resulted in an escape of sewage into the water pipes and for three days our neighborhood drank that water before the leak was discovered and stopped. This was after the epidemic had started. The truth was more shocking than my ingenious theory, and it never came to light, as far as the public was concerned.

Whatever the causes of the epidemic, that investigation, emanating from Hull-House, brought about the knowledge of the sanitary conditions of the Nineteenth Ward and brought about the changes that we enjoy today.

An incident that stands out in my memory is going with Dr. Hamilton to a rag shop not far from Hull-House to "gather some dust," as she put it. She was at the time making a study of tuberculosis, which was widespread in the neighborhood.[15] I saw a pile of damp rags on the floor of the filthy shop and asked one of the ragpickers where they came from. She told me that they had been brought from a garbage dump and that they would be dried and then sold. After all these years, I still recall how I shuddered at the thought.

The bathing problem in the neighborhood was no small matter. I still recall the huge kettles of water being heated on the stove and the washtub being dragged into the kitchen for our weekly baths. But we did get scrubbed once a week. There were, however, many people in the neighborhood who did not have the stamina for carrying kettles of hot water. This led to a discussion of public baths, one day. One of our German neighbors was telling my mother that in Germany she would go to a public bath whenever she wanted a bath. By this time I had the feeling that Hull-House was a place from which "all blessings flow," and I asked somebody if there were any public baths there. I was told where the public bath was. I found out later that it was through the efforts of Jane Addams that this public bath had been established.[16]

Miss Addams had for some time felt the need for public baths. But whenever the subject was brought before the city authorities, they argued that it would be a waste of public funds as people would not use the baths. And they cited as a horrible example the family who had used the bathtub as a coal bin.

So Jane Addams set out to prove that people would bathe if they had the facilities. She had three baths installed in the basement of Hull-House and opened them to the public. In her own words: "Our contention was justified by the immediate and overflowing use of the public baths. . . ."[17]

Armed with the proof that many people were clamoring for public baths, the Board of Health opened the first public bathhouse in Chicago. In fact, the lot on which the public bath was erected was donated to the city by a friend of Hull-House, and this made it possible for the city to erect the bathhouse for the small, almost insignificant appropriation of ten thousand dollars.[18]

Yes, Hull-House was an oasis in a desert of disease and monotony. And monotony can become a disease. The work at the factory, the making of cuffs, and more and more cuffs, had a dulling effect on all my senses. The only variation in this deadly monotony was that some days the cuffs would be blue and other days they would be green or pink or yellow. But the thought of going to Hull-House in the evening made the day's work bearable.

And then there was the possibility of seeing Jane Addams in action, a woman with that supreme faith that the world could be made into a better place for the whole human race. One evil condition after another was brought to the attention of city authorities, in a patient, simple, but resolute manner. The problems of the immigrants, who were to play a significant part in the pattern of American life, were brought to the surface, waking the conscience of Chicago.

Hull-House became a laboratory for experiments in human needs. These experiments were so ably demonstrated that the city fathers could not ignore them.[19]

The first playground in Chicago was one of these experiments.[20] Jane Addams had long felt the need for playgrounds, not only for Hull-House, but for the entire city. How to prove the need?

A rich young man who probably knew nothing about Hull-House inherited some property in the neighborhood. He came to look over his property and went to Hull-House to see Miss Addams. He told her he was mildly interested in what she was doing. People who were mildly interested when they first came to Hull-House became enthusiasts after talking to her for a while. So sure was she of what she was doing that she had no difficulty in inspiring her listeners and winning them over to what she was doing.

The man then told her of the property he had inherited and that he would like to help her with the work at Hull-House.

Jane Addams knew about the property in question. Not only was it not fit for human habitation, but it was being rented to people who used it for prostitution.

She suggested that he might begin right there by tearing down the rotting buildings.

He went away to think about it.

In a few days he returned and said he had decided to turn the property over to Jane Addams. Well, there was not much she could do with the property as it was. How would he like to have all the houses torn down, pay for the job, and turn the lots into a playground?

Well, he thought that was asking too much. But he finally agreed to do what Jane Addams had asked him to do and so the first playground was born in Chicago.

That playground became an example for the entire country. And today, not only has Chicago the finest system of playgrounds, but the city also supports the best system of social centers.

I remember the happy voices coming from that first playground; and no longer did children have to dodge horses.

Jane Addams was never condescending to anyone. She never made one feel that she was a "lady bountiful." She never made one feel that she was doling out charity. When she did something for you, you felt she owed it to you or that she was making a loan that you could pay back.

The most forlorn scrubwoman received the same warm welcome as the wealthy supporters of the house. I remember one day the daughter of a wealthy family had come to Hull-House to help in the reception room, and an old shabby woman came in and asked for Miss Addams. Looking down at the poor woman, the young lady started to tell her that Miss Addams was busy and could not be disturbed, just as Miss Addams was coming down the stairs. She quickly told the young lady that perhaps she had better go home. Then she took the old woman by the arm and said she was just going to have a cup of tea and would she join her. Then she led her to the coffeehouse, where she listened to a tale of woe.

America has not yet awakened to the realization of what it owes to Jane Addams. No one will ever know how many young people were helped by her wise council, how many were kept out of jail, how many were started on careers in the arts, in music, in industry, in science, and above all in instilling in their hearts a true love of country—a love of service.

My sister and I were now earning enough money so that we could allow ourselves an occasional visit to the theater. The only one we knew of was the Bijou on Halsted Street near Jackson.[21] This theater was within walking distance of our home, so that we did not have to pay carfare. Every penny counted in those days. As I look back on those hair-raising melodramas, I am comforted by the thought that they cost only ten cents. But they did introduce us to the theater.

Some of the plays we saw were called *The White Slave, East Lynne, Ten Nights in a Barroom, Bertha the Sewing Machine Girl, Two Orphans,* and many others.[22] In these plays the villain was always punished and the hero always married the beautiful golden-haired girl.

The posters in front of the theaters always fascinated me. I distinctly recall a poster of a beautiful girl, with flowing curly hair, dressed in rags, who was being threatened by the villain, and the caption underneath read: "Rags are royal raiment, when worn for virtue's sake."[23]

On Sunday afternoon we would go to the Haymarket Theatre.[24] This was a vaudeville house on Madison Street near Halsted. We would climb to the top gallery where we could get seats for ten cents. I can still see the sign on the wall: "No whistling or loud talking, or stamping of feet, or spitting permitted."

I think there were two or three large vaudeville theaters in

Chicago at the time. Two were in the Loop, and the other was the Haymarket. After the acts had played in the Loop, they would come to the Haymarket, and we saw some very fine acts in the almost forgotten Madison Street theater.

The one-act play that I remember most vividly was played by Mrs. Patrick Campbell in the star part.[25] The play was about a Russian general who had fallen in love with a beautiful lady, played by Mrs. Campbell. The play took place during a visit the lady paid to the general's home. She told him she had heard how cleverly he had disposed of the two men who had been arrested for talking against the czar. Yes, that was rather clever, he thought. He pointed to a post that was in the center of the room. He told her that he had had them tied to this post and after giving them the flogging they deserved, he had shot them. The lady seemed to be very much amused and said she would like to drink to that noble act. After the general had a few more drinks, she asked him to show her just how he tied the men to the post by tying her in the same manner. He obliged and after a moment he freed her, with great demonstrations of his love for her. She playfully suggested that he let her tie him to the post, just to see how those traitors looked. Being quite drunk by this time, he agreed and she proceeded to tie him, giving the ropes a few extra pulls. When he was firmly tied, she told him that she was the daughter of one man and the sister of the other man that he had shot. Then she whipped out a small revolver and shot him.

Memories of Russian oppression still fresh in our minds, this playlet made a deep impression on my sister and me.

I was making progress in the reading class, and Miss Landsberg suggested that I join the Shakespeare Club.[26] Harriet Monroe, who became the editor and I believe the founder of *Poetry Magazine,* was the leader of the class. I spent many rich evenings reading the plays. Several times Miss Addams came into the old dining room and quietly took a seat at the table. To me, the room always became warm with a feeling of peace when she was there.

Her presence was felt everywhere in the house. Whether we were reading Shakespeare, or working in the Labor Museum, or dancing in the dancing class, or listening to a lecture or concert, whenever she appeared, the room became brighter. Every time I saw her the thought came to me that if it had not been for her, I would not be enjoying all these things.

I remember Miss Addams stopping me one day and asking me if I had joined the dancing class. She thought I worked too hard and needed some fun. So I joined the dancing class and learned the waltz, two-step, and schottische. By this time I was able to pay the dollar that paid for ten lessons.

The dancing class was in the charge of a beautiful, understanding woman. Her name was Mary Wood Hinman and we all loved her.[27] She was always dressed in a gray accordion-pleated skirt, with a blouse of the same material, a red sash, and gray dancing shoes. She floated around that room like a graceful bird. We danced once a week in this carefree class, all winter. In June, the class closed for the summer with a gay cotillion, every bit as gay, if not as elaborate, as the ones staged today to introduce debutantes to society. No matter where the members of the dancing class came from, dingy hovels, overcrowded tenements, for that one night we were all living in a fairyland.

My sister and I next joined the gymnasium. We managed to scrape together enough money to buy the regulation gymnasium suit—wide bloomers and blouse—though if anyone could not afford the suit, she could attend anyway. Miss Rose Gyles was the teacher,[28] and she put us through the paces once a week.

The gymnasium was like an oasis in a desert on Halsted Street. Hundreds of boys, who had no other means of recreation, could go to the gymnasium and play basketball till they were so worn out that they could only go home and go to bed.

One evening, as I entered the reception room, Miss Addams called me into the residents' sitting room and asked me to join a class in English composition.[29] The class was just being organized and the instructor was to be Henry Porter Chandler, of the University of Chicago.[30] Not many students had applied, and Miss Addams asked me to register for the class as she did not want Mr. Chandler to feel that people were not interested in such a class.

I told Miss Addams that I had never written anything. But she insisted, and so I went into the dining room where four or five people were gathered. She introduced me to Mr. Chandler. Mr. Chandler outlined a course of work. He asked us if we had ever written anything. Most of us had not. He then told us that there were certain kinds of writing, such as book reviews, short stories, arguments, criticisms, and some others. He asked each of us to write anything that we wanted and to bring it to the class the following week. He then dismissed the class.

Mr. Chandler was the secretary to William Rainey Harper, the first president of the University of Chicago, and an instructor in English composition.

I could not sleep that night. Why was it that he did not tell us how to write? How could a person just write? Then the thought came to me that if you had something to say, perhaps you could write it down on paper. I kept thinking, Have I something to say?

During that week I did not attend any classes at Hull-House. Every evening, as soon as I reached home from work, I would hurry through with supper and helping with the dishes and then would sit at the kitchen table and write. I still have that "masterpiece."[31] Here it is:

"The Ghetto Market"

> Sociologists who are studying and seeking to remedy conditions among the wretchedly poor have done vast good. The poor may now be clothed; they receive medical attention and surgical care which none but the very rich could afford to pay for. They need not be ignorant, for schools are free and there are many devoted women in the social settlements who are laboring night and day to make up for whatever deficiency may exist in the capacity of the city institutions. But there is one injustice untouched; one wrong which is crying for immediate remedy. This is the unsanitary, filthy food which the poor in certain quarters are forced to eat. Not until the city takes the matter in hand and orders all vegetables, meat and fish to be sold only in adequate and sanitary rooms will this condition be entirely overcome; for as long as the old market of the Ghetto district exists, so long will the inhabitants of the district patronize it.
>
> Few people whose work does not take them into the neighborhood have any idea what the Ghetto market is like. I took a trip through it the other night for the purpose of observation. I soon came to Jefferson and Twelfth Streets. The illumination for the stands and shops is furnished by curious gasoline lamps nailed to the houses in an irregular line, so that when I followed the crowd of shoppers, the lights in the distance looked like a poorly organized torch-light parade. I walked along aimlessly for a moment till I saw a woman with an empty basket coming from a side street.
>
> The first stop that she made was at a poultry shop, where a great many women were gathered. This shop was about six feet in height, length and width. Trading was carried on in front of the shop. My "guide" carefully examined every fowl; she then counted the contents of her small purse and walked into the shop. I readily concluded that here everyone buys according to the size of her purse; for I saw the shopkeeper behind the counter take up the fowl and cut it into four pieces. One of these he wrapped in a newspaper and placed in the basket.
>
> We were soon near the fish traders. The fish were kept on the window sills of the shop, somewhat smaller than the one we had just left, and on stands and barrels arranged on the sidewalk.

The sills and stands were made of tin, with strips along the edge to prevent the fish from slipping to the ground. In each stand and sill a waste pipe was arranged through which the waste water from the ice took its course. But unfortunately this pipe reached the floor only, thus leaving the floor of the shop and sidewalk in front of it always covered with mud.

A man and his wife were the chief clerks, cashiers, and wrappers. The woman wore an apron which I thought at first sight was meant to protect her dress; but a second look showed me that it was tucked up on one side, letting all the slimy drippings from the fish fall unheeded on her skirt. Her head was covered with a shawl, which looked as if at one time it was black, but it had now turned green, yellow, gray, and various other colors.

The man wore a pair of overalls made of heavy blue cotton cloth, but from the constant wiping of his hands after handling the fish, looked like a leather of no particular color. The two seemed to handle their wares all day without washing their hands a single time. Not only that—I was amazed to see the man even re-fill his gasoline lamp and handle fish immediately after. The women who crowd around this stall are permitted to handle the wares to their heart's content. When they finally selected suitable portions of the fish, the shopkeeper weighed them on a dirty scale and wrapped them in a dilapidated newspaper, regardless of what substance may have been used in printing it or who handled it when it came off the press.

We next went to the cake stand which consisted of a long table standing on the edge of the sidewalk, over which was erected a heavy canvas. The table was covered with a miscellaneous assortment of cakes. These seemed to have a double mission in the world; not only did the buyers enjoy their delicious flavor, but the flies seemed very much at home, and from the constant buzzing I knew at first sight that they enjoyed the surroundings.

The woman I followed now turned to a stand opposite. Here were for sale prunes, raisins, nuts, beans, rice, salted herring, soda water, candles, matches, soap, and various other articles too numerous to mention. All these were uncovered except for the flies. Is it any wonder that this district has more typhoid fever than any other section of the city?

Nearby was a bench covered with old coats, vests, shoes, and trousers. Here second-hand shoes are bought without a thought as to who the previous wearer was. A woman will pay fifty cents for a pair of shoes and sixty cents for repairing them, whereas for one dollar her boy can be provided with a new pair that had never been worn and carried no possible taint of a contagious disease.

Is this question not well worthy of consideration? Cannot the poultry shop, fish stall and cake stand be kept off the street, free

> from the dust and the flies? Why should this class of people who work harder than any other be compelled to eat inferior food when they might be supplied with good food for the same money? Are there not plenty of men employed in building houses, ice boxes and various appliances for keeping provisions? Yet these people eat food sold on the street under the filthiest conditions.

Are you smiling? Well, I am.

The next time the class met, I brought the masterpiece, over which I had sweated five nights and a whole day Sunday, to Mr. Chandler. Each member of the class had brought a composition. Mr. Chandler did not look at the papers. He told us he would let us know the following week what he thought of our efforts.

Dena Miriam Faltz Satt, Hilda's mother, was born in Poland, birthdate unknown, and emigrated to Chicago in 1892.

Hilda as a young girl. (University of Illinois at Chicago, The University Library, Jane Addams Memorial Collection)

The Jewish Training School, which Hilda attended from 1892 to 1896, was maintained by philanthropic German Jews to educate newcomers from eastern Europe. (Joseph Regenstein Library, University of Chicago)

A typical scene in the Hull-House neighborhood, picturing the congested front and "rear" wooden houses. Maxwell Street area, ca. 1906. (Clark negative, Chicago Historical Society)

The Satt family probably lived in a house much like one of these, although the address of their first home in America is not known. (University of Illinois at Chicago, The University Library, Jane Addams Memorial Collection)

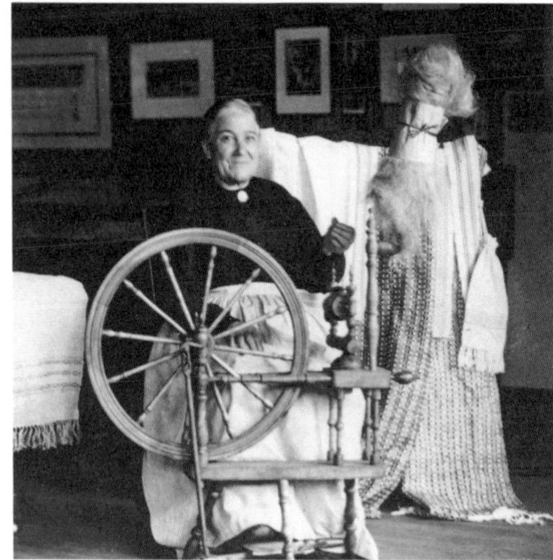

An Irish woman, probably Mrs. Brosnahan, spinning at Hull-House. (University of Illinois at Chicago, The University Library, Jane Addams Memorial Collection)

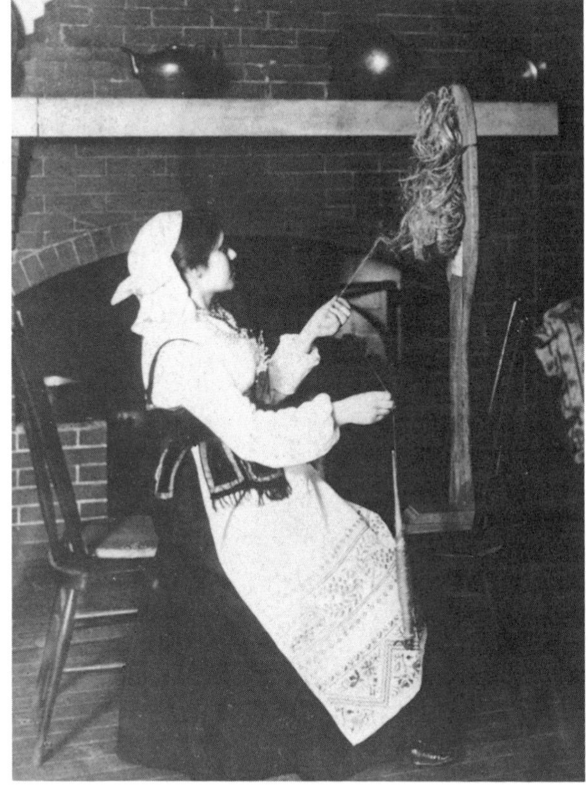

Hilda, ca. 1900, at a craft demonstration. It was customary for participants at the Hull-House Labor Museum to wear national costumes to stimulate pride in national tradition as a counterbalance to the humiliation usually meted out to immigrants. (University of Illinois at Chicago, The University Library, Jane Addams Memorial Collection)

Jane Addams, 1860-1935, co-founder of Hull-House. (University of Illinois at Chicago, The University Library, Jane Addams Memorial Collection)

The "octagon," Jane Addams's study, where Hilda learned of her scholarship to the University of Chicago. (University of Illinois at Chicago, The University Library, Jane Addams Memorial Collection)

Dr. Alice Hamilton, 1864-1972, author of *Exploring the Dangerous Trades,* whom Hilda assisted in "gathering dust" for tuberculosis studies. (University of Illinois at Chicago, The University Library, Jane Addams Memorial Collection)

Laura Dainty Pelham, 1845-1924, director of the Hull-House Players, criticized and directed Hilda's play, *The Walking Delegate.* (University of Illinois at Chicago, The University Library, Jane Addams Memorial Collection)

The ghetto market, in the Maxwell Street area, was the subject of Hilda's first writing, ca. 1904. (Barnes-Crosby photo, Chicago Historical Society)

Hilda (with the long braid) and her friends at Saugatuck, Michigan, 1911. (University of Illinois at Chicago, The University Library, Jane Addams Memorial Collection)

THE HULL-HOUSE PLAYERS

IN

The Walking Delegate

A play in four acts, dramatized from Leroy Scott's
novel of the same name by HILDA SATT

(*First presentation on any stage*)

April 10, 17, 20 and 27, 1912

Persons of the play in the order of their appearance

Tom Keating, a foreman	Stuart G. Bailey
Mrs. Keating, Tom's mother	Laura Thornton
Maggie Keating, Tom's sister	Debrah McGrath
Barry, a workman	Edward Sullivan
Pig Iron Pete, a workman	Frank Keogh
Mrs. Barry, Barry's wife	Laura Criddle
Buck Foley, a business agent	Louis Alter
Ruth Arnold, Mr. Driscoll's stenographer	Helen Silverman
Mr. Driscoll, a contractor	Wm. Z. Nourse
Bill, a workman	Jos. Marsolais
Connelly, secretary of the Iron Workers' Union	A. E. Rubenstein
Jake, a workman	Mr. Nourse
Smith, a workman	Sydney A. Hale
Johnson, a workman	Paul Grauman
Mr. Baxter, a contractor	Mr. Grauman
Mrs. Baxter, Baxter's wife	Maud Smith
Mr. Berman, a contractor	Mr. Hale
Mr. Murphy, a contractor	Mr. Marsolais
Mr. Bobbs, a contractor	Mr. Rubenstein

Time: The winter of 1900 Place: New York City

Act I. Kitchen in Mrs. Keating's home.
Act II. Potomac Hall.
Act III. Dining-room in Mr. Baxter's home.
Act IV. Potomac Hall.

Laura Dainty Pelham, Director L. Carter Lucas, Business Manager

The playbill for Hilda's play. (University of Illinois at Chicago, The University Library, Jane Addams Memorial Collection)

The West Side Turner Hall 12

The week that followed will ever stand out in my memory as a turning point in my life. The one thought that ran through my mind was, What would Mr. Chandler think of my composition? Would he toss it in the wastebasket? Would he laugh at it? Whatever the outcome, the fact that I had put my thoughts down on paper made a deep impression on me. Walking to work, sitting all day at the sewing machine sewing those endless cuffs, my thoughts were always with Mr. Chandler and "The Ghetto Market."

During that eventful week, on my way home from work, as I walked along dreaming of books and how they were written, a man handed me a leaflet. It was too dark to read it so I stuffed it into my coat pocket and forgot about it. After the supper dishes had been washed, I decided to walk to the corner to buy a newspaper. I put on my coat and instinctively put my hand into the pocket and pulled out the leaflet. In flaming letters, it announced:

MEMORIAL MEETING[1]
in memory of
THE FIVE MARTYRED ANARCHISTS
to be held in
THE WEST SIDE TURNER HALL.[2]

I had never heard of the West Side Turner Hall, nor did I know what the words "martyred anarchists" meant. But I was curious. I forgot about the newspaper. Maneuvering my sister into the bedroom, I showed her the leaflet. She read it and looked at me.

"What do you think it means?" she asked.

"I don't know," I answered. "How about finding out?"

"All right, let's go over and see," she said.

We told Mother we were going to visit a neighbor and we walked over to the hall.

The West Side Turner Hall was located on West Twelfth Street, a short block from Halsted Street. We walked up a well-worn staircase of a dilapidated two-story building. Many feet must have climbed those stairs, as the steps were worn down in the center. We entered a smoke-filled hall. Several hundred people were seated on folding chairs. Many were standing about, talking animatedly; others were leaning against the walls. Everybody seemed to be smoking.

My gaze wandered to the stage. There, five white plaster busts of five men were arrayed on a bench. Each bust was draped with a red band across the chest. I sat and stared wide-eyed. Who were these men portrayed by these busts? What did it all mean?

Soon a man mounted the stage and rapped for order. The people standing around took seats. For a moment there was absolute silence in the hall. Then the man on the stage announced that they would sing the memorial hymn.[3] Copies of the words were passed. A woman came to the stage and seated herself at the piano and played what I later discovered was "Annie Laurie." I remember some of the words and here they are:

> Chicago's soil is bloody
> For where three some years ago,[4]
> Five God-like heroes perished,
> For whom our tears still flow.

After the song was sung (it had many other verses that I do not remember), the man introduced the speaker of the evening. That was the first time that I saw and heard Emma Goldman.[5]

She was short and rather heavy, with thick black hair combed straight back. She was dressed in a black skirt and white shirtwaist, which was the fashion of the day. She wore thick glasses from which dangled a black ribbon. She looked like all the other women in the neighborhood.

The story of the Haymarket incident has been told in many books, as I later discovered.[6] But I want to give here the impression that it made on me that night. And I want to tell it as I remember it.

Emma Goldman started out by telling us that she knew that everybody in the hall knew the story of the martyred comrades, but like the story of the Exodus, it had to be told each year so that "we will not forget."

It is hard to believe that after all these years one can remember what was said that night, but I do.

In 1886 there was a determined effort made by the workers to get an eight-hour day. It was bitterly fought by the employers. On May Day of that year, more than forty thousand workers went on strike for the shorter day. There was bitter feeling about that strike and the employers demanded and were given police protection to prevent damage to property by the pickets. On May 3 a worker was shot by a policeman at the McCormick plant. The workers, incensed by this action, called a protest meeting for the following evening. Some of the workers were anarchists. That was another word I was to hear for the first time that evening.

The protest meeting was held at a place called Haymarket Square. Many thousands came to that meeting. The mayor, Carter H. Harrison, was so concerned with these events that he went to the meeting to see for himself what was happening. The meeting was orderly. After all, he felt that this was a free country and that the men had a right to their opinions. He also noted that it was beginning to rain and that many of the spectators were leaving on that account. He concluded that the meeting would soon break up, so he personally stopped at the police station and told the captain in charge that everything was under control and that he need not send any more police to the meeting. As soon as the mayor had left, the captain, contrary to the orders of the mayor, ordered a considerable number of police to the scene of the meeting. As the patrol wagon was nearing Haymarket Square, someone threw a bomb and several policemen were killed and some were wounded.

It never was established who threw the bomb nor where it came from. But a wave of hysteria descended on Chicago. The blame for the bomb throwing was fastened onto the anarchists. Eight of the most active were arrested. Only two of the eight were at the meeting. One of the eight was not in Chicago on that fatal night. But the eight were held responsible because they had been the most vocal in the demand for the eight-hour working day and their fiery speeches had incited the mob to riot, which ended in the bomb throwing. They were indicted on that charge.

As I sat there listening to the recital of these events, I kept thinking of the shirtwaist factory and the hours I worked, and I could not get myself to feel that asking for the eight-hour day was a crime. But I was horrified at the throwing of the bomb.

Emma Goldman was telling the silent crowd of men and women that of the eight indicted, these, and she pointed to the busts, became the martyrs to labor and the eight-hour day, which will come as an everlasting memorial to their heroism.

Of the five names I remember only two. I could do some research and give the other names, but I prefer to describe that night as I remember it. One name is Albert Parsons and the other is August Spies. There may be a reason why I remember these two; I will come back to that later.

The eight men were tried during an intensely emotional upheaval. Emma Goldman told us that the employers and the press had condemned the men before the jury found them guilty.

The presiding judge accepted the premise that six of the men on trial were not at the meeting and so could not have thrown the bomb. But in his instructions to the jury he stressed the fact that the men, by their speeches, had caused someone to throw a bomb and they were, therefore, guilty. The jury brought in a verdict of guilty.

There was a tremendous protest to this verdict. Emma Goldman said that protests came from all over the world. From abroad, people like George Bernard Shaw and William Morris sent letters condemning the verdict. In this country, William Dean Howells, Henry Demarest Lloyd, and many others tried to stop this "murder," as she called it. But arrayed against the sanity of Chicago were the mighty employers who demanded the death penalty. They thought that by silencing the leaders they could kill the demand for the eight-hour day. But the struggle goes on, Emma Goldman said that night so long ago.

Now to return to the two anarchists whose names I remember. Albert Parsons was somewhere in Wisconsin when he read of the bombing. After several days, a large reward was posted for his apprehension. So sure was he that he could not in any way be associated with the affair, he came voluntarily to Chicago and presented himself to the authorities. He was promptly put under arrest, tried, and convicted.

The eight men were offered clemency if they would sign an appeal for mercy. At first they all refused to sign the appeal, claiming they were innocent and that asking for mercy would be a confession of guilt. Three of the men were finally swayed by their families, and they did sign the petition. These three were given prison sentences. Six years later Governor Altgeld pardoned them. Emma Goldman spoke rather bitterly of the three who had escaped the fate of the other five.

The five men who were memorialized that evening were sentenced to be hanged.

Now I come to the other name that I remember. August Spies's beautiful wife came to prison the day before the hanging to say goodbye to her husband. She had long black hair which she wore in a sort of bun on the top of her head. In the bun she is supposed to have concealed a tiny bomb, which she gave to her husband. He put the bomb into his mouth where it exploded, killing him instantly.

The other four men died on the gallows.

With this the meeting ended.

My sister and I were pushed along in the crowd and soon found ourselves on the street. It was good to breathe the fresh air again. We walked along without saying a word. I am sure we were both stunned by what we had heard. As we neared the house I exploded: "It can't be true," I said.

"How could she tell it if it was not true," my sister said.

I walked to work the following morning with the events of the previous evening running through my head. I did not want to believe what I had heard at that meeting. My father had come to America, I kept saying to myself, because here in this wonderful country a man was free to say what he wanted, even if he was wrong. As far as I could understand, these anarchists, as they were called, had been hanged for something they had said and not for breaking any law.

I was troubled and confused.

Many years later I came across the biography of Henry Demarest Lloyd, written by his sister, Caro Lloyd, and I was deeply moved by the following:

> It will always be remembered that in the stillness of the jail, on the midnight before the execution, Parsons sang *Annie Laurie*. Was it to send a message of calmness and courage over the walls to his comrades? Or was he singing to the ideal of his dreams? Was it humanity perfected, whose "brow was like the snowdrift?" Was it the free man of the future "whose face was the fairest that e'er the sun shone on?" Was this the "bonnie Annie Laurie" for whom he was to lay him down and die?
>
> For the funeral on Sunday Lloyd wrote verses with the refrain of Parson's last words on the scaffold: "Let the voice of the people be heard," and I remember as Mrs. Lloyd sat at the piano and the family were singing them to the air of *Annie Laurie,* Lloyd wept. He abandoned the idea of using them, fearing to increase the people's feeling. No retaliatory blow was struck, Chicago resumed its normal whirl and the tragic story soon passed into the gloom of history.[7]

The University 13

After a miserable day at the factory, when everything seemed to happen, my machine had broken down and I had lost several hours of work, I arrived at Hull-House. The composition class was to meet that night. What would Mr. Chandler think of my composition? Would he pay any attention to it? He had probably thrown it into the wastebasket. It couldn't possibly be worth anything, I kept telling myself.

The class assembled and Mr. Chandler opened his briefcase and pulled out a mass of papers. He handed them to the various authors, without any comment.

My heart missed several beats.

Then he handed me my paper and said: "Very good." I do not remember anything else that he said that night. But as the class was being dismissed, Miss Addams came into the room and said that she wanted to talk to me, that I was to wait for her. She talked for a few minutes with Mr. Chandler, then she took me into the octagon[1] and said these magic words: "How would you like to go to the University of Chicago?" She was very calm, as if she had asked me to have a cup of tea.

She did not realize that she had just asked me whether I wanted to live. I just sat there looking at her.

"Did you say the University of Chicago?" I finally gasped.

"Yes," she said. "Mr. Chandler told me that your paper shows promise, and he will make all the arrangements."

"But that is impossible," I said.

"Nothing is impossible," said Jane Addams.

For some time I could not talk. I kept thinking, I did not graduate from grammar school. How could I hope to go to the great university?

Miss Addams, with her infinite patience, sat there holding my hand. I know she was living through my thoughts.

If this could happen, then all sorts of miracles could happen. But then, did not miracles happen in Hull-House all the time?

"But what about a high school diploma?" I asked. "I heard that no one can go to college without a high school diploma."

"Mr. Chandler said that you could come as an unclassified student," she said.[2]

"But what about money?" I was beginning to lose hope.

"You will be granted a scholarship," she said. "It will cost you nothing."

"But I must contribute to the support of the family," I said. "My wages are needed at home."

"Well, I thought of that, too," she said smiling. "We will make you a loan of the amount that you would earn, and whenever you are able, you can pay it back."

By this time tears were running down my cheeks. What had I done to deserve all this? She took my hand and said: "I know how you feel, my dear. I want you to go home and talk this over with your mother, and let me know what you want to do. But I want you to go, remember that."

I went home and found Mother and my sister sitting at the kitchen table, drinking tea. I sat down without removing my coat. My sister looked at me.

"What's happened to you?" she said.

I just sat there staring—then I blurted out: "Miss Addams wants me to go to the University of Chicago."

"But how can you?" my sister asked.

Then I poured out my soul. I told them what Miss Addams had said about a loan, how my tuition would be free, how my life would be changed.

"This can happen only in America," Mother said.

"Yes," I said, "because in America there is a Jane Addams and Hull-House."

The exciting events of the night before did not keep me from going to work the next day. I sewed cuffs all day. As soon as I had finished eating supper, I dashed off to Hull-House. I waited for Miss Addams to come out of the dining room.

She saw me at once and took me into the octagon. The walls were covered with the photographs of the great humanitarians of the world: Leo Tolstoy, Abraham Lincoln, Henry Demarest Lloyd, John Peter Altgeld, Susan B. Anthony, Peter Kropotkin, Eugene V. Debs, and a host of others. And while these faces were looking down at us, I told Miss Addams that my mother and sister had consented to my going.

It was with a great deal of satisfaction that I told the foreman of the shirtwaist factory that I was leaving.

Memories keep coming back. It must have been the winter term when I matriculated at the University of Chicago.[3] I remember that it was very cold traveling to the university early in the morning.

I was told to go to Mr. Chandler's office. He took me to the registration office and I registered for three classes.[4] I was to take English literature with Mr. Percy Boynton, German with Mr. Goettsch, and composition with Mr. Chandler.

From the fifth grade in the Jewish Training School to English literature, starting with Chaucer, was somewhat of a leap. Since I did not have to worry about grades, being an unclassified student, I could drink in all the fabulous information that came from Mr. Boynton's mouth. And reading the assigned books became a tonic to my soul. I soon came to know Ben Jonson, Alexander Pope, Beaumont and Fletcher, Keats, Shelley, and Shakespeare.

In 1904 there were separate classes for men and women. Most of my classes met in Lexington Hall.[5] It was a poorly constructed building and was drafty and often very cold. In the composition class, when we were told to write about anything, I became bold, and perhaps a little impudent, and wrote a paper on why women students were assigned to cold, drafty buildings while the men were in more solid ones.

I think I got a high mark on that paper, but Mr. Chandler made no comment.

The subject of the next assignment was a debate on "Woman Suffrage." We were asked to hand in an outline as to which side we would take. I don't know why, but I chose to be against woman suffrage. The next day Mr. Chandler asked me to stay for an interview and in short order he convinced me that I was not against woman suffrage and that there was no point in writing something that I did not believe. I am sure that he still remembered my previous paper on the discrimination shown to women students and he was not going to allow me to contradict myself as to woman's rights. He proved to be right.

When the university closed for the summer, I evaluated my work. The English literature course had opened all sorts of vistas to me. But I think I did not pass. The jump from the fifth grade in the grammar school to Chaucer was a little too much for me. But the course gave me an everlasting desire to read and study, so it was not a loss. I did pass in German and I think I fared well in the composition class.

That term at the University of Chicago opened a new life to me. And I have never stopped being grateful for having been given the opportunity to explore the treasures to be found in books.

I often wonder what sort of a life I would have lived if I did not have that short term in the university made possible by Jane Addams.

After the short but eventful term at the University of Chicago, I must confess I was at loose ends. I was determined not to go back to the factory to sew cuffs. But I knew that I had to earn my living and help support the family. I now felt prepared to do more interesting and stimulating work. The question was, What could I do?

The answer came sooner than I dared hope. Miss Addams was preparing to go to Bar Harbor for the summer and she suggested that I take the job of answering the doorbell and the telephone. In those days the door was locked and everyone who wanted to come in had to ring the doorbell. This work was usually done by volunteers, but most volunteers were leaving the city for the summer and I may have been the first paid worker to have had that job. I worked from four o'clock in the afternoon till nine at night, five days a week. On Saturday I did "toting."

The word "toting" I think was invented at Hull-House.[6] In Webster's dictionary the word "tote" is given, and it means "to carry or bear on the person, as a burden." But at Hull-House it did not mean that at all. Toting meant showing people through the house. And let me say right here that I never found it a burden.

I came in contact with people from all over the world. It seemed as if everybody who came to Chicago from some part of the country or the world came to see Hull-House. I know that there are people in Chicago who had not been there, but tourists came. I never tired of showing the wonders of the house on Halsted and Polk streets.

I was asked and answered thousands of questions. I would not be able to count the times that I was asked why Miss Addams had never married. At that time, I did not know. But if I had known, I would have felt that it was nobody's business.

Most of the classes were discontinued during the hot summer months. But there had been a great demand for English classes for adult foreigners. A delegation of the students called on Miss Addams and asked her to allow the classes to continue during the summer. Miss Addams agreed to try one class if a teacher could be found. I volunteered.[7]

As I look back on that momentous event, I realize how presumptuous it was of me to offer to teach a class at Hull-House, where the standards were very high. I had no training in teaching. But English had fascinated me from the start; I had worked very hard to learn it, so why could I not teach the immigrants what I had learned? I offered to teach the class and was overjoyed when my offer was accepted. I had a feeling that, after all, there was no one else around who was willing to take the class. So the people who wanted to continue studying during the summer were told that the class would not close.

Here my training at the Jewish Training School became a blessing. Mrs. Torrance had been very meticulous about pronunciation, and I used her method that summer with surprising and satisfactory results. Most of my students learned to speak without an accent. The great value of not having an accent, in those days, was that you could get a better job. And that was rewarding.

But the great reward came that fall, when Miss Addams told me that I could continue to teach the class for the winter. The day I picked up the *Hull-House Bulletin* and saw my name listed as a teacher of an English class equaled only the day when I was told that I could go to the University of Chicago.

New Horizons 14

Being allowed to teach English to immigrants at Hull-House did more for me than anything that I imparted to my students. It gave me a feeling of security that I so sorely needed. What added to my confidence in the future was that my class was always crowded and the people seemed to make good progress. From time to time Jane Addams would visit the class to see what I was doing, and she always left with that rare smile on her face; she seemed to be pleased.

There were no textbooks for adult beginners in English at that time. It soon became evident that it would be a waste of time to talk about cat, rat, mat, fat, sat to people who probably had been to high school in a foreign country.

This situation was emphasized for me one evening when Miss Addams brought a Greek professor to my class. He had come to America for the express purpose of learning English and had come to Chicago because he wanted to see relatives who were living near Hull-House. These relatives had suggested that he find out what Hull-House was doing about teaching English to adults. Miss Addams told me that the professor would stay one or two nights in my class to see what was being done. The crowning glory of my teaching was when he decided to join the class and attended all winter.

But to come back to the subject of textbooks, since there were none, I decided to use the Declaration of Independence as a text. It was a distinct success. The students did not find the words difficult; so in addition to learning English, we all learned the principles of Americanism.

I next introduced the manual on naturalization and the class learned English while studying how to become a citizen. It was all very exciting and stimulating.

My students were now beginning to confide in me. Classes at Hull-House were never just classes where people came to learn a specific subject. There was a human element of friendliness among us. Life was not soft or easy for any of them. They worked hard all day in shops and factories and made this valiant effort to learn the language of their adopted country. At times they needed real help, and they knew that somewhere in this wonderful house on Halsted Street they would get it.

I recall a special case in point. One evening, after the class had been dismissed, one of my students stayed behind. At first he seemed reluctant to tell me his story. But it soon came tumbling out; he had been ill and had gone to a doctor and was told that he would have to have a delicate and rather serious operation. And he had no money.

I looked at the fine young man and the first thought that flashed through my mind was that he must be saved. I told him that I would speak to Miss Addams and that he should see her the next night.

I went in search of Miss Addams. It did not matter that it was late. She was always available when there was a need. I told her about my student.

"Come in and see me before you go to your class tomorrow," she said. "I will write a letter to Dr. McArthur.[1] I think he will take care of the young man."

Dr. McArthur was at that time the outstanding surgeon in Chicago. The young man took Miss Addams's letter to him and he performed the operation. I don't believe that anyone could refuse a request from Miss Addams.

Hull-House had a unique arrangement for getting work done. No teachers or attendants were paid. It was all volunteer work.[2] The residents of Hull-House were occupied with outside work during the day, and each gave a certain number of evenings to teaching and directing clubs. The only people who were paid were those who devoted their full time to the house.

So in the fall, when volunteers returned, I decided to look for a job. I had learned to use a typewriter, so I decided to look for more "genteel" work. I still shuddered when I thought of those cuffs.

I started scanning the want ads, but now I looked under the heading "Office Help."

A large mail-order house, which shall remain unnamed, advertised for bill clerks who could operate billing machines.[3] Since the keyboard of a typewriter was the same as that of a billing machine, I decided to apply. I was pleasantly surprised when I was told to report for work on the following day.

Carrying my lunch, I set out for my new job. I was taken to a large room that was filled with long tables on which the billing machines had been placed. There were about three feet between the machines. I was assigned to a machine and an instructor came to show me how the work was done. She also told me the rules of the office. I was told that no talking was permitted during working hours. I could, however, do what I wanted during the lunch period, which was forty-five minutes, even talk.

In addition to the blank bills, carbon paper, pencil, and eraser, I was given a wire spindle and several cards of different colors. I believe there were seven of these cards. I was told that when I had finished a batch of bills and needed more work, I was to put up a blue card on the spindle. When I needed blank bills, the green card was to be put up, and the supply clerk would bring the needed items. The red card would bring a new pencil. The yellow card meant that I needed an eraser. The purple card was a signal that I needed carbon paper. When my typewriter ribbon was worn out, and I must be sure that it was worn out, the orange card would bring a new ribbon. If I needed cleaning fluid to clean the machine, a pink card would bring it. I was not to leave my machine unless it was absolutely necessary. Then I was told that the toilets were at the end of the hall, and I knew what she meant by "absolutely necessary."

I had no difficulty learning to do the work and at first it was new and exciting. About the third day my mother noticed that my voice was husky, and she wanted to know what was wrong. I suddenly realized that I had not been using my vocal chords for three days and that my voice was beginning to show the lack of exercise. I suddenly realized that "genteel" work can be as deadly monotonous as factory work.

I made a feeble protest. I saw no reason why I could not speak to the girl next to me once in a while. The next day I was told that I was "too smart" for the job, and I was fired.

Several years later I went with a group of people on a sight-seeing tour that took us to the state penitentiary at Joliet. As I walked through the overall factory, I saw a spindle and several colored cards at each machine. I asked the guide what the cards meant and was told that when a prisoner needed supplies he had to use the cards to indicate what he needed, as no talking was permitted during working hours.

I often wondered whether the mail-order house got the idea from the prison, or the prison from the mail-order house.

I was again looking for a job. Miss Addams suggested that I might try A. C. McClurg & Co., a publishing house and at the time the largest bookstore in Chicago.[4] With a letter of introduction from Jane Addams, I was given a very friendly interview and got the job.

Working among books was almost as good as taking a course in literature. It gave me the opportunity of knowing what books were being published. I was keenly interested in what books people were reading. And I had the great privilege of working at McClurg's when

The Quest of the Silver Fleece was published. It was the first time that I came across the name of W. E. B. Du Bois.[5] This book aroused a keen interest in the growth of cotton in the South and the part that the Negro played in the industry.

I still spent my evenings at Hull-House, and one evening Miss Addams asked me to help organize a social and literary club for young men and women about my age. We all needed an outlet for recreation. About thirty young people joined the club, which was named the Ariadne Club.[6] I don't know who suggested the name, but like the mythological daughter of Minos, who led Theseus out of the labyrinth by a thread, the club led many of us out of a labyrinth of boredom.

I now had the opportunity to come into contact with young men. The club met once a week, and how I looked forward to those meetings. The first order of business, after officers were elected, was to appoint a program committee, whose duty it would be to arrange weekly programs. Since this was a social and literary club, one week was devoted to dancing and the next to study. For the more serious evening, a member was usually assigned to write a paper and to read it before the club. This was followed by a discussion.

And what subjects we discussed.

Papers were written on the collection of garbage, grand opera, clean streets, single tax, trade unionism, and many others. I think our subjects were influenced by what was going on at Hull-House.

The Ariadne Club soon branched out and launched a series of debates. We would try to find another club that would accept a challenge. If we could not find a club, the members would form opposing teams. The subjects of these debates come back to me: Which is mightier, the sword or the pen? Should women be allowed to vote? Which is stronger, the desire for fame or riches?

The club's next endeavor was book reviewing. A member would be appointed to read a book, write a review, and read it at a meeting. Some of the reviews were of *David Copperfield, Ivanhoe, The Pickwick Papers, The Count of Monte Cristo, When Knighthood Was in Flower,* and the various popular books of the day.

It was about this time that I found a copy of *Uncle Tom's Cabin.* I was deeply moved by the misery of the slaves. For the first time I read about slavery. For the first time I found out that people could be bought and sold on the auction block; that children could be taken from parents; that fathers could be sold, never to see their families again.

When it was my turn to write a book review, I chose *Uncle Tom's Cabin.*

A great discussion followed this review. When it was time to adjourn the meeting, we were nowhere near finished with the discussion. It was decided to continue at the next meeting, even though it had previously been decided to devote that evening to dancing.

Most of the club members had no contact with Negroes. We even found that some of the members had never seen a Negro. Dr. James Britton,[7] who was the club leader, told us that most of the Negroes had lived longer in America than any of us present and were fully entitled to anything and everything that the country offered. I thought of all the racial hatreds in Poland, Germany, and Russia, and I was thankful that I was being cured of this disease of intolerance.

In this connection, I recall that shortly after I had arrived in Chicago, one of my playmates told me that I must cross the street when I approached the Chinese laundry on Halsted Street. When I wanted to know why, she told me that if you pass the laundry, the "Chinaman" will come out with a long knife and kill you. I realize now that my playmate must have been told this fantastic tale by someone. Until I found out that the Chinese man who operated this laundry was the soul of kindness, I was afraid to pass the laundry.

We also had music in the Ariadne Club. The members who could play an instrument, or sing, would perform; we heard some very good concerts. Many of the members who worked all day would study music at night. I recall when a piano lesson could be had for twenty-five cents. Some of the members attended the Hull-House Music School,[8] and I venture to say that not a few became successful musicians.

The Ariadne Club also produced plays. I recall taking part in *David Garrick,* in which I played a fussy and obnoxious old maid.

My interest in the theater was a direct outgrowth of the dramatics at Hull-House.[9] It was a preparation for life.

Jane Addams 15

During three of the four years that I worked for A. C. McClurg & Co., I taught English at Hull-House three evenings a week. Since I did not work on Saturday afternoon, I devoted the time to toting visitors.

While toting I came in contact with people from all over the world. They all asked the same questions: Where was Jane Addams born? How old was she? Why did she never marry? How did she happen to start Hull-House?

It must be remembered that at that time *Twenty Years at Hull-House* had not been written. Or rather it had not yet been published. Neither was there any biography of Jane Addams. So the questions were not surprising.

After a span of almost fifty years, I would like to answer some of those questions as I see them. In her two-volume autobiography, *Twenty Years at Hull-House* and *The Second Twenty Years at Hull-House*, Jane Addams devoted most of the space to Hull-House. The personal side of her life, I feel, was treated casually. In his biography of Jane Addams, her nephew James Weber Linn did go into a little more detail. But I want to give my version of the life of this great pioneer in the field of humanism, which is called social service.

Jane Addams was born in Cedarville, Illinois, on 6 September 1860, the year that Abraham Lincoln was elected president of the United States. These two events left their mark on American history.

The American people still do not quite realize that it was Jane Addams who woke the conscience of America to the debt that it owed to the great masses of people who were pouring into America. It was Jane Addams who pointed out that these immigrants were making the clothing that Americans wore. They knitted the mittens and sweaters to keep American children warm. They were making the bricks and cutting the lumber to build homes. They were growing the food and working in the stockyards to prepare the meat for American tables. They were digging the coal and making steel and iron. There was almost no phase of American life in which these immigrants did not serve.

It was Jane Addams who pointed out that to many people these immigrants were regarded as intruders. They were accused of bringing a blight to the fair American cities. They were bringing disease and pestilence to America.

Jane Addams saw these immigrants as bewildered people, uprooted from their native soil. In many instances they had fled from oppression. But in the midst of the oppression there was also music and gaiety. There were books and art museums.

What awaited these immigrants in their adopted country? Jobs at hard work with long hours and low wages. Jane Addams saw them crowded into unsanitary, dark tenements.

How did she happen to start Hull-House? It is well known now that, while traveling in Europe, she visited Toynbee Hall in London and was convinced that the most congested part of Chicago needed something like Toynbee Hall. I dare say, many Americans visited London and saw Toynbee Hall. It was the vision of Jane Addams that brought about the establishing of Hull-House.

This oasis in a desert of boredom and monotony became the university, the opera house, the theater, the concert and lecture hall, the gymnasium, the library, the clubhouse of the neighborhood. It was a place where one could become rejuvenated after a day of hard work in the factory.

Almost everybody who saw Jane Addams would marvel at the serenity of her face. I have heard people say that "there was a sermon in her face." One sweet little lady said to me: "No sorrow could possibly have touched Jane Addams; she is so well composed."

Personal tragedy as deep as any Greek tragedy that ever was produced in the Hull-House Theatre was a part of her life.

Jane Addams was two years old when her mother died. For six years she was given loving care by her sister Mary, who was about seventeen when their mother died. When Jane Addams was eight years old her father married Anna Hostetter Haldeman, a widow with two sons: Henry, who was seventeen, and George, who was seven years old, six months younger than Jane Addams.

From the very start a beautiful relationship sprang up between the little stepbrother and stepsister. Jane Addams speaks lovingly of him in her biography: "My stepbrother and I carried on games and crusades which lasted week after week, and summer after summer, as only free-ranging children can. . . . We erected an altar beside the stream, to which we brought all the snakes we killed during our excursions."[1]

The coming of the stepmother into the house was not the happiest event in the life of the small Jane. The new Mrs. Addams was not completely happy with the life of a small village in Illinois. Hers was a cosmopolitan outlook on life, and in her forced surroundings she often exploded into violent fits of temper.

In a pamphlet given to me by Marcet Haldeman-Julius, a niece of Jane Addams, she has this to say:

> Jenny, accustomed to the unfailing serenity and indulgent love of her sister Mary, resented alike the uncalled-for temper and the necessary discipline and training that were introduced firmly by her stepmother. The new head of the household was just and equal in her treatment of Jane and George, though she was too honest to pretend that she loved them equally. Both children felt the storm as well as the sunshine of her gracious but complicated character. Naturally, Jane was at times the more critical of the two; this attitude was augmented by the fact that she and my grandmother were temperamental opposites.[2]

The years went by. Jane Addams grew to young womanhood and traveled abroad. She was formulating her life and making plans for the future. George Haldeman grew to young manhood, brilliant in the field of biology. His was a sensitive nature that must have been scarred by the complicated life in the Addams household.

George fell in love with Jane Addams, and though she felt a deep affection for him, she either decided that her career was uppermost in her heart or that she did not love him sufficiently to marry him. To quote Mrs. Haldeman-Julius again:

> For herself Jane made the wise decision—and one for which the world is grateful. But for George it was tragedy. Brilliant, sensitive and profound in his attachments, George Haldeman was one of those rare persons who love but once and can be overwhelmed by their feelings. Added to this, when the emotional crisis came, he was in the midst of an intense period of postgraduate study in biology at Johns Hopkins and, shortly afterward, engaged in summer research work in Florida. He was so torn within himself and for the moment so indifferent to life that he neglected to take the usual precautions necessary to his work. Brain and body collapsed, and, after an acute illness and a slow, imperfect convalescence, he spent the remaining years (until his death at the age of forty-eight) as a semi-invalid and recluse in the Cedarville homestead.[3]

One can understand the bitterness that the stepmother felt toward Jane Addams. For years she blamed Miss Addams for the tragedy that came to her adored son. It can also be understood that it was no fault of Jane Addams that the man who loved her could not make an adjustment when he found that his love was not shared.

The years that George Haldeman lived as a recluse, practically cut off from the world, must have been tragic, heartbreaking years for Jane Addams. But at no time did I ever get an inkling of the turmoil that must have filled her heart, at least some of the time. She went about her work serenely, efficiently, with a determined compassion that I have never encountered in another human being.

It must have taken a great deal of money to operate Hull-House. But during all the time that I was intimately in contact with the settlement, I do not recall any public appeals for funds to help support it.

Of Jane Addams's personal income, Mrs. Haldeman-Julius gives us these facts:

> Grandfather Addams, who had helped draft the inheritance laws of Illinois, logically enough insisted upon making no will, and, as his widow, Anna H. H. Addams inherited one-third of his comfortable estate. The remaining two-thirds were divided among the four children. Aunt Jane felt that, had he lived, he would have been interested in helping her with her plans. Grandmother was not ungenerous and ordinarily would have seen the justice of this viewpoint. But now her grief and dislike were granite obstacles to any cooperation.[4]

I have no idea what "the comfortable estate" meant. But it must be remembered that two-thirds of it was divided among four. I would venture a guess that whatever Jane Addams inherited went into the operation of Hull-House.

Jane Addams had the magnetism to draw people to Hull-House who gave money and service. She had very high standards and would not tolerate teachers who, despite training, did not have a sympathetic approach to their work. All teachers did volunteer work and felt privileged to be allowed to teach at Hull-House.

It was also a great privilege to be allowed to live at Hull-House. The "residents," as they were called, were men and women of the highest ideals and devotion. It became a privilege to donate money to Hull-House.

But at no time did Jane Addams make a compromise to get the much-needed funds for Hull-House. I recall two instances where her convictions were put to the test.

When John Peter Altgeld died, Clarence Darrow asked Jane Addams to speak at his funeral.[5] Two clergymen had been asked to conduct services and had refused. Jane Addams was advised not to participate in the funeral services, as some of the support might be withdrawn from Hull-House. But Jane Addams did speak at the funeral of the man who had pardoned the anarchists. It is to be regretted that her words are not to be found among her papers or her writings. Perhaps she did make a compromise by not publishing the eulogy among the eulogies that she gave during the years, in her book *The Excellent Becomes the Permanent.*[6] But it did take great courage to appear at the funeral of the man who was hated at the time by most people who had money.

The other instance that I can recall was that a wealthy family in Chicago offered to donate a substantial sum of money to Hull-House if the photograph of the head of the family would be hung in the octagon.[7] It was well known that this man was anything but humane to his employees. I saw the photograph standing on the floor of the room for a long time. It was never hung.

On my last visit to Hull-House a few years ago, I saw the lovely painting in pastel colors of Mary Rozet Smith.[8] This portrait used to hang over the fireplace in Jane Addams's room. It now has a place of honor in the rooms of the main building.

Although I had very little contact with Mary Rozet Smith, her beauty and charm would pass a current of joy through me every time she passed me. All the gifts of nature and material wealth had been bestowed on this woman. Yet she was simple in her dignity. She was Jane Addams's closest friend, and Miss Addams spent as much time as she could spare from her work at the home of Miss Smith, on the Near North Side of Chicago.

I recall when Miss Addams expressed a desire to have a pipe organ installed in the theater. Some of my friends and I decided that we should give a play and earn some money for the organ fund. We succeeded in making two hundred dollars. When we brought the money to Jane Addams, she treated us as though we had just given her the entire cost of the organ.

Several months later it was announced that Miss Mary Rozet Smith had decided to donate the pipe organ in memory of her mother.[9] Whenever Jane Addams felt that Hull-House needed an addition for the welfare of the neighborhood, the addition miraculously came.

The Hull-House Woman's Club was one of Jane Addams's favorite endeavors.[10] It brought together women from all over the world. Once a week the women could leave their dreary homes and commune with other women and enjoy the hospitality of a cup of tea and a piece of cake. A cup of tea and a piece of cake may be trite things to most of us. But to sit down and have a cup of tea that you did not have to brew yourself and a piece of cake that you did not have to bake was an event in the lives of the women of South Halsted Street.

I believe that most of the women residents of Hull-House were members of this club. Mrs. Joseph T. Bowen, who was perhaps the largest single contributor to Hull-House, at one time was its president.

I have a feeling that the Hull-House Woman's Club was Jane Addams's pet activity. Here was a real venture in democracy. Women from England, Ireland, Germany, Russia, Poland, Sweden, and many other countries were members. Women who had reached the highest educational levels and women who could not read or write sat side by side at the meetings. Women of wealth and women who barely had enough to eat participated in the discussions of the club on an equal basis. Each had one vote.

Jane Addams was concerned that this unique organization did not have a suitable meeting place of its very own. It would have been futile for the members to try to build a clubhouse. The majority of the members were neighborhood women. So Mrs. Bowen donated a building on Polk Street, part of which was for the exclusive use of the Hull-House Woman's Club. The upper floor became the largest meeting hall in the house. The building was named Bowen Hall.[11]

From the many talks that I heard Jane Addams give, I concluded that the two men who had the greatest influence on her life were Abraham Lincoln and Leo Tolstoy. And so to honor these men, the walls of the Hull-House Theatre portrayed them on wall-sized murals.[12] But Abraham Lincoln was not portrayed as president of the United States. He was the young Lincoln pulling a flatboat down the Sangamon River. Tolstoy was not portrayed as one of the world's greatest writers at his desk or as a member of the Russian nobility, but he was shown plowing a field with a wooden hand plow. I do not know whether the artists who painted these murals were paid or donated their services. But the murals were painted because Jane Addams felt they belonged there. When I toted people through the theater, I liked to tell them that here was depicted the dignity of labor. Then I would turn to the rear wall, where a beautiful landscape of golden waving corn had been painted, and I would say, "And here is the dignity of rest."

Above the stage were the words: "Act well your part, there all the honor lies."[13]

How many of us were imbued with that spirit? Who will ever know? The greatest lesson I learned from Jane Addams was that no matter what your role is in the great drama of life, "Act well your part."

Jane Addams was about thirty-six years old when I first saw her.

Compared with the women of the neighborhood, she was always well dressed. Compared with the wealthy women who came to the house, I would say that she dressed in simple, good taste. I know that she gave very little, if any, thought to her clothes. When she needed a dress, she probably told her dressmaker to make her a dress; the selection of the material was probably left to the discretion of the dressmaker. I recall one instance when she was being fitted for a dress, and when the dressmaker left with her tools and material, Jane Addams said: "What a bother, to waste all that time being fitted."

In contrast to the simplicity of Jane Addams, there were the many "grand ladies" who came to Hull-House. I was greatly impressed with the rustling silks and satins and velvets that these ladies wore. My admiration of these visitors was dimmed one day by an incident that stands out vividly in my memory. I was on my way to Hull-House when an elegant carriage, drawn by two spirited horses, stopped in front of the house. A footman, dressed in purple livery, jumped down from the driver's seat and opened the carriage door. Out stepped a queenly-looking woman dressed in silks, satin, and lace. On her head rested an enormous hat with several ostrich plumes sort of dripping down. She turned to the footman and said: "James, take the horses home. The air is very bad for them down here. You may return for me in two hours."

From the first day that I saw Jane Addams till the day she died, she never changed what is today called her "hairdo." Her hair, which was a soft brown when I first knew her, was always combed back and twisted into a bun at the back of her head. She probably never spent more than five minutes arranging her hair. There was no time in her life for beauty parlors and the long hours spent under hair dryers, where hairdos are set.

As time went on, I discovered that Hull-House was the experimental laboratory for Jane Addams's interests and services. To create opportunities for young people of the neighborhood, to bring a little sunshine into otherwise bleak lives of older immigrants, to point out the evils of miserable housing; in short, to tell Chicago what its responsibility to the poor was, was just first aid to the problem. She traveled through America spreading the gospel of a better life than she had found on South Halsted Street. As a result, social settlements sprang up all over the country. Chicago became dotted with playgrounds. Social centers were added to these playgrounds and became the responsibility of the city government.

Jane Addams was not a forceful speaker. She spoke with conviction and sincerity and always held her audience. Without radios or television, the lecture platform was the only means she had of telling the American people about the work of Hull-House. America needed that information, for there was poverty, loneliness, tragedy everywhere in this great and wonderful America.

The world began to regard Jane Addams as the prophets of old were regarded. She was honored wherever she went. All the adulation heaped upon her did not at any time make her aloof or allow her to lose the common touch. I remember one evening, when I was on duty answering the telephone for someone who had been ill, it started to rain and the thunder and lightning were unusually severe. Miss Addams was visiting on the North Side. In the midst of the storm she called up to tell me that she did not want me to go home while it rained so hard; that I was to go up and sleep in her bed.

The almost daily contacts with Jane Addams gave me an abiding faith in the true principles of Americanism. She was a firm believer in freedom of speech, freedom of the press, and freedom of religion. She demonstrated her belief by her actions at Hull-House, where men, women, and children of many faiths came together. At Hull-House no religion was introduced into any of the clubs or classes, with the one exception of the annual Christmas party, which became a sort of folklore tradition. The religious side of Christmas was left to the various churches. The feature of the Hull-House Christmas party centered around the trees and the songs and the candy and popcorn balls.

As for freedom of speech, I cannot recall any time when anyone was denied the use of the hall for a meeting on political grounds. The incident that stands out in my memory was the time when a group of young anarchists arranged for a meeting at which Emma Goldman was to be the speaker.[14] When the owners of the hall found out who the speaker was to be, they canceled the use of the hall. A committee came to see Miss Addams and asked if the meeting could be held at Hull-House. I will never forget her reply.

"Of course you may hold the meeting if there is a vacant room," she said. "I will see if there is a room."

There was a room and permission was granted for the meeting.

After the committee left, she turned and said to me: "I do not believe in anarchy, but I do not think it can be stopped by silencing its advocates. It will eventually die of its own inadequacy." She was indeed a wise prophet.

Jane Addams was not a "professional patriot," though her love of country was as deep as her faith in America. But it took her very little time to discover the so-called patriot who made a business of patriotism. She did not believe in the axiom "My country right or wrong."

When there was wrong in the country she wanted it removed and right established in its place.

In one of her addresses she said: "There is probably no greater love in the human heart than the love of a mother for her child. But that does not mean that a child must not be corrected from time to time. And so it is with love of country: it is our duty to point out the wrongs inflicted on American people."[15]

In retrospect, I feel that Jane Addams was perhaps too optimistic in thinking that a better world could be created within the economic conditions that prevailed.

Well, we still have poverty; we still have slums; we still have injustice; we still have discrimination.

But it was Jane Addams who pointed out that these evils exist. And we are on the road to a better life because she pointed the way.

New Horizons (II) 16

I was still working for the publishing company. The work was interesting and, at times, even enjoyable. I was now earning more money, and my pay was now called a "salary" instead of "wages."

The amateur and professional plays given at Hull-House aroused my interest in the theater. I could now afford to go to the theater once a week. The gallery seats cost from twenty-five to fifty cents in those days. The ten-cent seat in the Bijou Theatre no longer satisfied me.

An event I will never forget was going to see Otis Skinner and Ada Rehan in *The Taming of the Shrew.*[1] It was being given at the Illinois Theatre, which was located on Jackson Boulevard near Wabash Avenue. This theater, which was demolished many years ago, made theatrical history in Chicago.

My sister and I had bought tickets for this performance for a Saturday matinee. When the great day arrived, the worst snowstorm of the winter hit Chicago.[2] The streetcars were not running as the snow drifts were piled to mountainous proportions. So we walked to the theater, a distance of about two miles. Needless to say, it was worth walking ten miles in the snow to see this memorable performance.

Several years later I saw Otis Skinner in *Kismet,*[3] and one line has stayed with me through the years: "To the Caliph I am dust, but to the dust, I am the Caliph."[4]

At Hull-House there was Mary Shaw playing Ibsen's *Ghosts*[5] and George Bernard Shaw's daring *Mrs. Warren's Profession.*

I will never forget when William Butler Yeats came to Hull-House to read his poetry.[6] Or when Morris Rosenfeld came to read his Yiddish poems.[7] His poem "The Sweat Shop" was translated into English by James Weber Linn and set to music by Eleanor Smith, the head of the Music School at Hull-House.[8]

Then there were always plays being given by the Hull-House Players[9] and by the Children's Dramatic Club.[10] It was sheer delight to see young children perform plays by Molière, Shakespeare, and Schiller. The little boy of ten still stands out in my memory when he said: "Here is my dagger and here is my naked breast."[11]

I don't know how many of these children and young adults made a career of acting, but it was great fun while it lasted.

The great and noble plays of the theater of that time brought spiritual uplift and gaiety to my life. I saw Sir Henry Irving and Ellen Terry in *The Merchant of Venice,*[12] Sarah Bernhardt in the French version of *L'Aiglon,*[13] and Maude Adams in the English version.[14] E. H. Sothern and Julia Marlowe in *Romeo and Juliet* was a soul-stirring experience.[15] Then there was Minnie Maddern Fiske in a memorable performance of *Becky Sharp.*[16]

I vividly recall seeing James O'Neill in the *Count of Monte Cristo* at the old McVickers Theatre on West Madison Street.[17] I was thrilled by the scene where the hero of the play escaped from prison through the raging water. I did not know that almost fifty years later I was to see *Long Day's Journey into Night* by the actor's brilliant son, Eugene O'Neill, in which was revealed the tragedy that that play brought to the family of the popular and adored actor.

I also began going to grand opera. There was the Castle Square Opera Company performing in Chicago at that time.[18] It was a sort of opera repertory. The company performed a different opera each week and the tickets in the gallery were twenty-five cents.

The very first opera that I heard was *Faust.* Then followed *Martha, The Bohemian Girl, Carmen,* and many others.

Later my sister and I graduated to the Auditorium.[19] The walls of that grand old building heard the greatest performances of opera ever given anywhere. We heard Caruso, De Reszke, Schumann-Heinck, Emma Eames, Emma Calvé, Sembrich, Gadski, and the great Chaliapin. What rich memories these names bring back.

We also started going to musical comedies. These plays were a good tonic after a day of hard work. We saw *The Merry Widow,*[20] *The Prince of Pilsen,*[21] *King Dodo.*[22] Through the years the words of a song from *The Spring Chicken,*[23] with Richard Carle, linger in my memory:

> Will someone kindly tell me, will someone whisper why,
> To me it is a riddle and will be till I die,
> A million peaches 'round me, yet I would like to know
> Why I picked a lemon in the garden of love,
> Where they say only peaches grow.[24]

I solemnly declare that I did not look up these words; I remembered them, word for word.

Another incident that stands out is the night my sister and I went to see Weber and Fields and the lovely Lillian Russell.[25] The rain came down in sheets; but that would not stop us after we had paid for the tickets. We reached the theater, a little damp but anticipating a pleasant evening. We waited and waited but the curtain did not go up. About nine o'clock someone came out from the back of the stage and said: "Ladies and gentlemen, we ask your kind indulgence. The rain has flooded part of the stage, and all the chorus girls had to be carried from their dressing rooms to the stage. We are now ready to begin. We hope you will bear with us."

Since there was just a certain amount of money on which to live, I had to economize somewhere to be able to go to the theater. So I economized on clothes.[26] I had to be presentable at work, but I bought no party dresses. My mother would chide me for not giving more attention to my appearance. She was worried that I would not get a husband. But I was not worrying about a husband.

I had my share of dates. The members of the Ariadne Club often organized theater parties; we went to dances; we heard lectures and concerts at Hull-House. As I look back, although most of us worked hard all day to make a living and help support families, the evenings at Hull-House were filled with happy times.

A good many of the boys and girls of the Ariadne Club did pair off and get married.

A disturbing event came into my life about this time. The cashier in the department where I worked became ill and had to undergo surgery. The day she left, I was asked to substitute for her. While sitting in the cashier's cage I would do some of my former work. The man in charge of the department saw an opportunity to eliminate an employee.

The cashier was away for about four weeks, and no one had told her that she was not to return to her job. So when she was well, she returned to work. She was allowed to work that morning, and while I was out to lunch, she was told that she was no longer needed.

That was a great blow to her, as she had used up all the money she had on her illness.

When I returned from lunch, she was gone and the people in the department would not speak to me. Finally, one of the men came up to my desk and told me that the cashier had been told that I had suggested that I would do her work and mine, too. She had been very bitter and said some harsh words. "Only a Jew could do that," she had said.

Without a moment's delay, I went to see the head of the department and in no uncertain words told him that I would never again enter that cage.

"Well, if that's the way you feel, you can quit," he said.

"All right," I said. "I quit right now."[27]

I went to the locker in a rebellious mood. I took my coat and hat and left.

The news of what I had done soon reached the cashier and I received a warm note of apology and an invitation to dinner. I look back on this incident with a certain satisfaction. I had established friendly relations between an Irish Catholic and a Jewess but faced the problem of finding a job.

I went to a meeting of the Ariadne Club that night and jokingly asked one of the girls if she knew of a good job.

"Yes, I do," she said, "if you are willing to live away from home."

"I don't mind," I said. "What kind of job?"

"I know they need an assistant superintendent at the Marks Nathan Orphan Home," she said.[28] "The superintendent's wife was his assistant, but she's going to have a baby. The job is for six months." I got the job. My only regret was that I had to give up the English class at Hull-House.[29]

There were about two hundred children in the orphan home. Some were full orphans, some had lost one parent. The children were well cared for. Every child had his or her own bed in a large dormitory.[30] The food was very good and plentiful. The children were well clothed. They had excellent medical and dental care. But the heartbreaking period was bedtime. How was one to tuck in so many children and give them that good-night kiss that means so much to a child?

When the six months had passed, I was again looking for a job.

I had met and formed a lasting friendship with Sidney Teller. He had given up a successful career as an engineer to devote his life to social service. And he was dedicated to what he wanted to do. He had studied at the Chicago School of Civics and Philanthropy and was now ready for his first job in the field that he had chosen.[31] He worked during the day for the United Charities of Chicago and had been offered the position of superintendent of the Deborah Boys' Club, a home for working boys.[32] He thought he could manage both jobs, as he would be needed only at night at the club. But he had to have someone who would be responsible for the place during the day. He knew I was looking for a job and he telephoned me and asked me if I would become his assistant and take charge of the food and general management of the club.

The job sounded attractive. A cook was in the club and a maid to keep the house clean. Sidney and I were both to live at the club, but the cook would act as chaperon. In fact, her room was between Sidney's and mine.

There were about forty boys between the ages of fourteen and eighteen. They were working boys who had no homes and did not earn enough to pay their way in private homes.

My job was of a supervisory nature. I was to see that the house was kept clean, plan the menus, buy the food, take care of everybody's laundry, and keep things mended. While it kept me fairly busy, the work was not hard. I have never found it hard to tell others to do the actual work.

The boys were served breakfast; they took their lunches, which the cook prepared. In the evening Sidney and I would have dinner with the boys in a homelike fashion. We really tried to make a home for the boys.

Most of the boys had left school after finishing a few grades, so Sidney organized evening classes for them. Some preferred to play games, but there were some who wanted to improve their English, so Sidney started a class in English. He found a volunteer who took charge of the class. The teacher was Julia Pines.

I had formed some pleasant friendships in the Ariadne Club and the various classes that I had attended at Hull-House, but the deepest and most lasting friendship was made when I met Julia Pines and Sidney Teller.[33] Through the years they have been loyal and steadfast friends, in joy and in sorrow.

I had been attending a series of illustrated lectures on "European Cities and Their Social Significance" at Hull-House;[34] on this particular evening the subject was Berlin. The lecture was over about ten o'clock and I returned to the club.

As I was going up the stairs to my room, Sidney's door opened and he came out and said that a friend was visiting him. I looked up and there in the doorway stood a very young-looking man. He was rather short, about five feet four inches in height. He had blond curly hair and wore glasses.

"I would like to have you meet William Polacheck," Sidney said.[35]

I mumbled something about being "happy to meet him" and started to go to my room. But Sidney stopped me; he wanted to know if I could find something to eat in the kitchen. I thought I could and went down to raid the icebox and pantry. I found some cold tongue and rye bread. I arranged this on a tray with a jar of mustard. Then I decided to make some cocoa, as Sidney did not drink tea or coffee. I hunted for something sweet, but the boys had eaten all the cookies and cake. But I did find some raisins and nuts. I brought the tray upstairs and poured the cocoa.

We sat around eating and drinking the cocoa and talking. Sidney wanted to know what the subject of the lecture had been. I told them that a very interesting feature had been that a street-washing machine was being used in Berlin, which had been invented and manufactured in Milwaukee, and while this European city was using it, not a single city in America had yet seen fit to use it.[36]

Bill was very much interested. He was from Milwaukee.

The next morning the three of us had breakfast and Bill and Sidney left. That meeting with Bill did not impress me.

I did not even think of him again until I received a short and very proper note asking me if I would go to the theater with him the following Saturday. If I would, he would come to Chicago for the weekend. Also, if I agreed to go, would I get the tickets for any play I wanted to see, and he would, of course, pay for the tickets when he arrived.

I wrote him a short and proper note saying that I would be delighted to go to the theater with him, and the play I selected was *The Passing of the Third-Floor Back* with Forbes Robertson.[37] By return mail I received another note asking me if I would meet him at the train or the theater, as he could not arrive in time to call on me. This was not considered proper by etiquette authorities, but I met him at the train and we walked to the theater.

The play made no lasting impression. After the play Bill suggested that we go to the College Inn of the Sherman Hotel for something to eat. We were seated in a corner of the large room and Bill suggested that we have broiled lobster.[38] I had never eaten lobster and I was not a bit ashamed to say so. I said that I was afraid I would not know how to handle it. This did not seem to phase him a bit, for he ordered the lobsters, specifying that he wanted plenty of melted butter. When the lobsters were set before us, he very carefully prepared my lobster, scooping out all the meat from the shell and handing it to me. He then calmly prepared his lobster. The thought kept running through my head that the lobster was not kosher, but it tasted heavenly.

I was beginning to like Bill.

The Forward Movement 17

As the summer approached I became restless. I was beginning to lose interest in the work at the club.[1] A persistent urge to write was asserting itself more and more. I went to see Miss Addams, my never-failing refuge, and talked to her about it.

"I was waiting for you to come to this stage," she said. "You have been working steadily for a long time. Why not take some time off and try to do some writing?" She took a book from the shelf and handed it to me. "I have been wanting this book dramatized. Why don't you try your hand at it?"[2]

I looked at the book; it was *The Walking Delegate,* by Leroy Scott.[3] I looked doubtful. She wanted to know whether I needed money. I had saved some money during the winter; enough to leave with the family for daily expenses but not enough to pay for a vacation.

"You know you could wait on table at the Forward Movement," she said.[4] "You would get your food and lodging for that, and it would only take an hour of your time at each meal. You could write the rest of the time. It is a beautiful place on the shore of Lake Michigan in Saugatuck. I am sure you would like it."

Miss Addams had persuaded me. I rented a secondhand typewriter, bought a ream of paper, and decided to go to Saugatuck for the summer.

When my friends at the Ariadne Club heard of my latest venture, several of them decided to go with me. There were many conferences between parents and children and soon a party of four boys and three girls and a mother had been lined up for the vacation. The mother was to chaperon the party.

It was an overnight trip from Chicago to Michigan, but we were as excited as if we were going to cross the ocean. For some of us it was the first vacation away from Chicago. We had reserved state rooms, one for the boys and one for the girls. There were four bunks in each room. There was little or no sleeping that night. We stayed up on deck, watching the lapping water as the big ship went skimming along. There was a small orchestra on the boat and we danced for a while. We were young and life was beautiful.

We arrived in Holland, Michigan, about five o'clock in the morning.[6] We were told that we would have to take a trolley to Saugatuck but that the first trolley would not leave for two hours. Leaving our baggage in the checkroom of the dock, we walked to the main street of the town and looked for a place where we could have breakfast. We soon found a small restaurant. We walked in and sat down at a large round table. Soon a rosy-cheeked girl came in and greeted us with a cheery good-morning and asked us what we would like to eat. One of the boys spoke up and said, "What have you got?"

"Oh, we have steak, chops, waffles, pancakes, eggs any style, fried potatoes with all orders," she said.

We looked at one another. We had not been in the habit of eating meat for breakfast. But the boys were brave; they ordered steak. I timidly ordered scrambled eggs. After the girl had taken the orders, she went into the kitchen and soon came back with an enormous plate on which rested about two pounds of butter. I often think of that breakfast when I see the thin slivers of butter served today in restaurants. She also brought a huge pitcher of milk, a smaller pitcher of cream, several bowls of jelly, and a big bottle of syrup.

Then the orders began to arrive. One portion of steak was enough to feed a family. She also brought dozens of hot biscuits and a big plate of hot toast. She placed a big pot of coffee on the table and said, "Have a good time."

How we did eat that morning!

I kept thinking and wondering what this would cost. We had been reckless on that wonderful morning and never thought of asking the price of anything.

When we had eaten as much as we could possibly hold, we asked for our checks. Those who had ordered steak were given checks of thirty-five cents. Those who had eggs were charged twenty cents.

Our first view of the Forward Movement Camp was a sight I can never forget. The lake was blue and calm that morning and the sandy beach seemed endless. We were assigned to our sleeping quarters; the three girls and the mother were given one tent and the boys another. I was quartered in a dormitory where the people who waited on tables lived. This dormitory was located on the top of a hill and was a four-story house.[7] I was on the top floor. When I looked out of the window on one side, I looked over the tops of "millions" of trees, their leaves and branches swaying lazily in the breeze. From the opposite window I could get a view of the ribbonlike Kalamazoo River, winding its way about the countryside.[8] Then the most overpowering view of all, the great lake. That day it was as calm as the sky above it. The angry whitecaps that I had often seen in Chicago during the stormy weather were hidden in the bosom of the lake. The clouds had been stored in ethereal bags; it was a perfect day!

I unpacked my one bag. My wardrobe was meager, but I was sure it would be adequate for the summer. I had bought a navy blue alpaca swimming suit, which consisted of wide bloomers and a blouse to match, with very proper short sleeves and long black hose. No nice girl would go into the lake with bare legs.

After my clothes had been stored, I went to look for a place where I could deposit my typewriter. I found a niche under the stairs that I decided would be just right; I would not be in anybody's way and it would be quiet. I soon found a discarded wooden box in which peas had been shipped and took it to my corner. I placed the typewriter on it, put the paper on a chair near it, and was ready to write. Then I went down to explore the camp.

There was still an hour before the dinner bell, so I walked about drinking in the beauty everywhere. The first things that caught my eye were the signs marking various roads and paths. There was a Ruskin Road, a Lincoln Path, a Tolstoy Hill, a Browning Path, and many others bearing the names of poets, writers, artists, and composers.[9]

As I walked along, intoxicated with the surroundings, a tall white-haired man came toward me. It was Dr. Gray, the guiding light of the camp. He was another rare human being who had been placed on this earth to make life a little more bearable for us who had to live in the world.[10]

The Forward Movement played a dual role. There was a camp for poor children, who were given a free vacation, and the camp for paying guests, whose fees helped pay for the children's camp.

I had set a rigid schedule for myself. I would get up early, eat breakfast, wait on table, remove the dishes to the kitchen, then set the table for the next meal. Then I would climb the hill and the stairs where my typewriter was waiting. I wrote till the first bell rang, summoning the waiters. I would eat dinner, which was served at noon, repeat the process of the morning, and then go back to the typewriter for two hours. I would then put on my overpowering swimming suit and go down to the beach, where my friends were waiting for me. I never learned to swim, so I missed the joy of gliding through the water, but I did enjoy getting into the cool lake and sitting on the sandy bottom with the water reaching my neck.

After supper I would write till dark. Several times I took time off to watch the sunset. At Forward Movement there was a sun-setting period. It was almost a religious rite. The people would gather on the beach, on benches, on the steps leading to the beach, to watch the sunset. There was no talking while the great ball of fire slowly descended into the lake, shedding its colors on the water as it slowly sank. No words could do justice to those sunsets. You had to live through the sight to know the power it had over us poor humans, sitting there, humbly small and yet feeling rich to be part of it.

After dark there were bonfires and marshmallow roasts. Once or twice a week we would go to the town of Saugatuck to dance. There was a large beautiful dance pavilion there, with a smooth floor and good music.[11] The pavilion was built on the edge of the river and had a veranda all around it. We would sit there between dances and watch the boats, with their twinkling lights, glide by. After the dance was over, we would go to the village drugstore and gorge ourselves on five-cent ice-cream sodas. And when we were reckless, we would order an angel's wing for ten cents. This fabulous dish consisted of a banana cut into four pieces which were draped over the sides of the dish. Then three scoops of ice cream, chocolate, strawberry, and vanilla, would be put on top of the banana. Over this would be poured a thick strawberry sauce and then a small mountain of whipped cream gracefully arranged. This would be topped with chopped nuts and a bright red cherry would top the whole concoction. I almost swoon when I think of them.

After one of these orgies we would stagger back to camp. We would have to cross the river in rowboats if it was too late for the ferry. Then we would walk up the road, carrying our lanterns. These lanterns were made of a circle of tin and a heavy wire handle that was clipped to the circle. In the center was a holder for a candle and over it was a glass chimney.

The vacation for my friends who had come to Saugatuck soon ended and they returned to Chicago. But I stayed on and worked on the play. I worked steadily and faithfully for the balance of June and most of July. During this time I had been receiving short notes at first, then long letters from Milwaukee. I wrote to Bill once a week, as I was reluctant to take any time away from my typewriter.

About the middle of July I received a letter from Bill saying that he would like to come to Saugatuck for a week; would I reserve a tent for him, as he would like to camp.[12] I wrote back that the tent was waiting for him.

He arrived the following Friday morning on the first trolley.

I asked to be relieved of waiting on table for that week, as I wanted to eat with Bill during his stay. We were together every day of that heavenly week. We walked through Browning Path, up Tolstoy

Hill, down Lincoln Path and Ruskin Road. We went to town several times to dance and walked home with our lanterns, holding hands. By this time I was very much in love.

The days passed, much too fast. He had rented a rowboat and we would row down the river, lazily. Bill would recite reams of poetry which he had memorized. He was very fond of German, which he knew well, and he would recite Heine fluently. How vividly I recall his saying:

> Du bist wie eine Blume
> So hold und schoen und rein . . .[13]

He never tired of reciting Browning. While the boat drifted he recited Yeats:

> I will arise and go now, for always night and day
> I hear lake water lapping with low sounds by the shore . . .[14]

I was becoming quite unhappy. I would not for the world have let him know how I felt. I made a heroic effort to be gay during the time I was with him, but when I climbed my hill it was with a heavy heart. After all, it was possible that he was not in love with me. And a nice girl did not come right out and ask the man if he loved her. That was forbidden by all the rules of what was proper.

The last Saturday night of his stay I wore the only white dress that I had brought. It was a nice dress with many little ruffles of lace; I wore two or three petticoats. My hair, which was almost black, was arranged in a becoming way. I put a small red poppy in my hair. I considered myself quite elegant.

We went to the dance and danced all evening together.[15] He did not leave my side for a moment. Several of the boys asked me to dance, but he glared at them and frightened them away.

Pretty soon the orchestra was playing "Home Sweet Home," which was the signal that the dance was over. We walked to our boat and rowed across the river. He lit the candles of our lanterns and we started up the road to the camp. When we reached Browning Path, we turned in. We had to walk very close to each other, as the path was narrow. He put his arm around my waist and we kept on chattering about how wonderful the evening had been, how he liked to dance with me; but that was all. No hint of a proposal.

When we reached the foot of the hill, he said good-night and went to his tent. In those days, a nice boy did not kiss a nice girl good-night.

It was raining the next morning. The elements were sharing my sorrow and weeping for me. But I appeared in the dining room with a cheery good-morning. He was sorry it was raining on his last day. After breakfast he suggested we take a walk in the rain. We put on raincoats and rubbers and started off. We pushed our way through the woods and found some new paths. The gentle rain was dropping on the leaves and on our rainhats. I tried to put out of my mind the thought that he would leave the next day.

By the time we had finished dinner it was raining very hard and he said that his throat was a little sore. So I suggested that he go to bed. He agreed and went off.

I climbed the hill to my room and stood looking at the angry lake. I tried to read my manuscript. The words seemed blurred.

The supper bell rang. I dressed in a blue calico dress. This time I did not care how I looked. After all, what did it matter? I was sure Bill did not love me. He liked me, yes, but that was all. I was quite sure that Bill would not propose to me. But I was determined not to let him know how I felt.

There was a plate of carrot strips, radishes, and green onions on the table. In desperation I ate several onions.[16]

When we had finished eating he asked me if I could get him some hot water and salt so that he could gargle.[17] He said he would go to his tent and finish packing and I should bring the water and salt to the tent.

I went to the kitchen, took a pitcher and filled it with hot water, put some salt into a cup, and went to his tent. He was standing between the flaps of the tent, looking at the angry lake.

I handed him the pitcher and the cup. He put them on the table and came back and firmly took my arms and pulled me into the tent. The next moment I was in his arms and his lips were pressed close to mine.

And I had eaten raw onions for supper!

When I think back to that rapturous moment of my life, I realize that Bill did not ask me to marry him in mere words. In 1911 no "proper" young man kissed a "proper" girl unless he meant to marry her. And Bill meant just that, and I knew it.

As soon as I had regained my breath I demanded: "Why didn't you do this last night or the night before or the night before that?"

"I wasn't absolutely sure that you would say yes, and I was not going to spoil my week," he said with a twinkle in his eyes.

I kissed him good-night and left him standing in the entrance of the tent, blowing me a final kiss. The lake was still angry.

I did not see Bill the next morning. He left the camp at six o'clock so he could catch the seven o'clock trolley.

It had stopped raining. The sun shone brighter than it had ever shone since the world began. The birds were singing a cheerful good-morning to me. It was a beautiful day and I was very happy.

As I stood in front of the mirror combing my hair, I said to myself: Shake the stars out of your eyes, there's work to be done. I went down to the dining room, ate my breakfast, and resumed waiting on table. Then I returned to my typewriter.

The Walking Delegate 18

I returned to work on the play in real earnest and allowed nothing to interfere with my work. I worked all day as long as there was light. The characters of the play began to live for me. After dark I would stretch out on my bed and ponder the situations described in Leroy Scott's novel.[1]

The central character of the book had been drawn from Sam Parks, the labor racketeer.[2] Parks had become a power in the building trades union in New York by leading a successful strike which had won a raise in pay for the workers. His success probably went to his head, and he began to dream of wealth for himself.

Some time later another strike was called, and by this time Parks was in complete control. There were rumors that he had been known to accept bribes, but the workers remembered only the raise in their pay envelopes and were willing to let Parks be their spokesman.

It was not until conclusive evidence was presented in court that Parks had "sold" the strike for a considerable amount of money that he was arrested, tried, and sentenced to a prison term.

Leroy Scott, a newspaperman in Chicago, was a resident at Hull-House. In his book *The Walking Delegate,* he developed the thesis that not only was there a conflict between the honest and dishonest elements in the trade unions but that there were honest and dishonest elements in the ranks of the employers. Wherever there was a bribe-taker, there was a bribe-giver. This was the point that most interested Miss Addams.

The central figures in Mr. Scott's book were Buck Foley, the dishonest labor leader, and Tom Keating, the honest foreman and leader.

In the book, Mr. Scott chose the Iron Workers' Union as the scene of operations. Buck Foley had led a successful strike and had become the hero of the workers. In a bitterly contested election, where Buck Foley and Tom Keating were the candidates for walking delegate, Foley won by a very small margin.

Shortly after the election another strike was called and Foley was in complete control. Tom heard rumors that Foley was known to accept bribes, but whenever he brought these rumors to the attention of the workers, the majority were still behind Foley.

But the day came when Tom Keating proved to the workers that Foley had "sold" the strike for fifty thousand dollars. And like his counterpart, he was sent to prison.

In the dramatization, I had the play end in a stirring meeting of the union, where Foley is exposed by Keating. The workers are enraged and are ready to lynch Foley, but he escapes.

In my pondering I kept thinking that while Sam Parks had been sent to prison, which he richly deserved, I had never heard of any punishment meted out to the people who had brought about his downfall.

Miss Addams and Mrs. Pelham, the director of the Hull-House Players,[3] had for some time wanted a play written by someone in the neighborhood; someone who had attended classes at Hull-House. They wanted the play produced by the Hull-House Players. And here was a perfect setup.[4] A book written by a resident; dramatized by a student of Hull-House; and performed by its own actors. It was the first time that such an event had taken place. I do not know whether it was ever repeated.

I had no illusions that the play would have any commercial value.[5] As I look back, I did the best I could. An experienced writer might have made a good play out of the book, though I doubt whether it would be a successful commercial play. The subject matter was not popular. There was too much corruption in the trade union movement and in industry to make the subject acceptable to the commercial theater. I was satisfied to write the play and to have it produced at Hull-House.

I continued working day after day in my corner under the stairs. Some days were very hot, but as there were no men permitted in the house, I would often work in a petticoat. The comfortable and sensible shorts had not yet been discovered.

The dramatization of *The Walking Delegate* was a tiny incident in Jane Addams's interest in the labor movement. Before she asked me to dramatize the book, there had been labor upheavals in which she had played an important part.

I recall an incident that sounds more like fiction than labor history. In the big clothing shops in Chicago, before there was a union, foremen and forewomen had the power to cut the pay of workers without consulting the employer. That is, they had the permission to do so. The lower the cost of operation, the higher the profit, and the higher the pay of the foremen. It was common knowledge that these foremen and forewomen could be ruthless in their greed for advancing their own pay at the expense of the workers.

The story was told of a young girl who was working in the largest clothing factory in Chicago. She was a seamer of men's pants, for which she received four cents a pair. The foreman got the brilliant idea of cutting the pay by a quarter of a penny. The girl became incensed and with several of her colleagues complained to the employer. When the girls were told that the foreman was in charge and had all the authority, a baker's dozen of the girls, led by the spirited girl who was the first to object to the cut in pay, walked out of the factory. It was entirely a spontaneous act. There was no union and hence no one could order them to strike.

No one paid much attention to the incident. Fourteen angry girls quitting their jobs was regarded as somewhat of a joke. But after all, little David's slingshot had killed the mighty Goliath and who could tell what might happen.

The next thing that happened was that the finishers in the pants department refused to finish the pants that had been sewn by the people who remained at the machines. Each day a few more people would leave their work, calling to the others to follow. In some cases the foreman would try to stop the workers, but they pushed him aside and kept walking out of the factory. This happened toward the end of September 1910. By the middle of October, eight thousand workers were on strike and had begun organizing what is today the mighty Amalgamated Clothing Workers of America.[6]

That winter was a bitter one for the workers. I recall many scenes and incidents that took place. Since the owners of the clothing factory were among the largest contributors to the Jewish charities, it was rumored that they had threatened to withhold their contributions if relief was given to the strikers. Winter put in its appearance far too soon that year. The men in their thin, threadbare coats and women in their long skirts and shawls picketed faithfully. I recall some residents of Hull-House who walked in those picket lines.

Since the days of Peter Stuyvesant, the Jewish people had taken care of the Jewish poor. But now it was not a question of accidental poverty; the Jewish strikers could have gone on working (long hours for miserable wages). If they did not work, why should they be given relief? So argued the employers.

Jane Addams and James Mullenbach, who was then superintendent of the United Charities,[7] and others set out to solicit money for food and coal for the strikers. In the two months at the beginning of that winter they were able to collect about twenty thousand dollars,

with which they set up milk stations and food stores. Many doctors treated the strikers, especially those beaten by the police, without charge. The strike had the complete support of the socially minded people of Chicago. The chief credit for all this good will must go to Jane Addams.[8]

Bill's heartwarming letters arrived daily. In my eagerness to finish the play I did not always take time to answer his letters. One day I wrote and asked him to send me a can of typewriter oil. What could have been more prosaic? This was his reply: "I have sent the oil. From now on *The Walking Delegate* will go smoothly. Knowing that this is my first gift to you, I have had it perfumed in Turkistan, wrapped in a can of gold, and there is a gleaming diamond in the can which is a part of the Star of Bethlehem. And it's good oil."[9] The play was finished the last week of August and I packed my belongings and returned to Chicago.[10]

I took my precious bundle of paper to Hull-House and turned it over to Miss Addams. It was a labor of love; the first offering that I could give her in return for having given me a life free from drudgery, boredom, and ignorance.

The play was read and re-read several times by Mrs. Pelham, the director of the Hull-House Players. She finally told me that the play had merit but that she wanted some scenes rewritten.[11]

By this time I found myself without funds, and the money that I had left with Mother for the summer had been used up. I was very eager to get back my job at the publishing house; I wanted to work there until such time as Bill and I would decide to be married. We had tentatively decided to wait a year. I pocketed my pride and went to see my former supervisor and asked him for my former job. I started to work that very day.

Every evening was given to rewriting the scenes that Mrs. Pelham wanted changed. I kept consulting with her and making changes till Christmastime, when she finally accepted the manuscript. After the holiday season the play was put into rehearsal.[12]

As I look back I get a warm feeling of satisfaction at the restraint I displayed in offering no suggestions or objections to Mrs. Pelham. I felt that she knew all about producing a play and I knew nothing.

My mother was overjoyed when I told her that I was engaged. The day after I told her the good news, this note arrived:[13]

> Dear Mrs. Satt:
>
> Hilda has told you that we are engaged to be married. We find that we love each other and our happiness is based on that prospect. But we want you to feel happy in our happiness.

> I am a young man, of good health and a fair capacity for making sufficient money to support Hilda and a most determined desire to make her happy. I love her dearly.
>
> So I ask you, humbly and affectionately, to accept me as a son. I am sorry that I can't speak so that you can easily understand me, but you will be able to feel my sincerity.
>
> We would like to be married in July.
>
> I hope you are well. I hope you will like me—and give us your blessing—that you will feel that you are not losing a daughter, but are gaining a son.
>
> Your loving son,
> William

My sister read the letter to Mother and translated each word. Mother was deeply touched, and I know that she loved him as long as she lived.[14]

That winter was enriched by the frequent letters from Milwaukee. How we did set the world to rights in those letters! He was in favor of the eight-hour day. He was even rooting for a five-day week. In those days the accepted facts of today were considered too advanced.[15]

I felt more and more how much indebted I was to Jane Addams. If it had not been for those few months, brief as they were, at the University of Chicago, I would never have attracted a man like Bill. I could not possibly have discovered the things that I was able to talk about unless I had that guidance. I had found out how and where to look for books. I had learned to listen to symphonies and enjoy them. And I felt greatly privileged to receive those letters.

When the rehearsals of *The Walking Delegate* were in full swing and dates had been set for performances, I shared my beautiful secret with Miss Addams. She looked at me for a moment, then asked me: "Is he Jewish?"

When I assured her that he was, she took me in her arms and kissed me.

She then explained why she had asked me that question. Personally she felt that marriage was only the concern of the two people involved. But an incident in New York had been very distressing for her. A Jewish girl who had been attending classes in a settlement there had married a non-Jew and the people of the neighborhood had blamed the settlement for the girl's "downfall."[16]

"I am very happy that you will be married, and I am happy that you chose a Jewish man," Jane Addams said. And then, with her generous understanding, she added: "I am happy for your mother's sake. I know she would be unhappy if you did not marry a Jewish man."

She then asked me to come to her room. There on a table was a pile of books. They were the first copies of *Twenty Years at Hull-House* which had been delivered to her. She picked up a copy and wrote on the fly leaf:[17]

To Miss Hilda Satt
Comp of the "author"
Jane Addams

"Here is a small gift," she said handing it to me. This *small gift* has become one of my most cherished possessions.

Now that there was no more work to be done on *The Walking Delegate,* I went back to teaching my class in English. When the Hull-House classes opened in January, I was assigned to a class. Most of my former students had gone into advanced classes. I was deeply moved when one of them insisted on coming back to my class for pronunciation.

When Bill came to Chicago for a New Year's Eve party, we decided to be married in April. We saw no good reason why we had to wait until July. So we set the date for April 17.

Bill had not told his mother of our engagement and our plans to be married. She had been a widow for some time and had leaned rather heavily on Bill. To her, he had taken the place of his father. Our marriage would bring a change in her life that she would not find easy to accept. So we decided not to tell her till one month before the wedding. We thought that if she was going to be unhappy, she might as well be unhappy a year later.

But the day arrived when she was told, and I had to pay my first visit to his home.[18] I was to arrive in Milwaukee on a Sunday morning and have dinner with my future mother-in-law, and in the afternoon I was to meet his grandparents.

It was the beginning of March and it was cold. My mother and sisters made a great to-do as to what I was to wear. They wanted me to make the best possible impression on Bill's mother, so I had to buy a new dress. It was a dark red broadcloth dress, the most expensive dress I had had since coming to America.

Bill met me at the train. I confessed to him that I was scared. But he assured me that his mother was quite ready to receive me and that he was sure that she was reconciled to the inevitable.

My first impression of Bill's mother was that she was very beautiful, very proud, and very cold. I do not recall whether she kissed me on that first meeting; I think not. But she said that I was welcome and that she hoped that Bill and I would be happy.

A simple dinner was served by a maid. Bill and his younger

brother kept the conversation going. I liked his brother from the start.

When the dinner was over, Bill's mother excused herself and said she would take a short nap. The brother had to go to study for an exam. Bill and I went to the living room and started looking at his fine collection of books. While looking at the books Bill told me a little of the history of his family. His grandparents had come to America in 1848.[19] His father [was then one year old] and his mother had been born in Milwaukee. His father had built up a successful lighting fixture business, where Bill was now working. His father died when Bill was about fourteen years of age, leaving his family in more than comfortable circumstances. His mother always insisted on spending much less than she could afford. She owned the two-story house in which they were living and wanted to live in the upper flat and rent the lower instead of getting a house.

Before long Bill's mother came out of her room, wearing her hat and coat, and said she was ready to go see her parents. We walked several blocks to the apartment building where the grandparents lived in a modern apartment.

I was greeted warmly by the grandfather and indifferently by the grandmother. They spoke German and when they heard I could speak German they became very friendly.

When supper was announced by a German maid we all went into the dining room, which was in the rear of the apartment. I was quite startled and horrified to see a huge platter of ham on the table. This was really an indication that they had come to America much sooner than I had. While I had by this time learned to eat nonkosher food, I still had an inhibition against anything that came from the pig.

Grandfather opened a bottle of champagne and toasted us in good German style with *"Hoch sohl sie leben."*

I wanted to catch a seven o'clock train, so Bill and I left right after supper. As soon as we were on the street Bill said: "How do you feel?"

"Well, I'm still alive," I said. "But it was an ordeal."

My mother and sisters now went to work feverishly to get me fitted out so that I would enter my married state in proper clothes. I had already announced that there would be no veil or any other "folderol" that goes with a wedding.

I had no idea at that time where all the sheets, pillowcases, towels, tablecloths, and napkins came from. I later found out that my generous sister Anna had paid for most of the things that I was to bring to my new home. I was also told to go to a tailor, where I had my first custom-made suit made. It was an elegant navy blue serge suit.

A dressmaker was brought into the house, and before long I was being fitted into several silk dresses. One was a beautiful white crepe silk, trimmed with some rare lace that Mother had brought from Poland.

The dates of the performances of *The Walking Delegate* were set,[20] and we discovered that a performance had been scheduled for the night when we planned to be married. We made no changes in our plans. We decided it would be fun to attend a performance after the wedding dinner that Mother had planned.

The first performance of the play was on 10 April.[21] I have no recollection of that performance. It was a week before the wedding and I suppose that event crowded every other thing out of my mind.

We were married in a rabbi's study. I wore my prized navy blue suit and a small navy blue straw hat trimmed with a small stalk of wheat. Bill may have sent me a corsage, but I do not remember.

After the "I do's" had been said and the ring had been placed on my finger, we went to my home where Mother and my sisters served an appropriate wedding dinner. Everybody said it was wonderful. I am sure it was, but I cannot recall eating anything.

When the marriage certificate was given to me, I suddenly realized that this precious document, in addition to making me Bill's wife, also made me a citizen of the United States.[22] It is curious that I should have thought of this at such an auspicious moment, but I did.

Had my father lived to become a citizen, the children would have been naturalized through his citizenship—that was the law before the Cable Act was passed. I did not feel it was important for me to apply for citizenship since I could not vote. Even in those days I felt that women were second-class citizens. They were expected to pay taxes but had no voice as to how the taxes were to be spent. But now I was a citizen of my adopted country, and I hope I have always been a loyal citizen, following the precepts of Jane Addams.

It is customary for a bride to change from her white dress to a suit. Well, I reversed the process. I changed from a suit to my lovely white silk dress, and we all started for Hull-House in automobiles, if you please, which had been rented for the occasion.

Miss Addams had invited all of us to a party to be given after the second performance of the play.[23] The play was well received by the audience. There were rounds of applause after each act, and I was quite the heroine of the evening. I was surrounded between the acts by my friends from the Ariadne Club.

When the curtain came down on the last act there were shouts of "Author!" and I was led to the stage; there I stood bowing, my heart just too full to say a word, and the tears were rolling down my cheeks. Someone handed me a tremendous bouquet of red roses and the curtain was lowered.

The party that followed made the deepest impression. I was a little dazed when I was being married and things are slightly foggy. But that party stamped itself on my mind.

The tables were set in the coffeehouse. All the residents, I believe, attended. I felt humbly grateful that this gallant group of men and women, who had come to live in the house that was to bring hope and some sunshine into the lives of so many people and so many reforms to the city, had come to honor me. The actors, who had breathed life into my characters, were all there. They were a fine group of friends, and they gathered around me and were very generous with their praise of the play.

When I finally was led to a table and seated between Bill and my mother, Jane Addams whispered in my ear that I must tell my mother that the chickens in the chicken salad were kosher.

That was the tolerant, generous, understanding heart of Jane Addams. She had gone to all that trouble to please my mother. But what she did not know was that the dishes, the butter, the cream in the coffee, the ice cream, and the small cakes baked with butter made everything not kosher.

PART IV

Family Life and Politics in Milwaukee, 1912–29

Milwaukee 19

The next day Bill and I left for Milwaukee. This was to be our new home, and though it was only eighty-five miles from Chicago, I looked forward to the trip as if I were going to Europe, or at least to California. For the present, this two-hour trip was all the honeymoon trip we were to have. But Bill was going to stay away from work for a whole week. His mother, having gone to New York, left us to live in her apartment, and for that one week we would forget the outside world and just create a small world of our own.

We reached Milwaukee about five o'clock in the afternoon. It was raining—a slow, pleasant, April rain. We stopped at a grocery store near the house and bought some food. We decided that we would fix our own supper—our first meal by ourselves. I selected a loaf of bread, some butter, a dozen eggs, and a quart of milk. I decided that would be enough for the time being and that I would do some shopping in the morning. I did not pay any attention to what Bill was buying. The grocer put everything into a large bag, Bill paid him, and we left.

When we reached the apartment I took off my hat and coat and went into the kitchen to cook our first meal. When I opened the bag a horrible odor greeted me and I called Bill to come and see what had happened to the food we had bought.

"I don't see how anything could have spoiled in so short a time," I said, "but this food simply stinks."

Bill came into the kitchen and, after one sniff, he burst out laughing. He pulled a small package from the bag. It was Limburger cheese. In those days that German delicacy was not packed in jars, so I was given the full benefit of its odor. This was my introduction to Limburger cheese, which Bill adored and which I detested.

I scrambled some eggs and made toast and we sat down to the first meal that I prepared. Bill ate his smelly cheese with great relish while I struggled to keep from holding my nose. When we finished Bill took me in his arms and said: "I will now repay you for having eaten raw onions on that never-to-be-forgotten day in Saugatuck."

His kisses were wonderful, even if they were flavored with Limburger cheese.

During that first enchanted week of our married life Bill told me a little about his family. His father had been brought to America as an infant from Bohemia, some forty years before I came. At the time there were two children in the family. They lived in a small house, which did not even have running water. Bill's grandfather supported the small family by buying and selling cattle. He would drive to nearby farms where he made his purchases and then would bring the livestock to Milwaukee where he would sell his cows or calves or sheep or lambs to the local butcher. The butchers did their own slaughtering in those days. In most cases this livestock had to be kept overnight or several days until they were sold. The pump was about a block from the house, so the grandmother not only had to pump and carry water for the family use, but water had to be carried for the animals.

"My grandfather had an idea that when he brought home the cattle, his job was finished," said Bill. "It was Grandmother's job to feed the cattle and supply them with water."

As the years went by, more children were born, and whenever it was necessary a wing was added to the small house. By the time the eighth child was born, it had become a big house.

Although I had never cooked anything at home, I had often watched my mother prepare food, and I had no difficulty from the very start in preparing meals. I took special delight in showing Bill that I could cook. I do not recall [except for one incident] ever spoiling any food, or allowing it to burn, or baking biscuits that could be used as bricks [probably because] I did not try to bake biscuits.

Bill returned to his work a week after we were married, and I was on my own as a cook. It was the custom in Milwaukee for the men to come home for a noon dinner, a custom imported from Germany, I suppose. This custom brought about the first and only disaster I experienced as a cook.

I had bought a thick, beautiful steak and I was going to broil it to a rare and juicy state, just the way Bill liked it.

He told me he would be home about twelve o'clock. I watched the clock and at exactly fifteen minutes to twelve I popped the steak into the broiler and watched it lovingly while it turned to a beautiful golden brown. The hands of the clock pointed to twelve. I had dinner ready on time. The table was set. The salad was crisp and inviting, with a small tomato cut into the shape of a flower. But there was no Bill to eat it. I did not want to take the steak out of the broiler, as I did not want it to get cold. So I just allowed it to keep broiling. It was now twelve-thirty, but there was no Bill in sight. Thinking he would be along any minute, I poured a glass of bubbly beer and put it next to his plate. Before long I realized that this was a mistake, as the beer began to look flat. The lettuce began to look droopy and I was on the verge of tears. It was now one o'clock and the steak was still in the broiler. At one-thirty I heard a key in the lock and a smiling Bill walked in. The steak was dry and almost burned, the beer was warm and flat, and my beautiful salad was limp.

"I'm sorry to be late," he said cheerfully, kissing me, as if nothing had happened.

"You said you would be home at twelve o'clock and to please have dinner ready," I said, choking back the tears.

"Well, I had a customer and he insisted on telling me the history of his life, and you know you must always listen to a customer," Bill said.

"Well, the dinner is ruined," I said, and I ran into the bedroom, where I indulged myself with hysterical weeping.

Never again did I put a steak into the broiler until Bill was in the house.

During the coming weeks Bill introduced me to Milwaukee. The most natural place to start was the Schlitz Palm Garden.[1] I really was impressed with that famous landmark.

It was an enormous room with artificial palms arranged against the walls all around the room. Small, medium-sized, and large tables were placed about in a homey fashion. The tables were covered with plaid tablecloths that gave a cheerful look to the room.

Families of father, mother, and even small children were seated around the tables eating pungent sauerbraten with fluffy dumplings and beautiful purple sweet-sour cabbage. Everybody was drinking beer from tall steins.

The headwaiter seated us at a small table with a hearty *guten Abend*. After he had left, I asked Bill if he knew the waiter; he had seemed so friendly.

"Oh, he greets everybody that way," Bill said. "Just plain good old German hospitality. Outside of being presented with a check, you feel that you are visiting." And that is just how it felt.

There was much visiting between the people at the tables. It seemed like a big party in a private home. There was a small string orchestra playing, and it was not at all unusual for someone to start singing to the music that was being played.

When another waiter came for our order, without a moment's hesitation I ordered sauerbraten and dumplings and sweet-sour cabbage.

"And will you have a stein or a bottle of beer?" the waiter asked hopefully. I will never forget the look on his face when I ordered coffee. He seemed to say: "Where did this barbarian come from?"

We spent many wonderful evenings at the Schlitz Palm Garden, and I was very sad when Prohibition ended its colorful life.

I was very much impressed the first time that Bill took me for a long walk down Prospect Avenue.[2] At that time the street was lined with stone mansions that served as homes for the wealthy residents. Some of the mansions looked like mausoleums. There was a stone castle built on a bluff, overlooking Lake Michigan. It was supposed to have been a copy of a *schloss* on the Rhine. Bill pointed out the homes of the brewers, the tanners, and other millionaires who lived here in German splendor. When we reached West Water Street, Bill took me to Martini's.[3]

Martini's had nothing to do with cocktails . . . or liquor of an intoxicating nature. It was a German bakery and coffeehouse. But simply to say that it was a bakery was like saying that the sunset was "nice."

The divine odor of freshly baked kuchen just naturally started the juices flowing in your mouth. On the wall hung a funny little framed German sign that read: *Hier wird English Gesprochen* (Here English is being spoken).[4]

The showcases were bulging with the greatest variety of German pastry ever displayed outside of Germany. There were coffee rings, with rich, thick frosting topped with chopped nuts. There were bund kuchens, with browned almonds peeping from the crust. There was streusel kuchen, with rich buttery streusel sprinkled generously over the top. Then there were horns filled with either nuts or fruit. The cheese torte was no measly thin layer of cheese. The cheese was about four inches high and had been made of real cream cheese, flavored with lemon and orange. Then there was mohn kuchen, a rich dough rolled with a mixture of poppy seed and honey and nuts.

Of the smaller variety there were berliners, bismarcks, schnecken, cream puffs, chocolate eclairs with rich, thick chocolate frosting.

The fruit kuchen case was a riot of color. There were apple, apricot, cherry, peach, plum, blueberry, and every kind of fruit that could be combined with rich kuchen dough. Near this case was a huge bowl containing a mountain of whipped cream. If you wished to take on the extra poundage, you could have your fruit kuchen smothered in the whipped cream.

In the rear of the store was a large room with marble-top tables where hot or iced coffee and chocolate were served. A waitress brought the coffee in a huge heavy cup, but you had to go out to the store to select your pastry. There was such a variety that it would take a yard-long menu card to list them all. So Mr. Martini solved the problem by simply having each person select the pastry and carry it back to the table.

If you ordered iced coffee you were served a glass holding about a quart of rich black coffee with a huge lump of ice cream floating in the coffee; this was topped with gobs and gobs of whipped cream. If you ordered chocolate it was served smothered in whipped cream.

In one corner of this room there was a large table. Until four o'clock in the afternoon the public was permitted to sit at this table. After four o'clock it became a *Stamm-tisch*[5] and was reserved for the German actors of the resident stock company and for German newspapermen. After rehearsals the actors would gather here for their coffee break. There seemed to be no staring or gawking at the celebrities. Everybody was used to seeing them at that table. They had become home folks. There was almost no English spoken at Martini's. I recall the first time I was there, I spoke in whispers to Bill, as everybody else was speaking German and I felt I might be conspicuous.

The German Theatre brings back rich memories.[6] The audience was composed mostly of season ticket holders. Going to the theater became a ritual. The audience seemed to be a large family meeting each week. There were performances on Sunday and Wednesday nights. Our season tickets were for Wednesday and we never missed a performance.

The first German play that I saw that week was *Die Versunkene Glocke* (The Sunken Bell). I loved the smooth, rich poetic German.

I recall a fine play called *Die Fünf Frankfurter,* a play about the Rothschild family, in which Hedwig Beringer, the only name I can remember, played the part of the mother of the five Rothschilds.[7] A sensitive performance of Hauptmann's *The Weavers* is a pleasant memory. There were plays by Shakespeare, Ibsen, Shaw—all translated into German. There were plays by Schiller and Goethe and many others. The first performance I ever saw of Shaw's *Pygmalion* was a German translation in the Pabst Theatre.[8]

Milwaukee had its social settlements. The one in the Jewish neighborhood was simply called "the Settlement." To me it was like a little sister of Hull-House. Bill was in charge of all boys' activities, and it was quite natural for me to feel at home there.

The Settlement had been started by a group of socially minded men and women and they had the responsibility of supporting it.[9] Mrs. Simon Kander, who had conceived the idea of the Settlement, now gave birth to another idea. She and some of her co-workers issued a small cookbook to help support their pet project. It was a very thin book at the time and sold for fifty cents. Today it is the world-famous *Settlement Cook Book.*[10]

Outside of Bill's family, the first person to invite me to a private home in Milwaukee was Mrs. Kander. This was during the second week in my newly adopted city. There were about twenty women invited to this party. What an array of home-baked kuchen and pastries was set before us! It was a miniature Martini's.

The women were warm in their welcome to me and made me feel at home. Each one assured me that I had married a wonderful man. I agreed with all of them. Before I left that party I had been made a member of the local section of the National Council of Jewish Women.

Being still imbued with the writing bug, I looked around for some kind of writing job. Bill suggested that I offer my services to the *Milwaukee Leader,* the Socialist paper of that day. Since it was a non-profit paper, and since it operated in the red most of the time, I offered to work without pay. I was given the job of dramatic critic.[11]

The Socialist paper was quite "respectable" in Milwaukee at that time. It enjoyed the second-largest circulation in the city and carried as much advertising as the leading paper. Milwaukee had a Socialist mayor, and it was well known that he was elected by many people who were not members of the Socialist party. The membership of the party was nowhere near as large as the vote cast for the mayor.

Though I did not get any pay, I did get two seats in the "fourth row center," a time-honored place for dramatic critics, so we saw all the plays that came to Milwaukee. But my adventure as "drama critic" was short-lived. I had been so imbued with being honest that when I saw a play that was both stupid and vulgar, I said just what I thought of it. The theater owner threatened to withdraw his advertisement if I was not removed. So I was removed.

The Socialist party and its paper did have a wholesome influence on the city. There were no crooked politicians, no "Hinky Dinks," no "Bathhouse Johns."[12] The city was clean and the services of very high quality. I recall an amusing incident that may illustrate the reaction to cleanliness in Milwaukee.

A group of young people had come up from Chicago for the day and one of the boys was going to play a trick on the streetcar conductor. So he handed him several Chicago streetcar transfers. The conductor handed the transfers back and the correct ones were produced. The Chicago boy then dropped the transfers on the floor of the streetcar.

"Young man, where do you think you are, in Chicago?" asked the conductor. "Pick up those transfers. We keep our streetcars clean."

Sheepishly the young man picked up the discarded transfers and stuffed them into his pocket.

During that first blissful week in Milwaukee, Bill insisted that we decide on a gift to take the place of the traditional diamond ring, which I had not received. The first phonograph without a horn had just made its appearance in a local music shop and we went to hear some records played on it.[13] It was a rare innovation and we were both thrilled with its performance. It was made in the shape of a box, with a door opening at the top. Inside was the turntable on which the record was placed. The tone was much richer than anything that had been played on the old phonograph with the ugly horn.

"This is the engagement ring that you have been worrying about," I said. And then and there we became the first owners of this new machine in Milwaukee. (So the man in the music store told us.) We spent the rest of the day selecting records. And what a galaxy of treasures we bought that day! Caruso, Melba, Alma Gluck, Fritz Kreisler, Slezak, Schumann-Heinck, De Gogorza, and Chaliapin were now members of our household. I was very much impressed when Bill wrote a check for five hundred dollars and handed it to the salesman, who was a little starry-eyed at the fine sale that he had made.

Music became a part of our lives like the air that we breathed.

It soon became known that I had written a play, and so people took it for granted that I knew everything that was to be known about the theater. When I attended my first meeting of the National Council of Jewish Women, I was asked to arrange a program. This was a first effort at community service. I was given complete freedom as to what sort of program it was to be. I thought a good deal about this and finally decided that since this was an organization of Jewish women, the program should concern itself with Jewish women.

I called up the chairwoman of the program committee and asked her what she thought of a series of tableaux depicting the women of the Bible.[14]

She was very enthusiastic about the idea, and I wrote a running commentary, using the text from the Bible whenever it was suitable.

The performance was a huge success, and I was established among the Jewish women of Milwaukee.

Milwaukee was a city of wholesome living and solid friendships. It was a city of song accompanied by the drinking of beer; there were many beer gardens and many singing societies. Bill's grandfather, on his mother's side, boasted that he sang tenor parts with the Milwaukee Liederkranz for fifty years.[15] At the age of eighty he was still attending singing sessions. And it was quite common to receive a case of beer as a birthday gift.

A delightful spot to which I was introduced that summer was Whitefish Bay.[16] It was a suburb of Milwaukee on the shore of Lake Michigan which was reached by a series of trolley cars. On a high bluff, small tables were set about where we were served the best planked whitefish I have ever eaten. The plank was circled by a border of delicately browned mashed potatoes. Of course, everybody drank beer. I still could not drink the amber liquid and was given furtive looks when I ordered coffee or soda water.

A string orchestra played German and Viennese waltzes, though I do not recall any dancing. Life was gay and carefree and seemed so far away from Chicago.

I had heard that there were saloons in Chicago where free lunch was served with a glass of beer, but I had never seen the inside of a saloon till I came to Milwaukee. After German Theatre, one memorable Wednesday, Bill decided he wanted some beer. So we went to a well-known saloon and there I saw a free lunch. One could hardly know where to begin. There was a stack of sliced cheese about three feet high. There were pickled herring, anchovies, imported sardines, ham, all kinds of sausages, roast beef, rare and well done. Then there was a variety of relishes and pickles and olives. Stacks and stacks of rye bread were piled up. With the purchase of one glass of beer, one could help himself to as much lunch as he wanted. But the capacity for drinking beer seemed boundless, and I venture to say that the owners of the saloon did not lose money.

In connection with the capacity for drinking beer, I recall a story that was told of a tourist who was visiting a brewery and asked the guide if it were true that he could drink a whole keg of beer at one time. The guide said: "Just a minute, lady, I'll find out." He went out and soon returned, wiping his mouth with the back of his hand and said: "Yes, lady, it's true."

In August Bill decided that he could get away for two weeks, so we went to the northern woods of Wisconsin. We stayed at a small hotel, located on a beautiful lake. It was pinewood country and it was very exhilarating to wake up in the morning and be greeted by the odor of pine trees. There was great excitement among the men about the big fish that had been caught. Bill did not care about fishing, so we spent a good deal of our time rowing on the lovely lake and hiking through the woods and reading.

In the fall of that year there was great excitement over the presidential election. Theodore Roosevelt, having failed to get the Republican nomination, decided to run on a Progressive ticket. Since the Republicans had the elephant as a symbol, and the Democrats had the donkey, the Progressives selected the bull moose; this symbol of the Progressive party vanished with the defeat of Theodore Roosevelt.

At the Progressive convention it was Jane Addams who seconded the nomination of Roosevelt.[17] This was before woman suffrage had been granted to women and was the first time that a woman was allowed to act in that capacity.

It is very hard for me, in looking back on events of that day, to understand how Jane Addams ever agreed to support Theodore Roosevelt. Mrs. Haldeman-Julius had this to say on this matter:

> It seems to me . . . that this was one adventure into which Jane Addams was mistakenly maneuvered by her attachment to the belief that progress must come through compromise. . . .
>
> Even so, it must always seem a grim incongruity that Jane Addams, advocate of peace and humanitarianism, should have pulled oars with such a man as Theodore Roosevelt: a raving Jingo—an execrator of birth control because he favored large families for the purposes of militarism.[18]

During the campaign, Theodore Roosevelt came to Milwaukee. Knowing that Jane Addams was supporting Mr. Roosevelt, I was keenly interested in the meeting. I was told by a newspaperman that there would be a tremendous crowd at the meeting, so Bill and I decided to get to the Auditorium early. We did not take time to eat supper that evening and reached the hall when the doors opened. I had brought some sandwiches from home, which we ate after we were seated.

Pictures of Jane Addams were nailed to every available spot. The edge of the stage was completely covered with her pictures. No matter which way I turned, there was the smiling face of Jane Addams.

The meeting had been scheduled for eight o'clock. It was now eight thirty and no sign of the meeting starting. After another fifteen minutes a man stepped in front of the curtain and said: "Ladies and gentlemen, I don't want to alarm you, but I must tell you that Theodore Roosevelt has been shot!"[19]

The audience rose as if an electric current had passed through the seven thousand people that filled the hall. The air was charged with horror and indignation. The man brought down his gavel with great force, and it was only after pounding the gavel again and again that he succeeded in getting the attention of the audience.

"Ladies and gentlemen, please be seated and listen to me," he shouted. "Mr. Roosevelt insists on speaking. We have been pleading with him to go to a hospital, but he is determined to deliver his address."

Just then Theodore Roosevelt walked out on the stage and stood before the great crowd. There was absolute silence.

"Ladies and gentlemen," began Mr. Roosevelt. "There may be some people among you who do not believe that I was shot, that I am perhaps staging an act for votes. So here is the evidence." And with these words he unbuttoned his coat and vest and showed the crowd the bloody shirt.

From all over that great hall came cries asking him not to speak but to go to a hospital. Several women fainted and had to be carried out. But Theodore Roosevelt said that if this was the last thing he did on earth, he would deliver his talk.

He spoke for about an hour and fifteen minutes. I do not recall anything that he said. (I was too upset emotionally to retain anything.)

When he had finished and had been taken backstage, the crowd became a wild, hysterical mob. The pictures on the wall and around the stage were loosened by the moving crowd and were lying on the floor. The muddy shoes were trampling on the face of Jane Addams. I picked up as many pictures as I could reach and put them on chairs. I could not bear to see them trampled and covered with mud.

I will never know how we managed to get out of that hall. The newsboys were already on the streets, filling the air with their shouts of "Extra papers!" Bill bought a paper and we walked home in silence.

The newspaper accounts were disturbing, to put it mildly. The newspaper that we read that night said that it was not surprising that such outrageous things could happen where there were so many Socialists and where their press influenced so many people.

It was not until the next morning that it was discovered that the man who did the shooting was some poor insane person who had come from New York and had traveled on the same train that had brought Mr. Roosevelt to Milwaukee.

The *Milwaukee Leader* demanded and got a retraction of what had been printed in the papers, in perhaps thoughtless haste. The retraction appeared and Milwaukee was vindicated as a city of law and order.

I was preparing to visit my mother; I had gone to Chicago for a day each month since coming to Milwaukee. I would bring my share toward the support of the family, which I could now afford without straining my budget. The night before I was to leave, Bill suggested that I stay a week in Chicago. I protested, saying I did not want to leave him for a whole week. But he told me that he had a great deal of extra work and that he would work almost every night and I would be alone much of the time. He seemed very insistent. So I stayed a week, and when I got home he met me at the train. I noticed a change had come over him. He seemed much more reserved when he greeted me, and instead of kissing me on the lips he kissed my cheek. He insisted on taking a cab. We usually walked the distance. He thought my light bag might be too heavy for the walk.

When we got home he handed me a card that had come from the state laboratory in Madison, telling him that his test for tuberculosis had proved positive. He then told me that he noticed that he had been running a slight temperature and, without telling me, he had seen a doctor and the doctor had sent a specimen of his sputum to Madison. And here was the answer. He had not wanted me to be home and receive that card while he was at work.

I was stunned, but not for long. I smiled at him and said that we would go to see Dr. Theodore B. Sachs in Chicago, as soon as we could get an appointment.[20]

The next morning I called Dr. Sachs's office and was given an appointment for that very afternoon. Bill called his office and left word that he would not come to work that day, and we went to Chicago without telling anyone.

Bill had the report of the laboratory of the State Health Department. He took it to the doctor, who put him through a very rigorous examination. The doctor told us that he evidently had just become infected; that it was not serious but needed immediate attention.

Bill was ordered to stop working at once and live very quietly. He was told that he could stay up till midnight once a week. At all other times he was to go to bed at nine o'clock. He was to have his windows wide open, no matter how cold it was, and he was to have rich food and a quart of milk a day. And he should come back in three months.

We left the doctor's office at about five o'clock. My heart was heavy but I was determined not to let Bill know it. I insisted that we go to our favorite nook in the College Inn and have some lobster. He smiled as the fragrant dishes were brought in.

"Shall I prepare your lobster for you?" he asked.

I smiled.

"Your smile is still radiant in the face of this," he said, squeezing my hand. "We will face this together."

We took the first train we could get and went back to Milwaukee.

The bright side of this illness which had come so suddenly was that we had no financial worries—and this helped. Bill's pay went right on, though I was prepared to go to work if it had been necessary.

When the three months were up, we went to see Dr. Sachs and he found that Bill was very much better, but if he could afford it, it would be very good for him to go to the country for the summer.

We immediately decided that we would like to camp somewhere for the summer. It would be cheaper and it would give us the privacy and quiet that Bill needed most of all.

His uncle owned a beautiful tract of land on Lake Nagawicka in Wisconsin, and we were given permission to put up a tent or shack. We had heard of something called a "Kenyon house," so we investigated and found that this sort of house was just what we needed.[21] It was made of heavy waterproof canvas and was divided by cloth curtains into three sections. It was equipped with a hardwood floor, screened windows and doors. For rainy days there were isinglass windows that could be rolled up when not needed.

Before leaving for the country we found an apartment for the fall, when we would be returning to the city. A two-family house was being built, and while it was half done we rented the lower apartment.

We had our Kenyon house set up, and as soon as the weather permitted, we packed up and went to the country.

We were no sooner settled than word came from Chicago that my mother had died.[22]

We settled down for the summer. In spite of everything that had happened, we often looked back on that summer with a nostalgic feeling. When we set out I had a faint idea somewhere in my head that I might do some writing. But the days went by and nary a word did I put on paper. I spent most of my time cooking nourishing, tasty meals and reading to Bill, while he was lying in the sunshine, drinking in all the health that he could absorb.

We returned to Milwaukee and went to Chicago to see Dr. Sachs. We had by this time learned to love him for his wisdom and kindness. He had not only been a doctor but a warm, kind friend.

Bill was given a complete examination and told that he was fine and that he could go back to work. We were both grateful that Bill had not been shipped off to a sanitarium. The private ones were very expensive and we were afraid of the municipal institutions. I had heard of the conditions prevailing in the Chicago sanitariums, and they were not pretty pictures. There had been talk that Chicago and Illinois tuberculosis sanitariums had become political footballs and were being kicked around to suit the politicians. The attendants who were supposed to care for the sick were political hacks instead of trained people.

These tragic rumors were confirmed several years later, when we were shocked to hear what had happened to our beloved Dr. Sachs. I know that I cannot do justice to describe the event, so I will let Jane Addams tell it, as it appeared in her book, *The Second Twenty Years at Hull-House:*

> . . . Theodore Sachs, whom we had known for many years at Hull-House through his skillful and unremitting efforts to reduce tuberculosis in our section of the city. One of the Hull-House residents, under his direction, had once made a careful study of one block—lung blocks we used to call them—in the Russian Jewish quarter in which the tuberculosis rate had been phenomenally high. Day by day we had been impressed anew with the universal testimony of gratitude and affection showered upon him by the poorest of his compatriots. We rejoiced with many people throughout the city when Dr. Sachs was made head of the Municipal Sanitorium for Tuberculosis. Although we knew that he encountered unending difficulties with the officials of a corrupt city administration in his efforts to care for his patients properly, we were all aghast one morning to learn that this brilliant, sensitive man had committed suicide as a protest against the entire situation.[23]

War 20

The apartment that Bill and I had rented before going to Nagawicka was now ready, and we spent days buying furniture and household equipment. We moved into our very own home in November 1913. Until then we had been living in Bill's mother's apartment while she was traveling.

In January 1914 our first child, a son, was born.[1]

At this moment this was indeed "the best possible of all worlds." And I had the most wonderful baby in it. When that tiny body was put into my arms for the first time, I felt that there could be nothing that was wrong in the world. A feeling of exaltation came over me. For nine months my little son had been growing in my body, nurtured by my blood. And now here he was in my arms, and I was being told that I could continue to nurture him and keep him alive with the over-generous supply of milk that filled my breasts.

Many gifts were showered on my baby, but the only one that I remember is the soft wool kimono that Jane Addams sent with her card, on which she had written in her own almost unreadable writing: "With affectionate greeting to Charles Lessing Polacheck and his mother."

Nature had endowed us with all these rich blessings of life. At what point had the madness of war and greed entered the hearts and minds of humankind? And how much heartbreaking work would it take to bring sanity back to the world? Who can answer that question? I only know that Jane Addams was in the front ranks of that gallant army for peace.

The peace and joy of life with my baby were soon shattered by the outbreak of war between Germany and France. It was a great shock to many people, and for a while I was overwhelmed with the tragedy. But Bill pointed out the futility of self-indulgence in grieving over something that I could not change. And I realized that I had brought a child into the world and that I had to go on caring for his needs.

The horror of war increased when England joined in the fighting.

Jane Addams was now a citizen of the world. It has often been said that there is nothing new in world history. Well, here was something new. Never before had women of different countries and cultures banded together and demanded peace while their men were fighting on the battlefields. In 1915 Jane Addams and a group of heroic women met in Washington and organized the Woman's Peace party, which later became the now-famous Women's International League for Peace and Freedom.[2] It was the wisdom and farsighted vision of these women that added the word "freedom" to the word "peace." For there can be no peace without freedom.

With the hectic days of talking peace whenever the opportunity presented itself and having a hopeless feeling that our own country might soon be involved, it was good to be able to come home and hold my baby in my arms. I felt that I needed this relief to be able to talk more peace the next day. We were asked to be neutral, but it was not easy to be neutral in Milwaukee. A hysteria was descending on the country and it was felt more keenly in Milwaukee, where the German population was so large and where many had relatives fighting on the battlefields.

There were many brave voices lifted against the war. Since a state of neutrality had been declared, William Jennings Bryan, who was secretary of state, felt that American bankers should make no foreign loans to countries that were at war. He felt that would be inconsistent with the spirit of American neutrality. Shortly after this declaration Bryan was relieved of his post.[3]

On the morning of Thanksgiving Day 1916 our second child was born, a dimpled girl whose eyes were as blue as gentians.[4] We had much for which to be thankful. But our joy was dimmed by the threatening war clouds.

Then debate started in Congress as to whether we would enter the war. When the final vote was taken, Jeannette Rankin, of Montana, voted against the war. When the vote came to the Senate, to the glory of the state of Wisconsin, Robert M. La Follette voted against war.[5]

In April 1917 America entered the world war.

Immediately things began to happen in Milwaukee, where the population was predominantly of German extraction.[6] People stopped talking to old friends. I suppose hatred is an outgrowth of war. If rulers could not whip up enough hatred in people's hearts, maybe we could not get men to fight. But it seemed out of all proportion to begin to hate a former neighbor or friend.

I was invited to a tea one afternoon where one of the guests innocently asked if anyone would like to go to a concert to hear Johanna Gadski, the great German soprano. Several of the women rose to their feet and told the guest in no uncertain terms what they thought of a traitor who would be willing to hear a German sing. And one of them actually stalked out of the house.

Our beloved Frederick Stock, the conductor of the Chicago Symphony Orchestra, stopped conducting.[7] He had to retire for the duration of the war. The German Theatre soon closed down. It was considered unpatriotic to listen to plays written by Schiller, Goethe, Sudermann, and Hauptmann. Not only was Dr. Stock retired, but all German compositions were barred from symphony programs.

It was indeed a time when "Justice had fled—and men had lost their reason."[8]

The funny little sign in Martini's was removed from the wall; it was no longer proper to laugh at so ridiculous a statement. The Germania Club changed its name to the Wisconsin Club. Even harmless plebeian sauerkraut had to be changed to "liberty cabbage."

It must be remembered that many voices were raised against America's entry into the war. On June 15, 1917, Congress passed the Espionage Act, making it illegal to talk against the war.[9] Between that time and July 1918, about a thousand people were arrested and tried in the courts for antiwar activities. The outstanding opponent to the war was Eugene Victor Debs. He said: "The American people did not and do not want this war. They have not been consulted about the war and have had no part in declaring war."[10]

For opposing the war, Eugene Victor Debs was sentenced to prison for ten years. He became convict no. 9653.[11]

Every organization with which I had affiliated since my coming to Milwaukee cooperated with the war effort. Everybody was selling so-called liberty bonds. The schools were asking children to bring prune and peach pits to school to use in making gas masks. Since my babies needed my care, I promised Bill that I would not say anything in public that might endanger my freedom. But I stopped going to meetings and resigned from every organization that supported the war.

In July 1918 our third child was born, our second son.[12] And what a blessing he proved to be! I was now forced to breastfeed a child and help care for a nineteen-month-old child who was slow in learning to walk. My home and my family kept a good deal of the turmoil of the world away from me. But no one could escape the ravages of war.

Bill's younger brother, Stanley Polacheck, had left the University of Wisconsin to enlist in the navy. After winning his commission as an ensign, he was assigned to a ship that transported troops across the

Atlantic. That meant that every ten days or so he had to cross the treacherous waters, with torpedo-filled submarines under the water and bomb-filled airplanes above. Every time he left for one of those voyages Bill and I would just look at each other. Our hearts were too full for words. And we would wait for news that the ship had arrived in France. Then, when the ship left France, we would just wait and wait and wait till we heard that the ship had arrived on our own American shore.

During all that time I never heard Bill talk just of his own brother. He always included all the boys that were being taken across.

The size of our family made it necessary that we find a larger home. We soon found a comfortable house with a large yard in Shorewood, a suburb of Milwaukee.[13]

We settled down to a quiet life. One could not be gay in a world at war. I consoled myself by the thought that, like Jane Addams, I would devote as much energy as I could muster to the cause of peace.

We saw many of our friends become conscientious objectors and go to prison.[14] I hugged Thoreau to my heart; he had written: "Under a government which imprisons unjustly, the true place for a just man is also in prison."[15]

In November hopeful rumors were beginning to reach us that peace was near.

Evening after evening we would sit hopefully waiting for the glad tidings of peace. Bill would read out loud, and among the things he read, I remember a poem:

> Here in this leafy place
> Quiet he lies,
> Cold, with his sightless face
> Turned to the skies;
> 'Tis but another dead;
> All you can say is said.
>
> Carry his body hence—
> Kings must have slaves
> Kings climb to eminence
> Over men's graves
> So this man's eye is dim—
> Throw the earth over him.

I do not know who wrote the lines.[16]

The tenth of November was Bill's birthday.[17] In the hope that peace would be declared that day, I gave a party. By one o'clock there was still no news of peace. So our guests went home and we went to bed.

But I did not sleep. I still felt that peace would come that night. At two o'clock in the morning of 11 November, I heard the joyous whistles and I knew that peace was again in the world.[18]

How can I describe the joy that gripped the people on that memorable morning. Bill and I took our four-year-old son, who was carrying a small flag, and we went to the main street of Milwaukee and joined the crowds that just walked, singing and shouting for joy. The shops and stores were open, but there was no one in them.

On a side street we saw an elderly Italian wine dealer roll out a barrel of wine to the sidewalk and offer wine to anyone who wanted to drink it.

It was a spontaneous demonstration that no people wanted war, that war had been forced on the people by the rulers. Then the thought came to me that here in America we have no rulers. As citizens who had the vote, we had somehow failed to elect the right people.

All sorts of thoughts kept crowding my mind that day. I kept thinking that the first thing we must do is to get all the conscientious objectors out of prison.

We came home that afternoon more dedicated than ever to the thought that the greatest need of the world, as Jane Addams had pointed out, was world peace.

Hilda in 1912. (University of Illinois at Chicago, The University Library, Jane Addams Memorial Collection)

William Polacheck, ca. 1912.

The Kenyon house, in which Hilda and Bill spent the summer of 1913. (Photo by Stanley Polacheck, Bill's brother)

Hilda and her children, 1926. *Left to right:* Dena, Hilda, Charles, Jessie, Demarest Lloyd.

The Hull-House fortieth anniversary reunion, 1930. *Seated, left to right:* Dr. Alice Hamilton; Rose Gyles; Jane Addams; Enella Benedict, head of the Art Studio; Edith de Nancrede, director of dance and children's theater. *Standing, left to right:* Jessie Binford, director of the Juvenile Protective Association; Dr. Rachel Yarros, social hygiene pioneer; Esther Kohn, active in fund raising; Victor Yarros, law partner of Clarence Darrow; Ethel Dewey, teacher of English and citizenship; George Hooker, secretary of the Chicago City Club; Adena Miller Rich, of the Immigrants Protective League. (University of Illinois at Chicago, The University Library, Jane Addams Memorial Collection)

Jane Addams's funeral in the Hull-House courtyard, 24 May 1935. (University of Illinois at Chicago, The University Library, Jane Addams Memorial Collection)

Hilda and Dena at a May Day parade, ca. 1936.

A Polacheck family reunion at Mountain Lakes, New Jersey, July 1953. Hilda's daughters Jessie and Dena are seated to her right; sons Demarest and Charles are in the back row (*left* and *center*).

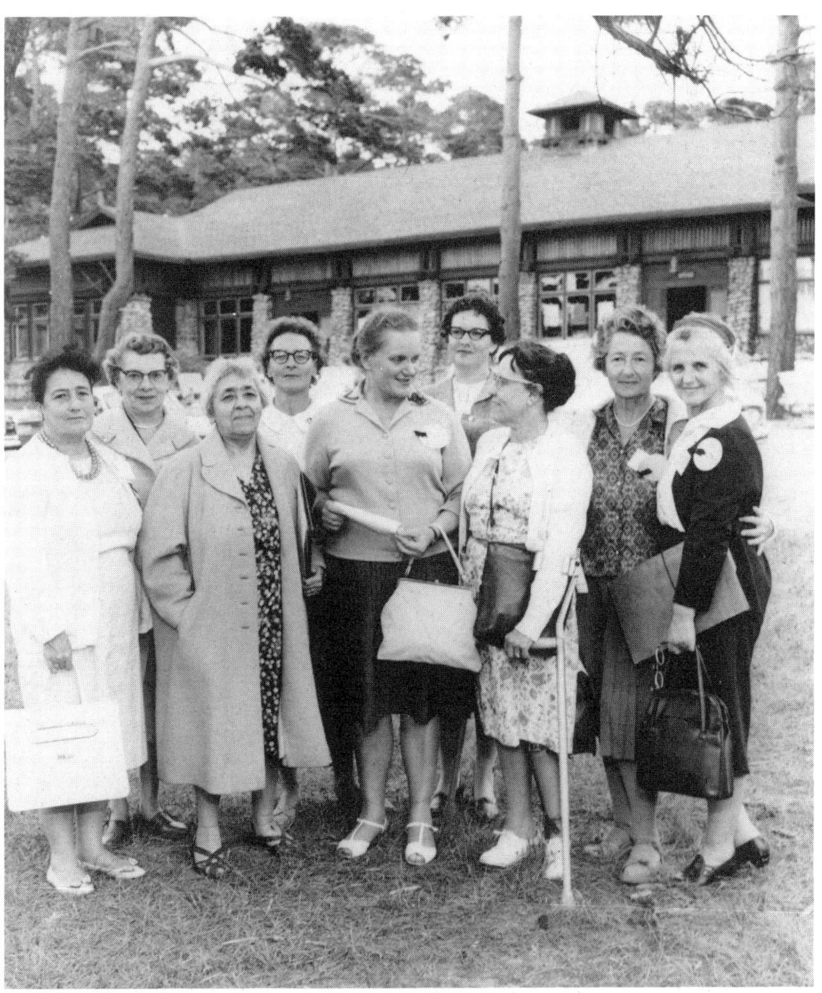

Hilda attended the Fifteenth International Congress of the Women's International League for Peace and Freedom, 8-13 July 1962, Asilomar, California. She is pictured here with Stanislawa Zawadeska-Nussbaum *(center)* of Warsaw, Poland, who was her roommate, Ava Helen (Mrs. Linus) Pauling *(far right)*, and several unidentified women.

Hilda as a grandmother, ca. 1960s. (Photo by Dr. Joseph T. Sheridan, a Chicago surgeon)

Peace 21

> I join with you most cordially in rejoicing at the return of peace. I hope it will be lasting, and that mankind will at length, as they call themselves reasonable creatures, have reason enough to settle their differences without cutting throats; for in my opinion, there never was a good war or a bad peace.[1]
>
> —Benjamin Franklin

With the coming of peace, people everywhere began feverishly to organize peace societies.[2] There were many wild ideas advanced in those exuberant days. Not only were organizations being formed, but plays were being written around the peace motif. One such one-act play was played in variety theaters by Alla Nazimova.[3] The theme of the play was that women should refuse to bear children unless the men agree to eliminate war.

Milwaukee had its share of people who advanced impossible ideas. An otherwise intelligent woman who had recently moved to Milwaukee was the prime mover in organizing a peace society.[4] Many of my friends and I were eager to join any peace movement. After several meetings an organization was formed.

The next thing we knew, the somewhat erratic lady, in an interview with the papers, had given out that this new organization proposed, first of all, to mobilize the women of the country to refuse to have children.[5]

The papers came out with screaming headlines: "Women to go on childbearing strike," or some such nonsense.

We were at the time holding our meetings in the public library,[6] and at once some of us were called by the head of the library and told that it had been besieged by telephone calls demanding that we be ousted from the library.

We organized a committee of women with the largest families and went to see the librarian, who, I think, was somewhat amused by the whole affair when we assured him we had no such intentions.

The sensational publicity had a very bad effect on our organization, so we decided we had better start over again. We wanted the confidence and good will of the community.

So we met and decided to become affiliated with the Women's International League for Peace and Freedom.[7] We all felt that peace could not come to the world unless it was organized on an international basis. It seemed quite simple to us at the time.

But life is not simple. We get ourselves enmeshed in all sorts of webs. We complicate our lives with intrigue, greed, deceit; in the end we do not know how to get out of all our difficulties, so we stage a war.

When the Milwaukee group was ready to join the Women's International League for Peace and Freedom, I asked Miss Addams to come to Milwaukee to give us the final push. She came and inspired us all with her clear thinking and sane reasoning.

I will never forget the description that Jane Addams gave us of the conditions she found in Germany after the war.[8] The innocent bystanders, the women and children who had nothing to do with bringing on the war, suffered the most. She said that she had found no envy or malice on the part of the women. All that these subdued women wanted was bread and milk for their children. She felt that no country, not even our recent enemy, should be blockaded and left to starve.

Her vivid descriptions of the soup kitchens that she had visited are still with me. She described one such kitchen where a tremendous soup kettle was filled with water. Into the water were thrown a few dried vegetables and a piece of margarine the size of an egg. This was the soup that was fed to starving children. The bread served at that time was made of dried bark and sawdust.

After listening to Jane Addams's description of the devastation caused by the war, the women at the meeting voted unanimously to affiliate with the Women's International League for Peace and Freedom.

A source of personal satisfaction and pride for me was Jane Addams's coming home with me for dinner. It was the first time that she had visited me in Milwaukee. She was most generous in her praise of the children and insisted on holding the baby in her lap. She wanted to see all of the house that Bill and I now owned.

"You have a fine family and a very nice home," she said.

"I'm certain that I would not have all these blessings if it had not been for you and Hull-House," I said. "Bill would not have noticed me if I had not learned what I did at Hull-House."

"Now, now, Hilda," she said, "give yourself some of the credit."

When I asked her if she was disappointed that I had not written anything since I had married, she said: "Hilda, my dear, one baby is worth a dozen books, and you have three, so have no regrets."[9] Then she stroked my hair and said: "Some day, when the children are grown, you will write. I know it."

I hope I am now fulfilling her prophecy.

Bill and I worked in all peace endeavors started in Milwaukee. We also participated in many civic activities. The one that gave us the most satisfaction was the Milwaukee Open Forum, as it was then called.[10] We helped in its organization and it was one of our pet projects.

For several years I served as chairwoman of the program committee. While this office entailed a great deal of work it also brought rich rewards. As chairwoman I had the privilege and honor of having the speakers as my guests for dinner preceding each meeting.

What a galaxy of world-famous people graced our dinner table!

There was the memorable evening when Bertrand Russell was the speaker at the Forum. Bill and I were to meet him at the train and take him home for dinner. We had a Model T Ford, at the time, and Bill had forgotten to remove some metal casts and other junk from the car. I met him at the railroad station and we escorted Sir Bertrand Russell to a car filled with junk. I was furious with Bill, but Mr. Russell paid no attention to the rattling in the back of the car as we drove along. He was charming, human, and enthusiastic about Lake Michigan.

He was a warm, friendly dinner guest. Just before leaving for the meeting I told the children they could come down and shake hands with Bertrand Russell.[11]

My youngest son, who was then about three years old, said: "I hope your speech will be a great success."

Mr. Russell laughed heartily and said: "I hope so, my boy, I hope so."

Jim Tully, the author of *Beggars of Life* and other books, had been engaged to be a speaker at the Forum.[12] Some enterprising but ill-advised agent booked a number of lectures for him. Since Mr. Tully could not arrive in time for dinner, we had invited a group of people to come to the house after the lecture to meet the speaker.

Poor Jim Tully; he could write, but he could not speak. The lecture would have been a nightmare if Bill had not been chairman that night and turned the lecture into a question-and-answer period. And Bill answered most of the questions.

But in the living room Jim Tully was delightful. He had no

difficulty talking to people in an informal way. The lecture platform was not for him. He gave up lecturing, I believe, as soon as his contract expired.

Through those memorable years, when Bill and I were identified with the Open Forum, the person that left the most lasting impression was James Weldon Johnson.[13] He was a noble-looking person with a fine head and a sensitive nature. In addition he was a polished and cultured gentleman; it was a great privilege to have him sit at our table and talk to us of the various countries he had visited. I will never forget two sentences from his address at the meeting that night: "When a man is lynched, the suffering, though inhuman, is of short duration. But think of the searing effect on the people who commit the outrage and the moral degradation of those who watch a lynching."

In addition to working on the Open Forum I resumed my activity as chairwoman of the Peace Committee of the National Council of Jewish Women.[14] One program of the year was devoted to peace. I conducted a class within the council on "The Causes of War and the Way to Peace."

I suppose as each grain of sand has a part in forming the mighty dunes, so each tiny effort will help in bringing about ultimate peace. I'm afraid that I was muddled and often overoptimistic in my beliefs. But they were honest beliefs, perhaps flavored with wishful thinking.

How wonderful it was to be alive and at peace. Our children were normal, happy, healthy children with a variety of interests and many playmates. The street we lived on was just one block long, and before long the families living on the block became a happy family. One summer the children busied themselves publishing a newspaper.[15] One of the neighbors was a representative of a multigraph machine company, and he loaned a secondhand machine to the children for the summer. The machine was installed in the basement of another neighbor's house and they started on their publishing venture.

I recommend this activity as a preventative for juvenile delinquency, about which we hear much these days.

The children wrote the articles, laid out the copy, got ads from the butcher and the baker; if there had been a candlestick maker, he would have been compelled to advertise. Then they went from house to house and sold the paper.

When the summer was over and the children had to return to school, they had earned the enormous sum of $4.30.

The Shorewood schools were a joy both to children and parents.[16] They were conducted on a progressive, sane basis and there were many extracurricular events planned for the children. I had the privilege of arranging such a series one year, when we brought such programs as the Chicago Symphony Orchestra, Tony Sarg's Marionettes, the excellent pianist Guy Maier, and a lovely singing lady by the name of Edna Thomas; Carl Sandburg came and read his *Rutabaga Stories* and played the guitar. He delighted everybody. Then we brought him home to dinner. As there were several hours before dinner, I gave him a bottle of wine and a glass and told him to do anything he felt like doing until dinnertime. He had several glasses of wine, stretched out on the couch, and slept blissfully until we were ready to eat.[17]

Woman Suffrage 22

The National Woman's Suffrage Amendment had been introduced in Congress in 1878.[1] Even before that time voices were raised in favor of woman suffrage. In 1774 Abigail Adams, the wife of one president of the United States and the mother of another president, wrote to her husband: "In the new code of laws which I suppose it will be necessary for you to make, I desire that you would remember the ladies, and be more generous and favorable to them than your ancestors. . . . If particular care and attention is not paid to the ladies, we are determined to foment a rebellion, and will not hold ourselves bound by any laws in which we have no voice or representation."[2]

Woman suffrage (as it was called in 1908) was a subject often debated at Hull-House. I recall when such a meeting was planned and Miss Addams gave me a bundle of leaflets and asked me to distribute them on Halsted Street. I took a position on the corner of Halsted and Taylor streets and gave everyone who passed a leaflet.[3] It was a windy day and the dust settled on my face and turned the color of my blouse from white to gray. By the time my last leaflet had been disposed of, I was filthy.

When I came home my mother looked at me and there was disgust written all over her face.

"Where have you been?" she asked. "Your face is black, your blouse is dirty—were you cleaning a chimney?"

"I was distributing leaflets for a suffrage meeting," I said.

"A what meeting?" she asked with disgust.

"A meeting that will help bring the vote for women; Miss Addams will speak at the meeting," I said.

"Why do you waste your time and get your face so dirty?" she asked. "You ought to know that women will never be allowed to vote."

The group that met at Hull-House was rather polite in asking for the vote. It was considered best to be a "lady" and not offend the men who had the power to give the vote to women. So meetings were held and petitions were signed and submitted to Congress. And nothing happened. Women still had no vote.

But the "fomenting of the rebellion," which Abigail Adams had predicted, was beginning to appear. The women of England, led by Mrs. Pankhurst, began to show a militant demand for the vote. And the fever spread to America.

A group of more aggressive women organized the National Woman's party, whose policy was not to ask for the vote but to demand it. I joined this group.[4] I am quite sure that Miss Addams did not approve of this new organization. But I still think I took a step forward when I joined the militant group.

The policy adopted by the National Woman's party was to bring the subject of votes for women before the American people in dramatic form. Some of their acts may have been undignified, but they were good newspaper copy and the question of woman suffrage became a live one.

President Woodrow Wilson, while campaigning for the presidency, had promised to consider woman suffrage and to give it his support. After he was elected and there were signs that he might have forgotten his promise, Inez Milholland, a beautiful woman dressed in flowing white robes, held up a torch, in a very dramatic gesture, and burned Mr. Wilson's words.[5] It may have been a flamboyant gesture, but all the papers carried Miss Milholland's photograph and quoted her words. It was just another way of arousing the American public.

And the time had arrived when the public should be aroused to the fact that the majority of the women of America wanted a vote, so the women started on a campaign of picketing the White House.[6] This was often embarrassing for the president, and the police were given orders to stop the picketing. Naturally, the authorities thought that when a policeman would say to a picket "Move on," the order would be obeyed. But the police and the authorities did not know the determination of the dedicated fighters for a just cause. They refused to "move on." They felt that they had the constitutional right to petition their government for redress of a wrong. So wholesale arrests started.

Now when an ordinary picket is arrested, it is not newspaper copy. But when a woman like Mrs. Gilson Gardner was arrested, that was another story.[7] Mrs. Gardner was the daughter of Frederick Hall, who had been editor of the *Chicago Tribune,* and the wife of the Washington representative of the Scripps papers. Stories began to scream from the front pages of the newspapers. Mrs. Florence Bayard Hilles, the daughter of Thomas Francis Bayard, who had been an ambassador to England and the secretary of state under President Cleveland, was arrested and sentenced to sixty days but was pardoned after serving three days.[8] I was told that when Mrs. H. O. Havemeyer, the widow of the sugar king, was arrested for taking part in a watchfire demonstration, she was put into a patrol wagon carrying the American flag.[9] She insisted on sitting near the opening of the wagon, and as the patrol wagon dashed up Pennsylvania Avenue, she unfurled the flag and it proudly waved in the breeze, as if to support the women in their fight for freedom. A spectator took off his hat as the patrol dashed by and sang:

> Long may it wave, o'er the land of the free,
> And the home of the brave.

All this made juicy newspaper copy. Hardly a day passed without some front-page story. Women in long flowing robes were shown burning speeches of the president; the press photographers were kept busy. Women being put into patrol wagons became a daily feature. Pictures began to appear of women coming out of prison after hunger strikes, women being carried out of prison on stretchers or being just able to walk out of prison.

About 170 were at various times arrested and sentenced to prison and they refused to pay any fines.[10] They took the position that they were not guilty of any crime and therefore should not be penalized.

These women, of varying position, wealth, age, and education, were really heroic figures. They endured filthy jails, vile food, and even hunger strikes to get what they felt was their inalienable right.

In Milwaukee, one of the chief objections we heard to woman suffrage was that it would bring Prohibition. Perhaps this was a compliment that the women did not deserve, as Prohibition came before woman suffrage. But the brewery interests certainly did not want Prohibition and they were sufficiently strong to create a strong opposition to woman suffrage.

To arouse public opinion further, the National Woman's party chartered a train that was named the "Prison Special."[11] The women who had been imprisoned made a tour of the country in this train to tell the people everywhere of their experiences. Each woman wore a badge of honor consisting of a pin made to depict the iron bars of a cell door.

I recall very distinctly when the "Prison Special" came to Milwaukee. In order to save money the travelers were entertained in the homes of local members. Mrs. W. D. Ascough, of Detroit, was assigned to my house.[12]

Mrs. Ascough was a beautiful, stately woman. She had studied for the concert stage in France and England and was on her way to a brilliant career when she decided to abandon her music and to devote her talents to the cause of woman suffrage.

The Milwaukee section had arranged a mass meeting at the old Majestic Theatre, which was at that time the leading vaudeville house in the city.[13] The meeting was to be held at noon, while people were out for lunch. I am sure many people were late for their return to work that day. No one could leave while those eloquent women told of their harrowing experiences.

I recall an amusing incident while Mrs. Ascough was my guest. She came downstairs in the morning, dressed in a beautiful lacy chiffon robe, looking "every inch a queen."

I had a small table set near a window overlooking my neighbor's yard. As we sat down I noticed my second son, who was then about five years old, talking to my neighbor.[14] I could not hear what he was saying, but I did see my neighbor look at him with a horrified expression.

Now what is he telling her? I thought.

I soon found out. While Mrs. Ascough was upstairs dressing for the meeting, I went out to investigate. He had told my sweet, good, genteel, and very proper neighbor that "there was a lady at our house who just came out of jail."

When I explained who the lady was, my neighbor dashed into her house to get dressed to go to the meeting.

It was a very hot 26 August when the secretary of state proclaimed the Nineteenth Amendment to the Constitution a law.[15]

All the members of the board of the Milwaukee section had gone to their summer homes for the summer. I was the only board member in Milwaukee on that auspicious day. All the publicity, photographs, and newspaper mats had been left with me, just in case the good news came.

When word finally came from Washington over the press wires, a reporter from one of the newspapers called me and asked for copy.

I called a cab and made the rounds of the newspapers. The Nineteenth Amendment to the Constitution had become a law of the land. It read as follows:

> The right of citizens of the United States to vote shall not be denied or abridged by the United States or by any state on account of sex. Congress shall have the power, by appropriate legislation, to enforce the provisions of this article.[16]

It is ironic that when I was given the right to vote for the first time, only one candidate on the ballot stood for peace and he was in prison.

It is clear that many peace-loving people who were not Socialists voted for Debs. The Socialist party, according to some figures, never had more than 117,984 members.[17] Debs received 900,000 votes in that election.[18]

Warren G. Harding, the successful candidate, took office in March 1921. On Christmas of the same year he pardoned Debs.[19] The two outstanding deeds for which Warren Harding will be remembered are: on the debit side, the Teapot Dome episode; on the credit side, the pardoning of Eugene Victor Debs.

In September 1923 our lives were enriched once again by the birth of our fourth child, another daughter.[20] So now we had two boys and two girls!

Women's International League for Peace and Freedom

23

The two great endeavors in the life of Jane Addams were Hull-House and the Women's International League for Peace and Freedom. On her tombstone above her grave are engraved the words:

JANE ADDAMS
of
HULL-HOUSE
and
The Women's International League
for
Peace and Freedom[1]

Jane Addams felt that it was not enough to make this world a better place in which to live if the world was constantly being torn apart by war. And so, after Hull-House was established on a firm basis, she was willing, in her later years, to leave the work of Hull-House in competent hands.[2] She then devoted herself to world peace.

Her work and travels in the cause of peace are well covered in her book *Peace and Bread in Time of War.* There she tells us what the Women's International League for Peace and Freedom stands for and what it is:

> It is a federation of women with organized sections in 21 of the most important countries, and scattered members and correspondents from Iceland to Fiji; women pledged to do everything in their power to create international relations based on good-will, making war impossible; women who seek to establish equality between men and women, and who feel the necessity of educating the coming generations to help realize these principles.[3]

Several congresses of the league were held in Europe. I want to tell about the only congress held in America, at which I was present.[4]

This congress was held in Washington, D.C., in May 1924. To get some idea of the scope of the congress, it is in order to note the various countries represented. In addition to the American delegates there were women from Australia, Austria, Belgium, Bulgaria, Canada,

Czechoslovakia, Denmark, France, Germany, Great Britain, Greece, Hungary, Ireland, Italy, Japan, Netherlands, Norway, Poland, Sweden, Switzerland, and the Ukraine.[5] There were also fraternal delegates from Bolivia, British Antilles, China, Cuba, Ecuador, Guatemala, India, Liberia, Mexico, the Philippines, and Turkey. Many national groups from the United States sent observers.

It is hard to imagine at what great sacrifice some of these women from war-torn Europe and Asia came to this congress. Some of them spent their last dollar to come to tell us what the women of other parts of the world were doing to further peace. Many did not have any money but the women of their community had laboriously raised the money so that they could come.

For a whole week Jane Addams was on her feet, presiding at the meetings with wisdom and gentle firmness. There were sessions morning, afternoon, and evening. She was then sixty-four years old, and we all marveled at her endurance.

The message that these women from all corners of the earth brought us was that women were demanding peace, even if their governments still continued to pursue policies of war and destruction, which brought nothing good to anyone, devastation and misery to everybody.

The Wisconsin delegation, which was a large one, had special cause to be proud. The wife of our congressman and the wife of our senator attended the congress and I believe were members of the league. It was a great event for my delegation when we were honored by being allowed to give a luncheon for Mrs. Victor Berger and Mrs. Robert La Follette.

It was a great day for all of us when we were told that President Coolidge would give a reception for the delegates.[6] The reception was a silent one. The president shook each hand without saying a word. To me it seemed to be an insult that Mrs. Coolidge did not consider the reception of an importance to be present to greet the women from so many countries.

The event that has stayed with me through all these years was the concert given for the delegates at Howard University. As I look back I have a feeling that the guest of honor that night was Mrs. Fanny Garrison Villard.[7] I remember her standing near the bronze bust of her famous father, William Lloyd Garrison. She was dressed in a soft white dress with a black velvet ribbon around her neck and a small black velvet bow pinned to her snow-white hair. She was seventy-six years old at the time but full of life and vigor.

After singing for two hours the choir seemed as fresh as when they started. Most of the audience left, but a few of us stayed behind and were treated to more singing. The choir was ready and willing to give another concert, just for Mrs. Villard. She requested that they sing "Ain't Gonna Study War No More." There she stood, the dainty, energetic woman, in the midst of the group of singers, singing with great gusto. We all sang that song many times over.

Through thirty-five years I have carried that vision in my mind: a great daughter standing beside the bronze bust of her great father.

December 1927 — 24

I look back on my years in Milwaukee as years of a good life; years of love, fulfillment, and service. I had all that any woman could ask for: a loving, devoted husband, beautiful children, a host of good friends, and the health and strength to render whatever service my adopted city and country would ask of me.

Bill and I never had wealth, as wealth was counted in those days and as it is counted today. But we had the wealth of love and contentment and a burning interest in music, poetry, literature, and, above all, in peace and freedom.

Although a poet by nature and inclination, Bill had been forced into the business world.[1] His father had died when he was quite young, and [when he was] sixteen or seventeen his mother influenced him to leave school and go into the lighting fixture business that her husband had established and that was being managed by his brothers.

Bill had withdrawn from the firm when his mother died and had gone into the lighting fixture business for himself. While he never made a great deal of money, he made enough for every comfort that we wanted. We attended all the concerts that came to Milwaukee. We rarely missed going to the plays that came to the city.

The concerts in those days were held at the Pabst Theatre. For years, while the German Theatre was in existence, Bill supplied the theater with lamps and fixtures that were used as props. He was well known backstage and the doorkeeper never stopped him, so he would find a couch in the property room and stretch out and listen to the concerts. I preferred sitting out in front with friends.

I will never forget the night we went to hear Schumann-Heinck. She was a very large woman, with a well-developed bosom. Someone had sent her a huge, round bouquet of flowers in a hatbox. And when she came out to take bow after bow, she held this huge bouquet in front of her bosom and made it look twice as large as it really was. After the concert I went backstage to meet her; she was oozing friendliness. She shook hands with everybody who came to her dressing room, and when I spoke German to her she took me in her great arms and kissed me.

When it came to going to concerts Bill was like the pony express: "Neither snow nor rain nor heat nor gloom of night" could keep him from going to a concert. I recall one of the heaviest snowstorms in the history of Milwaukee, when the Chicago Symphony Orchestra was to give a concert. I looked out of the window and decided against going, but Bill started off. He did reach the theater, but he did not get home till some time the next morning. Some friends had come in from a suburb and had tried to go home on the streetcar.[2] The car got about halfway home and stopped at a shelter. They had to spend the night in that shelter.

When Frederick Stock, the conductor of the orchestra, heard about the incident, he said that there were not many cities in the country where people showed such devotion to music.

In the midst of this good life Bill died suddenly in December 1927.

As I look back, I know that something snapped within me. I was unable to think or make decisions. I still do not know how the year following his death passed. I was surrounded by loving friends and relatives. I was given advice as to what to do about continuing the business, about making investments with insurance money, and other pertinent things. But I simply did not function. That year stands out as a nightmare. There was only one thought that stayed with me: Bill was gone.

During the summer that followed I do remember sending a substantial check to Jane Addams. I had not heard from her after Bill's death, and I did not know that she had been very ill. In reply to my check I received the following letter written in her own handwriting:[3]

> My dear Hilda:
>
> I am just recovering from an attack of the "flu"—delayed to thank you for your letter and to tell you I would be glad to have you at Hull-House whenever you can come. I do hope that you will let me do anything I can.
>
> It was so good of you to send the check to the W.I.L. I have long wanted a new piece of international printing, may I use it for that and send you a copy?
>
> With assurance of my sympathy and affection, I am devotedly yours,
>
> Jane Addams
>
> July 16, 1928

There was a carton full of letters that came from friends. I still do not know the contents of any of those letters. But the letter from Jane Addams was saved.

I also saved one obituary written in a Milwaukee paper. I want to give part of it:

> He was best known in art, literary, and musical circles and was considered one of the most widely cultured men in the city. He was particularly a lover of poetry and his deep study and knowledge of the world's classics made him a most welcome visitor in many homes in the city. He was a quiet unassuming man whose life was bound up with every progressive movement that aimed to ameliorate and to advance human society. His wife, Hilda Satt Polacheck, whom he married about fifteen years ago, shared his enthusiasm in his cultural interest and both were closely identified with the movements for world peace, civil liberties, women's rights, Zionism and political liberalism.
>
> Their home was the rallying place for local artists, writers, thinkers of all creeds and they entertained distinguished visitors to the city, among the most recent being Jane Addams and Bertrand Russell who lectured here. The Polacheck home was the birthplace of many local movements of an educational, cultural and spiritual nature, and William Polacheck, in his retiring but congenial manner, inspired others to nobler thoughts and actions.
>
> Hardly any worthwhile lecture, drama, or concert took place here without the familiar presence of William Polacheck and his comment after the event was always eagerly sought by his friends.[4]

During the fall of 1928 I accepted Miss Addams's invitation to visit Hull-House. My children had never seen the house that helped make my life what it was. I took the four children and we went to Chicago to see Hull-House. I would now show my children what I had shown to thousands of tourists. The day stands out vividly in my memory.

Jane Addams was the perfect hostess. The children and I arrived at Hull-House about noon and Miss Addams at once took us to the coffeehouse for lunch.

The food was served cafeteria-style, but she insisted on bringing the food to the children herself. She waited on them as if they were her own children.

Jane Addams had no children of her own, but the children of the whole world belonged to her.

The advice and counsel given me by my friends and relatives were soon made meaningless by the coming of the Depression. I do not know what happened to all the money that I inherited. All I know is that I found myself at the end of 1929 with four children and very little money.

PART V

Return to Chicago, 1929–35

Going Back to Chicago 25

By 1929 my sanity had slowly come back. During those dark days of depression, the one comforting thought that stayed with me was that I was better prepared to meet hardship than my mother had been. The years I had spent at Hull-House, under the influence of Jane Addams, were now my strength and support. I had been taught to think clearly and to meet events with courage. I kept thinking of the many tragedies enacted day after day in the reception room at Hull-House. The immediate task before me was to earn enough money to care for the children.

Although every dollar counted at that time, I could not deny myself the privilege of going to Chicago to attend the fortieth anniversary of the founding of Hull-House.[1]

Jane Addams moved among the great and the humble just as any mother would when her far-flung children returned to the old home for a reunion. She knew everybody's name. She asked after children of the former children who had come to Hull-House years ago as bewildered, uprooted little immigrants. She would straighten a picture or move a chair into place just as any housewife would when company was coming. I felt that all the people who had come to that reunion were her family.

That evening at a meeting in Bowen Hall, some of the former residents spoke of the early days at Hull-House and how the years had taught them that they had made mistakes. One of the speakers recalled how she had put in a great deal of time and effort to teach the immigrant women what to feed their babies. They were told not to give babies most vegetables, bananas, and many foods that were found necessary for the growth of children. "So after forty years," she said, "I have come to the conclusion that the immigrant mothers knew much more about feeding children than we specialists did."[2]

I do not recall seeing Jane Addams after the reunion. But I will never forget how she seated me at her table in the dining room. I know that many celebrities sat around that table that night, but I only remember Jane Addams at the head of the table, carving a roast, as if she were serving a family.

I left Hull-House that night with a feeling that no matter what was in store for me, I could face it. I had been given a sort of transfusion of hope and courage that helped through the dark days that lay ahead.

Through the efforts of a dear friend, whom I had known years ago at Hull-House, I secured a job of managing an apartment hotel that had gone through bankruptcy. It was an everyday occurrence in those days to have people lose the earnings of a lifetime. People who had invested in large apartment hotels found their apartments vacant and income cut off and so could not keep up the payments. In short order the hotels were put into the hands of receivers until such time as it would be decided by the courts whether the former owners could salvage any of their investments. The receiver had the authority to appoint the managers of these hotels; I was given such an appointment.

I sold the house that had seen and heard so many happy times, and the children and I prepared to move to Chicago.[3] Then there was the heartbreaking ordeal of disposing of most of our furniture. We deliberated carefully what we would give up. We had gathered hundreds of books and records during the eighteen years in Milwaukee. We now sorted the books and records and decided which we would take with us. We knew that we were going from a roomy house and plenty of playspace to a small apartment with no playspace. Space in our new home would be limited and we had to plan carefully.

As living quarters go in Chicago, we were fairly comfortable. We had a five-room apartment in the hotel, so that I did not have to leave in the morning to go to work. I always managed to prepare a good breakfast for the children before they went to school. Some time during the morning when I had a few free moments I would prepare lunch. Very often dinner was late; very often, just as I was preparing to serve dinner, my telephone would ring and someone wanted to see an apartment. So the dinner would get cold and often it was served cold when it should have been hot. The children's understanding and cooperation made life bearable in those days of readjustment.

I recall an old woman who lived in the hotel. She had a modest income on which she could live in frugal comfort. She had gone to Florida to visit a relative before I became manager of the hotel. She had not heard of the black day when all the banks closed, as she was on the train on her way to Chicago.[4] When she arrived in Chicago she had one dollar and five cents in her purse. She took a taxi to the bank to get some money before coming to the hotel. She paid the cab driver the dollar and as she alighted from the taxi she saw a beggar sitting in front of the bank. She dropped the nickel into the beggar's cup and walked into the bank; it had closed. She fell to the ground and was identified by a card in her purse. She was carried into the hotel and taken to her small apartment. I called a doctor and notified her daughter. In a little while she had regained consciousness and slowly began to realize that her entire income was gone and that she had nothing on which to live.

"When I gave that beggar my last nickel, he was five cents richer than I am now," she said to me.

My new job gave me an insight into the lives of the people who worked in the hotel. There were sixteen maids employed to clean and service the apartments. They were paid forty-five dollars a month. Out of this meager sum they had to pay carfare. The first month in my capacity as manager, I had to hand out the paychecks. I was enraged to think how hard these women were working and what small wages they were getting. Jobs were at such a premium that a woman took any job, at any pay, just to be able to buy bread. Most of the women were married and had children to feed. Of the sixteen who worked at the hotel, only two had husbands who worked. The others told me that their husbands trudged around day after day, wearing out shoes looking for jobs that did not exist.

I was on duty from nine in the morning till nine in the evening, six days a week. When the older children did not have too much homework, they would wash the dishes. But when the homework was heavy, I told them to do the homework. So after the long twelve-hour day, I had the dishes to wash and the mending of clothing.

Clothing was a big item in those days and had to be kept mended. The children wore their clothes until they either outgrew them or they were utterly worn out. Every penny counted.

But I was paid a very good salary for those days and kept thinking of the maids, with their measly forty-five dollars a month. The receiver of the hotel was living in the building, so one morning I stopped him as he was going to work and asked him if his conscience did not bother him to pay such low wages. I expected that he would tell me to mind my own business, but he was very understanding and told me to give each maid a five-dollar raise. I did not tell the maids until the following payday when I called them together and told them of their raise. From that day, no maid quit her job while I had charge of the building.

In 1931 Jane Addams and Nicholas Murray Butler of Columbia University shared the Nobel Peace Prize.[5] I still do not know what

Nicholas Murray Butler did to advance the cause of peace. Among all the recipients of that coveted honor, no one deserved it more than Jane Addams.

When the news of the award came, Jane Addams was in the hospital awaiting surgery. Cables, telegrams, and letters poured into the hospital congratulating her. In James Weber Linn's biography of Jane Addams, he said: "And a distinguished woman statesman wired: 'Three cheers this is certainly good news although I wish Nick might have been eliminated'."[6]

For the operation Jane Addams had been given some new anesthetic which did not agree with her.[7] She was in the hospital for a full month and could not go to Oslo to accept her award. The American minister at Oslo accepted the awards for Miss Addams and Mr. Butler, and Professor Halven Koht made an address in their honor. He devoted the major part of the address to Jane Addams; again I quote from Mr. Linn's book:

> She is the foremost woman of her nation, not far from being its greatest citizen. . . . When the need was greatest she made the American woman's desire for peace an international interest. . . . In Jane Addams there are assembled all the best womanly attributes which shall help us to establish peace in the world. . . . She clung to her idealism in the difficult period when other demands and interests overshadowed peace. . . . She was the right spokesman for all the peace-loving women of the world.[8]

The award of sixteen thousand dollars was turned over by Jane Addams to the Women's International League for Peace and Freedom.[9]

More and more during those dark days of depression I felt that the influence of Jane Addams had entered the lives of all Americans, perhaps of people all over the world. This feeling was reaffirmed not long ago when I read an article by Eleanor Roosevelt. She compared Franklin Delano Roosevelt's ability to make decisions in time of crisis as opposed to some present-day politicians who hesitate to take a stand.

Mrs. Roosevelt said in the article that when she was a young woman she was doing volunteer work at the Rivington Street Settlement in New York City. On one particular day Franklin Delano Roosevelt came to take her home. But one of the children in the class or club had become very ill and had to be taken home. Mr. Roosevelt carried the child up several flights of dark stairs into a dark unsanitary tenement flat. And for the first time he saw how some people were forced by circumstances to live. It must have left a lasting impression on him.

Perhaps he felt like Abraham Lincoln did when he saw for the first time a slave being sold. He said to his companions: "If ever I get a chance to hit that thing, I'll hit it hard."[10] Perhaps Franklin Delano Roosevelt was imbued with that spirit in the Rivington Street Settlement. Would there have been a Rivington Street Settlement if it had not been for the vision of Jane Addams? And did he not share Jane Addams's philosophy when he said:

> I believe that we are at the threshold of a fundamental change in our popular economic thought, that in the future we are going to think less about the producer and more about the consumer. Do what we may have to do to inject life into our ailing economic order, we cannot make it endure for long unless we can bring about a wiser, more equitable distribution of the national income.[11]

The work at the apartment hotel kept us fed and housed. But the day came when the control of the hotel passed into the hands of a bank, and I was told that my services were no longer required. In the common language of that day, I was fired. Not because my work was unsatisfactory; the bank was very magnanimous in offering to give me a recommendation. In those days of the Depression, only those who knew the right people were able to get jobs. I had known the right person, but now he no longer had the authority to keep me in the job.

After spending a month trying to get some other job, I finally applied for a job on the Writers' Project of the WPA.[12]

WPA 26

Every day for a month I sat on a miserable hard bench, in a dilapidated, filthy building, waiting to be certified. Getting certified was almost as difficult as finding a job.[1] Some of the workers in the department realized how filthy the walls were and what a depressing influence they had on the unfortunate people who were sitting there waiting. So one kindhearted person must have found some colorful posters advertising trips to the Orient, to Europe, to South America. Beautiful boats were gliding down the waters of the blue Mediterranean. The posters fairly shouted to us how wonderful a cruise could be. And there we sat, asking for a job, a chance to work, a chance to feed hungry children. It has truly been said that the nearest thing to tragedy is comedy. And here was depicted a tragic farce.

Finally my certification came through. I was now a member of the Illinois Writers' Project of the WPA.

In a scene in Pearl Buck's wonderful movie *The Good Earth,*[2] the hero, Wang Lung, says: "I hear there is a revolution in the big city."

"What is that . . . a revolution?" asks his companion.

"I don't know exactly, but it has something to do with bread," says Wang Lung.

The WPA also had something to do with bread. It was the bread that averted revolution in America and saved the American way of life.

And yet I do not know of any agency that was more maligned by some of the American people.[3] Men who worked at digging ditches, repairing sidewalks, and a host of other much-needed public works were called "shovel leaners." While "leaning on the shovels," they repaired sewers, built roads, prepared the beaches for summer, cleaned the streets, and did other jobs too numerous to mention. For a forty-hour week they received the munificent wages of from $50.00 to $65.00 a month.

The cultural projects, namely, the writers, artists, and musicians, were paid $96.00 a month.

The people employed on the cultural projects of the WPA were artists who had lost their markets because no one had money with which to buy pictures. They were musicians and actors who had lost their jobs because people could no longer afford to pay $1.10, $2.20, or $3.30 for a seat in the theater or concert hall. They were writers who had been employed on newspapers and magazines and free-lance writers who could not sell their work. These people were not lazy, they were not loafers, as they were often called; they were the blood that flowed through the veins of cultural America.

Many of them had bought homes in which to raise their families and which they lost because they could not keep up the payments. Many were not wealthy people; they were average Americans living in comfort.

Then they found themselves compelled to seek work with the WPA. Thanks to our lawmakers, this was made as humiliating an affair in which any self-respecting person ever found himself. All applicants had to be certified. In plain good old English this meant that they had to prove that they were paupers and could not find jobs in private industry.

The transaction of hiring a WPA worker was never put on the dignified basis of a man or woman offering to sell his or her talents for an amount of money that could keep a family alive.

Personally, I never saw any reason why WPA workers did not enjoy the same status as civil service workers. But we did not. Our lives were circumscribed by congressmen and senators; we were told we had to live on the $96.00 a month, no matter how many people there were in the family.

The $96.00 a month that I earned would only pay for rent, food, transportation to the job, and a very limited amount of clothing. A WPA worker had to decide whether to buy a pair of shoes for himself so he could go to work or to buy shoes for a child so he could go to school. It was very plain which WPA worker had a family. He always looked shabby.

There was never any money with which to repair furniture or replace towels or sheets. I want to cite one case that came to my attention. A young girl, whose father was on WPA, found a job that paid very little. But it was enough to have the sofa repaired. There was not a comfortable chair in the home, and she had hesitated to ask her boyfriend to come to the house to meet her family. She asked her father not to report to the WPA that she had the job, but her father, being a law-abiding citizen, said he had to notify the WPA. The girl left home. I know that the disruption of family life among WPA workers was a common occurrence.

To harass WPA workers further, Congress passed a law that all

WPA workers had to quit their jobs after eighteen months and be recertified.[4] The argument advanced by Congress was that after working for eighteen months it would be a good idea to discharge the person so that he might get an incentive to get a job in private industry. I don't know where the congressmen got the idea that anyone really wanted to work for the WPA. The congressmen who pushed this law through Congress did not hear President Roosevelt when he said: "Millions were denied the opportunities to better their lot."[5] When was there a time when an American would not jump at the chance of getting a better job?

Every time a worker lost his job on account of the "eighteen months" clause, it would take from one to six months to be reinstated. No congressional committee ever investigated how people lived during those six months of enforced idleness.

None of the benefits allowed civil service workers were accorded to WPA workers. Yet the pay of both came out of the taxes of the American people. WPA workers were not supposed to need vacations; yet the vacations of congressmen and senators and civil service workers were paid. WPA workers were not allowed to get sick; there was no sick-leave allowance. WPA workers were never given a holiday, either national or religious. All time lost on a holiday had to be made up by working longer hours during the following weeks. Unemployment compensation provided by the Social Security Act did not exist for WPA workers. In short, WPA workers were denied all benefits that other government employees enjoyed.

Funds for the WPA projects were voted each year by Congress. Only enough money for one year was ever voted. Each year a debate would be staged in Congress as to whether the cultural projects were needed. WPA workers never knew when Congress would vote them out of their jobs. They never knew what security meant. To most congressmen we were just frittering away good tax money. And yet Mr. Bernard De Voto, writing about the Writers' Project in *Harper's Magazine,* summed up the situation in these words:

> The achievement of the Project has been remarkable. One could not easily overstate the handicaps under which it has operated. It has never known what funds it might expect, whether it would continue past the next quarter-day, or when caprice or hostility might fundamentally change the regulations set for it. . . . But in spite of all this, the Project has done work of the greatest importance and has made contributions to the national culture which the writers and commercial publishers of the United States had not undertaken and probably could never undertake.[6]

The supervisors of the cultural projects were experts in their fields. Yet they were always at the mercy of congressmen, who set themselves up as judges of the arts.

In 1940 the Dies Committee started investigating the Federal Theatre [Project]. One of the members of this committee was Congressman Starnes, who became worried that the Federal Theatre [Project] would overthrow the government. In her book *Arena,* Hallie Flanagan recorded for all time the intellectual caliber of Congressman Starnes. During the investigation he said:

> "You are quoting from Marlowe. Is he a communist?" The room rocked with laughter, but I did not laugh. Eight thousand people might lose their jobs because a Congressional Committee has so pre-judged us that even the classics were "Communistic."
>
> "Tell us who this Marlowe is, so we can get the proper references, because that is all we want to do." This from Congressman Starnes.
>
> "Put it in the record that he was the greatest dramatist in the period of Shakespeare," said Miss Flanagan.[7]

Congressman Starnes, who was to pass judgment on the Federal Theatre [Project], did not know that Christopher Marlowe died 346 years before the Dies Committee started to investigate him.

Congress had the power to decide whether the work of the Federal Theatre [Project] was of service to America. Congress had the power to vote the project out of existence, which it did.

During those trying times, when there was no money for any kind of recreation, the morale of all of us was lifted when we could listen to a symphony concert on the beautiful campus of the University of Chicago. These concerts were provided by members of the Music Project. The concerts made it possible for thousands of people to face the days of want and privation. In his book *The Worlds of Music,* Cecil Smith had this to say:

> The years of the depression brought a general sobering-down. Many composers could not afford to go to Europe. Others were swept into new and serious attempts to justify the art of music in a difficult economic period. The WPA music project in the 1930s was an incalculable help to native composers. Not only did it keep many of them alive on relief allocations, but it also set up orchestras and chamber music groups which made the performance of new American works a primary concern. The 1930s were largely a period of conscious Americanization. All this time music based on

> folk lore, which today seems a bromide and an evasion of personal creative responsibility, attained its peak production.[8]

The accomplishments of the cultural projects speak for themselves. No congressman will be able to destroy the record of their achievements. Just as Hitler could not destroy the culture of the world by burning books, so the cultural projects were not destroyed by voting them out of existence. The work will remain a contribution to American life. Long after the congressmen who fought President Franklin Delano Roosevelt on the WPA issue are forgotten, the books that were written on the Writers' Project, the pictures painted on the Art Project, the music composed and performed on the Music Project, and the plays created and acted by the Federal Theatre Project will stand the test of time.

May 1935[1] 27

The time spent on the Writers' Project were days and weeks and months of deprivation. A time of heartbreak and constant worry as to whether the money would stretch to buy the needed food and pay the rent. But it was also a time of hope and even some satisfaction. I was living in a country where the government cared enough, at least, to give one a chance to earn the bare necessities of life.

The children were still going to school, and here too the government helped by setting up Federal Aid to Education.[2]

On the Writers' Project we were permitted to choose the subjects that interested us the most. It was natural for me to choose subjects connected with Hull-House.[3] I wrote a paper on the famous story of the "The Devil Baby." Then I wrote a paper on the history of the juvenile court, the typhoid fever epidemic, the day nursery, and many others. I do not know what became of the things we wrote. They were filed and forgotten. The State Guides, of course, are well known to everybody. I do not know what part I had in the writing of these guides. I was never told.

To refresh my memory for this writing I would go down to Hull-House, but Miss Addams was ill most of the time and I never saw her during those days.[4]

Then came the shattering news that Jane Addams had died.[5] It was on the twenty-first of May, in 1935, and at first I felt that I had lost the last prop of life.

The words kept coming over the radio—"Chicago's first citizen. . . ." For a long time I just sat there looking at the little box that had transmitted the message that brought to a close the life of the one person who had made such a difference in my life.

The next day I went down to the old familiar neighborhood and walked about the streets, as in a daze. I walked over to the house that had been my first home in America, where I had been brought as a child. It was still there. Whatever paint was left was peeling. It seemed old and worn with the years. My heart was old and worn too.

Then I slowly walked to Hull-House.

Shops and stores owned by Italians, Greeks, Mexicans, Irish,

Jews, Poles, Russians, all were draped in purple and black cotton cloth. As I stood in front of an Italian grocery store the owner came out and said to me: "Purple for the nobility of her life; black for our great loss."

Small groups of people were gathered on Halsted Street on that day; they just stood there. You did not have to hear them talk to know how they felt. It was written on their faces.

Children are usually insensitive to death. But I do not recall any children playing on the street that day.

I entered Bowen Hall, where the body of Jane Addams was serenely resting in a coffin, with a glass over the top, as if she was at last being separated from her neighborhood where she had brought life to so many.

She was leaving the house that had been the opera house, the university, the theater, the concert hall, the gymnasium, the library, and the clubhouse for millions who would never have seen a play or heard a concert or read books if it had not been for her.

She was dressed in a light blue dress, her hair arranged in the familiar style.

An endless line of men, women, and children were passing the casket to see for the last time the face that had brought light into many dark homes.

We all said farewell to Jane Addams that day.

The next day I attended the simple funeral service in the court of the Hull-House group of buildings. The grass was beginning to green after the long winter and the leaves and buds were beginning to appear on the trees. It was the only place in the neighborhood where grass grew and flowers were given a chance to bloom. Here in this quiet spot, disturbed only by the occasional rattling of a streetcar, sat as distinguished a group of people as ever gathered to do homage to a departed friend. The people of the neighborhood stood in silent reverence as far as the eye could see.

Her body was not taken to a church; there was no church that embodied her tolerance. She belonged to all creeds, to all races, to humanity.

Afterword

Dena J. Polacheck Epstein

About 1953 my mother, Hilda Satt Polacheck, wrote her autobiography at my home in New Jersey, relying principally on her memory, for she had no diary. She felt it was important to tell how an immigrant Jewish girl from Poland became an American at Hull-House, Chicago's first and most important settlement house. It was a way to repay, in part, her debt to Jane Addams and the other people at Hull-House who had done so much to change her life for the better. Although she probably did not know it, her story is the only known description of Hull-House written by a woman from the neighborhood.

When the manuscript was finished she wrote to Dr. Alice Hamilton, asking her to write an introduction. Dr. Hamilton replied that she would be happy to write one as soon as publication arrangements were made. When Dr. Hamilton died in 1970, at the age of 101, three years after Hilda's death, a publisher had not yet been found.

The editors to whom Hilda had introductions rejected the manuscript. "Who wants to read about an obscure woman like you?" she was told. "Write a biography of Jane Addams. We might be interested in that." She made several attempts to rewrite the manuscript to meet their requirements, but eventually she gave up, deeply disappointed. She knew she had lived through important events; she knew she had a story that needed to be told. Three months after her death on 16 May 1967, Hilda's family and friends held a memorial gathering in the second-floor dining room at Hull-House. Excerpts from her autobiography were read by her granddaughters and some friends. I promised myself then that I would try to complete the task she had left unfinished.

Years passed before I could turn to Hilda's manuscript. What I found were loose sheets of various kinds of paper. The first step was to sort this jumbled mass into coherent manuscripts. Eventually seven different versions emerged, all of them incomplete. Some had whole chapters missing, possibly the result of attempts to publish them separately, although none of them were published as far as I know. Others were mere fragments, as though she had tried to begin again but had given up after a few pages. A supposedly complete version had been given to Hull-House by one of her grandsons, but it too proved to be incomplete. All the versions shared an ambiguous chronology and a casual attitude toward dates.

When the sorting was finished I tried to assemble a complete version from seven incomplete ones. Incidents included in some accounts were omitted in others, and statements of her age were inconsistent. Fortunately, two more versions turned up, one in my sister's house and one in the hands of a nephew, carbon copies that had not been changed. With their help I was able to assemble a complete manuscript, although not necessarily the original version.

For the sake of historical corroboration, I tried to find outside documentation for as many statements in the manuscript as I possibly could. In casting about for likely sources, I remembered a box of letters Hilda had given me many years before, letters that she had exchanged with my father during their engagement. For the first time the box was opened and the letters were put into chronological order. What emerged were virtually two parallel diaries, one written in Chicago and the other in Milwaukee from the spring of 1911 until their marriage in April 1912. They wrote almost every day, letters that were wide-ranging in the topics they discussed—the fight for woman suffrage, settlement work, plays, music, family problems, socialism, sex, morals, and business.

According to my birth certificate, my mother was two years older than my father, but the letters hinted that she was either four or six years older than he was.[1] She wrote on 31 October 1911 that she had been cautioned, ". . . don't marry a man six years younger than yourself. . . . young men, even boys, have worshipped older women until they reached a certain age, then they (the men) realized that they were poorly mated." On 2 November she wrote: "I have such good news to tell you. . . . I looked up the history of the Brownings today and found that E.B.B. was 41 years of age when she married R.B. while he was 35. Shall we wait until I am 41 and you 37?"

Ascertaining her true age was important for evaluating her statements of age at various stages of her life. Different versions of her manuscript gave her age on coming to America as five, six, or seven. I estimate she must have been almost ten—an age that would explain how she remembered so much of Poland and why she was permitted to do things a five-year-old would probably not do. Establishing her true age also helped in estimating the date when she left school to go to work. While she described her first job in clear detail, she did not give a date or her age at the time. After many false starts I was finally able to get a credible statement of her birth date from the University of Chicago Archives: her registration form from 1904.[2] Hilda was born in 1882, not 1886 as she had later claimed.

It seemed likely that this was not the first time she had tinkered with her age. Although she gave conflicting stories of her age when she left school, circumstantial evidence leads to the conclusion that she probably changed her age to get working papers when she was thirteen, before she was legally qualified for them. Altering one's age had been common among the poor of eastern Europe as a means of survival under autocracy, and the practice was easily transferred to America when a poor family needed the wages of its children.

The death of Hilda's father only a year after the family arrived in this country was a disaster. Hilda, at age eleven, was too young to grasp fully her mother's plight, but the impact of the tragedy was evident to her. Her mother had been torn from a comfortable life within a large extended family that viewed life as she did and brought to a strange country. Here she found dirty streets, foul smells, and strange faces. If her husband had died in Poland, she could have depended on informal social patterns that would continue to include her and her children in the Jewish community, while her male relatives saw to her well-being.

My grandmother was a conservative woman who accepted wholly her traditional role of Jewish wife and mother. With her husband's death, her links to the Jewish community died. She was left not only poor and widowed but isolated. When circumstances forced her to become the breadwinner for the family, she retreated into herself. Her piety became profound. In 1912, when Hilda's fiancé proposed sending her a book, Hilda discouraged him, writing, "She only reads her Bible."[3] The fact that she never learned to speak English symbolized her dislocation in America.

In contrast, Hilda was adventurous, forward-looking, eager to try new things; their relations must have been stormy at times. But as long as Hilda lived at home, she respected her mother's wishes and did not write on the Sabbath. Her letters include such lines as, "Just a note because it is Friday and Mother does not want anyone to write on the Sabbath."[4]

The family remained isolated from the activities of the Jewish community in which they lived. Hilda never referred to attending religious services or being a member of a congregation. Perhaps it was not expected that a widow would participate in largely male activities.

Hilda did describe her mother's efforts to enroll her sons in a heder (Hebrew school), but they refused to stay, going in the front door and out the back. Coming to America as small boys, they would have remembered very little of their life in Poland and most likely wanted to grow up as Americans. Apparently they were more interested in athletics than in Hebrew school. The youngest, Max, became a star basketball player on the Hull-House team.

It is curious how little space Hilda devoted to her three brothers. Only the oldest, Willie, is even mentioned by name. Apart from their participation in Hull-House athletics, the boys seem to have displayed little interest in Hull-House and its more intellectual activities. Their interests diverged from Hilda's, and they did not share her enthusiasm for education and social causes.

Hilda's description of her years spent working in a knitting factory are brief, but the years between thirteen and eighteen must have seemed endless while she lived them. The money she and her sister earned could have provided only a bare subsistence, while her mother's narrow horizons limited the family's social life and recreation. The future must have looked utterly bleak: more drudgery, more poverty, more monotony. During these years she remained unaware of what the city of Chicago had to offer to enrich her life. No one in her family knew what lay beyond their immediate neighborhood, and Hilda's naturally quick and inquiring mind lay fallow from the time she left school until she rediscovered Hull-House in 1900 after she was fired from the knitting factory.

Her brief encounter with the union movement was not repeated. As she wrote, her father and mother had never been inside a factory and would have nothing to offer on the subject. After she was fired from the knitting factory, none of the places where she worked were organized. The garment workers' strike of 1910 did not affect her directly; she described it from the outside, concentrating on the help the strikers received from Hull-House residents and other supporters.

Hilda was fortunate in coming to Hull-House when its earliest experiments were over and the "creative years" were beginning.[5] She was receptive to everything that Hull-House had to offer, and the settlement had by then enough experience to plan programs that responded to the needs of the people in the neighborhood. The Labor Museum had been open only a short time, but its success was already apparent. Hilda's response to the museum when she was eighteen is a measure of the wisdom of the people who planned it. Although she had learned to sew at the Jewish Training School, she did not learn the sources of the materials on which she worked. Geography as she learned it did not include discussion of agricultural products and how they are used.

The classes Hilda was able to attend at Hull-House played a seminal role in her growth. She never ceased to marvel at her good fortune in progressing from the fifth grade in elementary school to the University of Chicago. Her registration information in the University Archives gives Hull-House as her previous school, the only example I could find of a settlement house being cited in this way. For Hilda, Hull-House served as school, social center, and source of moral support, taking the place in some measure of her dead father. Her uncritical picture of Jane Addams was a sincere expression of her feelings toward the woman who had substantially changed her life. Hilda was not prone to dispassionate analysis of those she loved. The people she admired—Franklin Roosevelt, Jane Addams, Eugene V. Debs—she admired wholeheartedly.

Hilda was drawn to the theater from her teens, acting in amateur plays and attending every play she could possibly afford. To her the theater represented all the finer things in life—art, drama, escape from drudgery, glamor, excitement, education, and the solution to social problems. At Hull-House the theater was valued as both entertainment and education, a view she consistently accepted. For Hilda, having a play of her own produced by the Hull-House Players was the culmination of every dream she had ever had. It made her feel that she was capable of anything she wanted to do.

After her marriage on 17 April 1912 to William Polacheck, a young businessman who shared many of her idealistic social and political ideas, Hilda moved with him to Milwaukee, a city she found congenial. She no longer had to maintain the routine of a job, for now she lived with a sympathetic and loving husband in relative comfort amid pleasant surroundings. No wonder she saw the city through rose-colored glasses. A Socialist administration was in office when she arrived. The streets were clean, city services good. Circumstances must have seemed perfect for implementing some of her cherished ideals that had grown in her mind during her Hull-House days.

From the outset of her married life Hilda was involved in the intellectual and social life of Milwaukee. Her reviews of plays for the *Milwaukee Leader,* her activities in many organizations, and the many warm friendships she made all demonstrate her joyous participation in the community. The First World War interrupted many of her activities, as her outspoken opposition to the war raised the possibility of charges of sedition. Hilda frequently remarked that she promised her husband she would not do anything to provoke her arrest because her young children needed her. When the war ended, her activities on behalf of woman suffrage and peace, her primary concerns, grew more prominent; at the same time she took part in lesser activities like the Open Forum, the PTA, and various Jewish organizations.

The astonishing breadth and depth of the disarmament movement in the early 1920s demonstrated that Hilda was not alone in her horror of war. By July 1922 a "No More War" movement was sponsored by organizations as diverse as the Girls' Friendly Society of America, the Chautauqua Association, the National Milk Producers' Federation, the Conference of American Rabbis, the Veterans of Foreign Wars, the National Grange, and Christian Endeavor.[6] Rotary International voted for disarmament at its Edinburgh Congress, while petitions demanding international disarmament poured into the U.S. Congress. Hilda must have felt that her long-cherished dream of a peaceful world was at hand. But opinion was not unanimous. When a conference of social workers voted against a disarmament resolution, Hilda was interviewed as a member of the Wisconsin League of Women Voters. "I think that the action of the social workers . . . was cowardly," she said. "True men and women would not do such a thing, let alone persons who are pledged to relieve humanity's sufferings. . . ."[7]

Knowing Hilda's love of a good story, I am surprised she omitted one of her favorites—the Milwaukee lecture by birth control advocate Margaret Sanger in 1923.[8] The lecture was sponsored by the Milwaukee Open Forum, and Hilda was directly involved in publicizing the event by talking to groups and clubs. Mrs. Helen Raab, the forum's organizer, engaged St. John's Auditorium for an unidentified lecturer, and when Mrs. Sanger's name was announced, the lease was canceled. Conservative women's groups called on the mayor to ban this "indecent and degrading" lecture; an alderman moved to ban this "tendency toward paganism." Various civic leaders were asked to comment on the fuss. The superintendent of schools replied, "I never heard of her." Hilda, a member of the Milwaukee branch of the Women's International League for Peace and Freedom, took the opportunity to call for "a federal law sanctioning birth control. She directed attention to the fact that a similar law is in effect in Holland, where there are birth control clinics. . . ."

Despite the protests a larger hall was rented and the lecture was given as scheduled. Where the usual Open Forum lecture drew an audience of several hundred, a crowd of 1,200 filled the hall to capacity and the police were forced to close the doors and turn away scores of latecomers. It was reported in the *Leader* that "two hours before the lecture, women were already clamoring for admittance." Yet when Mrs. Sanger returned the following year, there was no excitement and no overflow audience. Two months later, a birth control clinic was announced without protest.

Beginning with the early 1920s, I can remember events described in Hilda's manuscript, like being allowed to come downstairs to meet Bertrand Russell and Carl Sandburg. I can remember hearing many stories of Hilda's childhood and youth, of her Hull-House experiences and the wonderful people she knew there. Throughout her married life she did not feel constrained by her status as a woman; nor did she feel that she lived in her husband's shadow. Domestic help was available, and Hilda was able to participate in many civic, social, and political activities, even with four children at home. I remember her description of an all-day conference she chaired, excusing herself when it was time to nurse the baby. She enjoyed cooking, baking, even making wine, and did them all with great skill, but they were never the center of her existence. Her intellectual curiosity about new ideas and her energetic approach to solving problems, the qualities that had attracted her future husband, stayed with her throughout her life.

I had just turned eleven when my father died. I remember the grief that overwhelmed my mother, which I was too young to understand. She could not be comforted for a long time. Her years as a widow paralleled to some extent her own mother's life, but Hilda never retreated into herself. I remember vividly our visit to Hull-House and Miss Addams. We were warmly received, not only by Miss Addams, but by many older residents who remembered Hilda even though she had been gone for sixteen years. In particular, I remember Eleanor Smith, the head of the Music School, who asked about my piano lessons in the most friendly way. We ate lunch with Miss Addams in the coffee shop, and she cleared away the dirty dishes.

Hilda fought for a good life for her children, buying us theater tickets in the depths of the Depression by financial stratagems I still cannot understand. She seemed to budget by objectives, deciding what she was going to do and then somehow finding the money. At a time when many of our classmates did not go on to college, Hilda encouraged us to take scholarship examinations and get part-time jobs but never to give up school.

The casual treatment of dates and ages seems to have been typical of Hilda's generation, which was more concerned with action than records. The autobiographies of Jane Addams and most of her associates, including *Twenty Years at Hull-House,* gave few dates. Like all autobiographers, Hilda was also selective in the experiences she recounted. A few incidents were re-created for narrative effect and could not have taken place when and where she described. For example, the incident during the Spanish American War may have represented to her a lifelong opposition to war, while lopping four years from her age made it creditable that she was still in school in 1898 (if, as she wrote, she was five in 1892, she would have been eleven in 1898). This incident illustrates how she wished to be perceived: a consistent opponent of war and an advocate of woman's rights from her childhood. Some other events could not be documented, although there is no reason to doubt that they happened. The landing in Montreal and the providential meeting with Rose Woldenberg were stories I heard many times during my childhood, whenever the adult Rose Woldenberg visited Hilda in Chicago.

Similarly, Hilda frequently told her children about the memorial meeting for the Haymarket martyrs, singing the memorial hymn which, as a child, I assumed was well known. It came as a great surprise when I discovered that no one, not even Pete Seeger, had ever heard of it. The episode of the children publishing a newspaper is fresh in my memory, for I played an active role in the venture. These and other incidents are clearly identified in the endnotes. Most of the events in Hilda's narrative have been documented, testimony to the authenticity of her account and the accuracy of her memory.

Appendix A

Time Line of Events in Hilda Satt Polacheck's Life

12 October 1882	Hilda is born
Spring 1892	Departs from Poland; arrives in Montreal
16 June 1892	Arrives in Chicago
[Fall 1892]	Begins school at Jewish Training School, probably second grade
4 March 1894	Father dies
[December 1894 or 1895]	Christmas party at Hull-House
[Late winter 1896]	Leaves school to go to work
1900	Hull-House Labor Museum founded
1901	Meets Prince Kropotkin at Hull-House
1902	*Hull-House Bulletin* reports meeting of the Ariadne Club, "Hilda Satt, Secy."
[November 1903]	Memorial meeting for Haymarket martyrs
Spring 1904	Attends the University of Chicago
[Summer 1904]	Works at Hull-House; teaches English class(?)
1905	Katarina Breshkovsky visits Hull-House
[1905]	Begins work at A. C. McClurg & Co.
13 May 1906	Marks Nathan Jewish Orphan Home dedicated

1907	Deborah Boys' Club established (Sidney Teller, superintendent)
[1907 or 1908]	Meets William Polacheck
1909	Publishes articles in *The Butterfly*
191112	Works at McClurg's (for a second period?)
June 1911	Goes to Saugatuck
April 1912	*The Walking Delegate* is produced by Hull-House Players
17 April 1912	Marries William Polacheck
19 January 1914	Charles Lessing Polacheck is born
30 November 1916	Dena Julia Polacheck is born
13 July 1918	Demarest Lloyd Polacheck is born
14 September 1923	Jessie Polacheck is born
December 1927	William Polacheck dies
December 1930	Moves her family to Chicago
17 January 1938	Leaves employment with Jane Addams Houses
1938	Earliest date on her work for the Federal Writers' Project
11 April 1940	Recertified for work on the Federal Writers' Project
18 May 1967	Hilda dies

Appendix B

The Writings of Hilda Satt Polacheck

Hilda enjoyed writing throughout her adult life, but she did not reveal the extent of this accomplishment to her children or her grandchildren, who were more conscious of her prowess as a cook and baker. Her letters and her autobiography are written in a rough-and-ready style, a reflection of the kind of woman she was—direct, unpretentious, honest, at times blunt, almost totally lacking in subtlety and delicacy—a style more characteristic of the early twentieth century, when she was young. Most of what she wrote remains unpublished; some of it was not preserved.

Of Hilda's student work, only "The Ghetto Market," the paper she quoted in her autobiography, has survived. The next earliest work that has been found is "The Old Woman and the New World," published in *The Butterfly* in 1909. Other brief articles may also have appeared in *The Butterfly*. In 1911 two articles were published in *The Sentinel,* "a weekly newspaper devoted to Jewish interest" issued in Chicago.

In a letter postmarked 22 February 1911, Hilda wrote to her future husband:

> I decided to write this to-night because I would have spent the evening writing for *The Sentinel,* and I don't want to break myself of the habit of writing on Tuesday evening. . . . I had my talk with the gentleman of the *Sentinel,* and he offered to pay for my work, but I felt a certain feeling of repugnance rising in that spot where the conscience is supposed to rest, so I concluded to part with the paper. I believe that if a person engages in the dangerous art of reaching the moral and uplifting sense of man, that he is entitled to make his bread and butter thereof. But I do not believe that a man should become a writer and pretend to better and uplift the community, when in reality he is just going into the writing business. Commercialism should become artistic, but save me from the well known "commercial art." I would rather

> write on wrapping paper, and mean what I say, than write on "good form" paper, and say pretty things because they sound good.[1]

Her first attempts at play writing were reported in *The Sentinel* in April 1911:

> A dramatic performance, which will introduce Miss Hilda Satt in the capacity of playwright will be given Sunday, April 23, at the Chicago Hebrew Institute. Three one-act plays will be presented: "The Kind Lady," by Hilda Satt, "The Committee on Matrimony," by Margaret Cameron, and "Case No. 29,129," by Hilda Satt. The plays are under the personal direction of Mr. Louis Alter, of the Hull-House Dramatic Association. . . .
>
> The playwright and the players have a great many friends in all parts of the city, and a large audience is expected.[2]

No trace of these plays has been found. *Case No. 29,129* was performed again in Milwaukee after her marriage, prompting the *Milwaukee Leader* to announce, "Play Slams Out Home Run in War against Tenement Homes."[3]

In a letter postmarked 13 March 1911, Hilda wrote to Bill: "I find it loads of fun to have people speak my lines with the care and tenderness bestowed on rare events. . . . I hope you will be able to come and help make my first appearance as a play-write a pleasant memory. I am quite shaky about it. It seems a responsibility to put your thoughts before an intelligent public for consideration."[4] It is unclear whether or not he was in attendance, but he must have asked some questions in a lost letter, for she responded on 12 April 1911: "About my plays—. . . To be really frank with you—I consider my plays alive—timely—dramatic. They are worthwhile—still they are only practice work, for what I hope will follow. . . . By the way, both my plays deal a little bit with the chance a young person has for honesty after his father has amassed a fortune by hook or crook. Of course, after everybody dies, all ends happily."[5]

A few months after the first performance of her plays, Hilda was asked to dramatize Leroy Scott's novel, *The Walking Delegate,* for the Hull-House Players. A copy of the original version, written in Saugatuck, was sent to Bill Polacheck, who had it bound in limp leather. That copy is now in the Special Collections Department of the University of Illinois at Chicago Library. The revised version, performed at Hull-House in April 1912, apparently was not preserved.

The following is a list of Hilda's known writings, in chronological order:

"The Ghetto Market," in pencil on lined tablet paper, untitled, 1903–4

"The Old Woman and the New World," *The Butterfly* 3, no. 10 (October 1909): 4–5.

"The Marks Nathan Jewish Orphan Home," *The Sentinel* 1 (11 February 1911): 7–8, 18.

"Woman's Loan Association: A Practical Charity," *The Sentinel* 1 (18 February 1911): 13.

The Kind Lady and *Case No. 29,129,* two one-act plays performed at the Chicago Hebrew Institute, 23 April 1911.

The Walking Delegate, a play in four acts, dramatized from Leroy Scott's novel of the same name, performed by the Hull-House Players, 10, 17, 20, 27 April 1912.

Reviews of plays for the *Milwaukee Leader* signed by H.S.:

1 November 1912, "A Good Actress in a Flimsy Play" (*A Night Out*)

4 November 1912, "Talker at Schubert" (*The Talker*)

11 November 1912, "*Blue Bird* Not Spoiled by Glare of Footlights"

20 December 1912, "*Only Son* Lukewarm"

23 December 1912, "*Officer 666* Davidson [Theater]"

30 December 1912, "An Excellent Play" (*Fine Feathers*)

3 January 1913, "*The Wall Street Girl*"

6 January 1913, "A Lot of Weary Actors": "The play is a musty, creaky old comedy, of the 'parlor variety' often inflicted on a fond public. . . ."

10 January 1913, "*Robin Hood*"

13 January 1913, "Fine Millinery Display" (*The Pink Lady*)

10 February 1913, "*The Attack*"

17 February 1913, "*The Girl at the Gate*"

21 February 1913, "*The Real Thing*"

10 March 1913, "A Mountain Romance" (*The Trail of the Lonesome Pine*)

15 March 1913, "Wisconsin Dramatic Society," three one-act plays

24 March 1913, "*Bought and Paid For*"

8 April 1913, *Julius Caesar,* with William Faversham

2 May 1913, *The High Road,* with Mrs. Fiske

An article on "The Hull-House Players," signed "Hilda Satt," appeared on 1 February 1913 in the *Milwaukee Leader.* The review of their performance on 4 February was unsigned.

A series of short sketches, ghostwritten probably in the 1930s for

Anna Heldman, a social worker in Pittsburgh, were found among Hilda's papers. These sketches, based on Miss Heldman's experiences with clients, describe incidents in the lives of Jewish immigrants in a style characteristic of Hilda:

"Old Maid" (6 pp.)
"A Stormy Life" (6 pp.)
"No Luck" (8 pp.)
"A Daughter of the Levites" (13 pp.)
"Breach of Promise" (7 pp.)
"The Last Laugh" (10 pp.)
"The Untamed Shrew" (9 pp.)

Material written for the Federal Writers' Project included six short plays, now in the Illinois State Historical Library, Springfield:

Ordering Breakfast (8 pp.)
The Facts of Life (5 pp.)
The Gold Fish (8 pp.)
The Spy (9 pp.)
Mushrooms (8 pp.)
George Washington (16 pp.)

Items in the Manuscript Division, Library of Congress, as part of the Folklore Project, WPA Federal Writers' Project, Container A608—Life Histories, include:

"Christmas at Hull-House," part of "American Folk Stuff, 1937–38" (4 pp.)
"Dust," 1937–38 (8 pp.)
"Pack on My Back," 1937–38 (2 versions, 9 pp. and 10 pp.)
"Little Grandmother," 26 January 1939 (1 p.)
"A Prince Comes to Halsted Street," 26 January 1939 (2 pp.)
"The Air Is Bad," 26 January 1939 (1 p.)
"The Ghost of the Convent," 26 January 1939 (2 pp.)
"Children's Jump Rope Games," 10 April 1939 (1 p.)
"The Hull-House Devil Baby," 13 April 1939 (8 pp.)
"Song Games for the Small Child," 20 April 1939 (2 pp.)
" 'Blues' Songs," 11 May 1939 (2 pp.)
"Singing Games," 11 May 1939 (4 pp.)
"Spontaneous Stories by Young Children," 11 May 1939 (8 pp.)
"Songs and Yells of Steel Workers of South Chicago," 16 May 1939 (5 pp.)
" 'I Sell Fish' " 22 June 1939 (4 pp.)
"The Dybbuk of Bunker Street," 8 July 1939 (5 pp.)

In Container A866—Special Studies and Projects—Radio Scripts:

"The Story of Maxwell Street," 8 January 1941 (12 pp.)

"A Night's Lodging," for the series "Legends of Illinois," 8 January 1941 (14 pp.)

Found separately among the Chicago manuscripts:

"The Hull-House Labor Museum," 1937–38 (8 pp.)

There probably are others that have not yet been located among the 400,000 manuscripts left unpublished by the Federal Writers' Project. Of all those listed, only two are known to have been published, one of them twice: "A Pack on the Back" was included on pp. 51–54 in Ann Banks's "Making It Through Hard Times," *The Atlantic* 246 (July 1980): 40–57; "I Sell Fish" was published under the fictitious name "Louis Kurland" and "Pack on My Back" as "Morris Horowitz" in Ann Banks's *First Person America* (New York: Alfred A. Knopf, 1980; rpt., New York: Vintage Books, 1981), 29–35.

Two articles Hilda mentioned in her manuscript (history of the juvenile court and the day nursery) have not been found, but several manuscripts were found among her papers after her death that probably were written for the Federal Writers' Project:

"The Derby," describing Chicago's notorious First Ward balls (6 pp.)

"Christmas Dinner" ("#33"), (4 pp.)

"The Birth Certificate," a radio script (30 pp.)

A radio script headed "eon-610-1" but lacking a title, mimeographed, possibly for performance (41 pp.)

"The Seder" (12 pp.)

"A Week at Grandma's" (2 versions, 9 pp. and 12 pp.)

"Housing and the Typhoid Fever Epidemic" (4 pp.)

"Good Dishes Make Good Neighbors" (8 pp.)

Probably not written for the Federal Writers' Project:

"A Guinea Pig Evaluates WPA" (13 pp.)

Notes

INTRODUCTION (Lynn Y. Weiner)

I would like to acknowledge with thanks Dena J. Epstein and Peg Strobel of the University of Illinois at Chicago for their help in the preparation of the introduction.

1. See, for example, Sydney Stahl Weinberg, *The World of Our Mothers: The Lives of Jewish Immigrant Women* (Chapel Hill: University of North Carolina Press, 1988); Marie Hall Ets, *Rosa: The Life of an Italian Immigrant* (Minneapolis: University of Minnesota Press, 1970); Anzia Yezierska, *Bread Givers* (1925; rpt., New York: Persea Books, 1975).

2. Weinberg, *World of Our Mothers,* 74.

3. Ibid., 96.

4. Hilda Satt, "The Old Woman and the New World," *The Butterfly* 3, no. 10 (October 1909): 4–5.

5. Weinberg, *World of Our Mothers,* 15. See also Charlotte Baum, Paula Hyman, and Sonya Michel, *The Jewish Woman in America* (New York: New American Library, 1975). For the story of the Satt brothers and Hebrew school, see the Afterword to this volume.

6. U.S. Bureau of the Census, *Occupations of the Twelfth Census* (Washington, D.C.: Government Printing Office, 1904), cxlvii. Hull-House residents Florence Kelley and Alzina Stevens published an essay on wage-earning children in 1895 in the pioneering book *Hull-House Maps and Papers,* which was the first systematic investigation of an immigrant community in America. The essay is reprinted in Allen F. Davis and Mary Lynn McCree, eds., *Eighty Years at Hull-House* (Chicago: Quadrangle Books, 1969), 45–50.

7. Lynn Y. Weiner, *From Working Girl to Working Mother: The Female Labor Force in the United States, 1820–1980* (Chapel Hill: University of North Carolina Press, 1985), 28–29; Baum et al., *Jewish Woman in America,* 109–10.

8. This was a common fear of Jews living among Gentiles, based on the reality of pogroms in Europe during Christmas holidays. For other accounts of the lessening of this fear in America, see Amalie Hannig, "Christmas at Hull-House," *Ladies' Home Journal,* December 1911, 31, reprinted in Davis and McCree, *Eighty Years at Hull-House,* 91–93, and Weinberg, *World of Our Mothers,* 96.

9. Michael B. Katz, *Class, Bureaucracy, and Schools: The Illusion of Educational Change in America* (New York: Praeger, 1971), 119.

10. Alice Kessler-Harris, "Where Are the Organized Women Workers?," *Feminist Studies* 3, no. 1/2 (Fall 1975): 92; Elizabeth Anne Payne, *Reform, Labor, and Feminism: Margaret Dreier Robins and the Women's Trade Union League* (Urbana: University of Illinois Press, 1988), 89.

11. Interview with Dena Polacheck Epstein, 20 May 1988.

12. Jane Addams, *Twenty Years at Hull-House* (1910; rpt., New York: New American Library, 1961), 89.

13. See Louise de Koven Bowen, *Open Windows* (Chicago: Ralph Fletcher Seymour, 1946); James Weber Linn, *Jane Addams: A Biography* (New York: D. Appleton-Century Co., 1935); Marcet Haldeman-Julius, *Jane Addams as I Knew Her* (Girard, Kans.: Haldeman-Julius Publications, 1936).

14. Allen F. Davis, *American Heroine: The Life and Legend of Jane Addams* (New York: Oxford University Press, 1973), chap. 11.

15. See, for example, Anzia Yezierska, "How I Found America" and "The Free Vacation House," in *Hungry Hearts* (Boston: Houghton Mifflin Co., 1920).

16. Philip Davis's autobiography, *And Crown Thy Good* (New York: Philosophical Library, 1952), is excerpted in Davis and McCree, *Eighty Years at Hull-House,* 117–19.

17. Kathryn Kish Sklar, "Hull-House in the 1890's: A Community of Women Reformers," *Signs: Journal of Women in Culture and Society* 10, no. 4 (Summer 1985): 658–77.

18. For a discussion of the ideology of the settlement house, see Sheila M. Rothman, *Woman's Proper Place: A History of Changing Ideals and Practices, 1870 to the Present* (New York: Basic Books, 1978), 112–27.

19. Weiner, *From Working Girl to Working Mother,* 6, 89.

20. For a discussion of Jane Addams and the Women's International League for Peace and Freedom, see Davis, *American Heroine,* chaps. 12–15.

21. On the National Woman's party, see Christine A. Lunardini, *From Equal Suffrage to Equal Rights: Alice Paul and the National Woman's Party, 1910–1928* (New York: New York University Press, 1986). On the split between advocates of equal rights and protective labor legislation, see Rothman, *Woman's Proper Place,* 157–65.

22. See Kathryn Kish Sklar, ed., *Notes of Sixty Years: The Autobiography of Florence Kelley* (Chicago: Charles H. Kerr Publishing Co., 1986).

23. For examples of these autobiographical accounts, see Anzia Yezierska, *Red Ribbon on a White Horse* (New York: Scribner, 1950); Emma Goldman, *Living My Life* (New York: Alfred Knopf, 1931). For an overview of Yezierska's life, see Alice Kessler-Harris, "Introduction," in Anzia Yezierska, *Bread Givers* (New York: G. Braziller, 1975); Louise Levitas Henriksen, *Anzia Yezierska: A Writer's Life* (New Brunswick, N.J.: Rutgers University Press, 1988).

24. Yezierska, "How I Found America," 281–82.

25. Rothman, *Woman's Proper Place,* 119–20.

26. Interview with Dena Polacheck Epstein, 20 May 1988.

CHAPTER 1

1. *Encyclopaedia Judaica,* s.v. "Wloclawek"; Lucjan Dobroszycki and Barbara Kirschenblatt-Gimblett, *Image before My Eyes: A Photographic History of Jewish Life in Poland, 1864–1939* (New York: Schocken Books, 1977), 259. In 1803 the Jewish population in Wloclawek numbered 208; by 1897 it had reached 9,595, or about 20 percent of the total population of under 50,000. The city's name in Yiddish is Vlotslavek, the form Hilda invariably used.

2. Different versions of the manuscript give different ages for Hilda when she arrived in America, ranging from five to seven, whereas I estimate that she was almost ten. Her children were unaware that she had trimmed four years off her age at the time of her marriage, a circumstance that must have given her some trouble in writing her autobiography. Her true age was established from her registration form, "Matric. No. 19069," a transcript for Hilda Rifka [*sic*] Satt, University of Chicago Archives.

3. Louis Satt probably attended the Jewish elementary crown school in Wloclawek, one of four in Russian Poland, supported by the Jewish community. Isaac Levitats, *The Jewish Community in Russia, 1844–1917* (Jerusalem: Posner & Sons, 1981), 48.

4. "Polish-Jewish funerary art . . . developed over the centuries a complex system of symbols reflective of those values and virtues which Polish Jews considered of importance to memorialize on their tombs, such as scholarship, philanthropy, and ancestry. Books or a Torah crown meant scholarship; an alms box, charity; running water or musical instruments, Levite ancestry. Cut trees symbolized an early death; leafless branches, parents without children. Various animals indicated the name of the deceased: e.g., a deer (*Hirsch*), a dove (*Johan*), a stag (*Zev*), a sheep (*Rebecca*), a fish (*Fischle*)." Earl Vinecour, *Polish Jews: The Final Chapter* (New York: McGraw-Hill Book Co., 1977), 45.

5. This is Hilda's only reference to an education in Europe. It would come as no surprise if she had not been sent to school in Poland. According to Stephan F. Brumberg: "Because of the gender-related role differences encoded in traditional Jewish religious practices, the education of females was limited or wholly neglected. Some, not all, women learned the Hebrew alphabet and a few prayers, many learned to read Yiddish (or 'jargon' as it was called), but rarely did a woman advance to the study of Talmud. Males, on the other hand, had to learn to read Hebrew and recite the extensive prayers of the traditional liturgy, or they would be unable to discharge their holy obligations." Brumberg, "Going to America, Going to School: The Immigrant–Public School Encounter in Turn-of-the-Century New York City," *American Jewish Archives* 36 (November 1984): 92.

6. Hilda's suspicion that the pogroms were instigated by priests was only partially correct. Evidence points to a secret group of high officials in the Russian government, arch-reactionaries and anti-Semites who encouraged this program of violence. Louis S. Greenberg notes, "This government . . . could have put a quick stop to the pogroms had it seriously wished to do so." Greenberg, *The Jews in Russia: The Struggle for Emancipation, 1881–1917* (1944–50; rpt., New York: Schocken Books, 1976), 2:23–24.

7. Bella Chagall shared Hilda's feelings: ". . . father and my brothers . . . go to eat supper in the *sukkah.* Neither mother nor I nor the cook goes there. . . . Do they give a thought to us who have been left in the house?" Chagall, *Burning Lights* (New York: Schocken Books, 1946), 103.

CHAPTER 2

1. Louis Satt was probably more aware than his family was of the changing conditions for Jews in the Russian Empire and their probable impact on the Jews of Poland. The May Laws of 1882, which had caused wholesale expulsions of Jews in Russia from areas where they had been permitted to live for years, had not yet been applied to Poland, but their impact was anticipated. The U.S. Commissioners of Immigration, on their tour of inspection in Europe in September 1891, reported from Warsaw: "The Jews of Poland have thus far been spared from the rigorous orders which forced their race from Inner Russia to the Pale . . . but the more intelligent look upon their advantages as only of a temporary character. . . . It is . . . the belief of well-informed persons that it is but a question of a short time when the same pressure will be brought to bear on the Jewish population of Poland that now crushes them elsewhere. In consequence . . . commercial transactions are all made with reference to the crisis believed to be approaching." *Report of the Commissioners of Immigration upon the Causes Which Incite Immigration to the United States* (Washington, D.C.: Government Printing Office, 1892), 1:93, 95.

2. The date the family left Poland is unknown, as is the length of time it took for them to reach their destination. The typical time for the voyage reported in the ship registers for the Port of Quebec was ten or eleven days. For example, the SS *Sardinian* sailed from Liverpool on 26 May 1892 and arrived in Montreal on 4 June. Thirty years earlier the voyage would have taken six weeks.

3. Lutkin was dean of the School of Music at Northwestern University from 1895 to 1928 (*Baker's Biographical Dictionary of Musicians,* 1978 ed., 1053). Some Lutkin papers survive in the Music Library at Northwestern, but there is nothing on his trips to Europe.

CHAPTER 3

1. The name of the ship that brought the Satt family to the New World has not been determined. The microfilm copy of registers for ships entering the Port of Quebec, the entry point for Montreal, was provided by the Canadian Archives in the National Library of Canada. Registers for April-July 1892 do not mention Dena Miriam Satt and her six children, but some of the pages were torn, some illegible because of fading, and some entries incomplete, such as "Mrs. —— and two children." Thus, the evidence is inconclusive. The index to the Hamburg Staatsarchiv Auswanderungsamt I, Fach VIII, B.S. bd. 49, provided by the genealogical collection of the Church of Jesus Christ of Latter Day Saints in Salt Lake City was also searched with disappointing results: no mention of the Satt family, but again some pages were illegible and there is no way of knowing whether the entries were complete.

2. There is some inconsistency with Hilda's statement that her mother did not worry about money since she expected to be cared for by relatives in New York; she already knew they were headed for Montreal. Her pride, which later prevented her from asking for help after her husband's death, may explain her generous tipping. The arrangements made for meeting the Satt family on their arrival are unknown. Louis Satt probably felt he could not afford to take the time from work to meet them in New York and thus relied on relatives for that service. Uncertainty about ship schedules played a role as well. It could not be expected that one would know the exact date when people would arrive from Europe.

3. The Woldenberg family was not listed in the available Montreal city directories: in any case, they did not live there long, and by 1894 they were in Chicago. A biography of their son, Max, states that he was born in Wloclawek, Poland, on 23 August 1887 and arrived in Chicago in 1894. Hyman L. Meites, ed., *History of the Jews of Chicago* (Chicago: Jewish Historical Society of Illinois, 1924), 345; see also *Who's Who in Chicago* (1926). Since Max would have been about seven in 1894, it seems probable that he came with his family. Rose Woldenberg visited Hilda and her children many times, retelling the saga of the Satt family's arrival in Montreal. The Woldenberg family was not listed in the Chicago city directory until 1897: "Woldenberg, Jacob, tailor. h. 444 W. Division."

4. The cheating of immigrants by ticket agents was widespread. Pamela S. Nadell, "The Journey to America by Steam: The Jews of Eastern Europe in Transition," *American Jewish History* 71 (December 1981): 269–84; Samuel Chotzinoff, *A Lost Paradise: Early Reminiscences* (New York: Alfred A. Knopf, 1955), 39–45.

5. There is no way of verifying the date of the Satt family's arrival in Chicago, but there is no valid reason to doubt the date Hilda gave as it is consistent with every known fact.

CHAPTER 4

1. There is no listing for Louis Satt, either residence or shop, in the *Lakeside Annual Directory of the City of Chicago* in 1892 or 1893; nor can the "steamship ticket agency" over which the family lived be identified from the 1892–93 city directories. The earliest listing for any member of the family is in the directory for 1894, after Louis Satt's death: "Satt Dora [*sic*] wid Louis, h. 114 Bunker." City directory listings may have been hit or miss in the crowded ghetto of non-English-speaking immigrants on Chicago's West Side.

2. Dora Aaron, later Mrs. Harry Rabe.

3. "Chicago [in 1893] had two thousand miles of streets. Fewer than a third were paved, mainly with huge blocks of wood, but also with macadam, with gravel, asphalt, cinders, cobblestones, or with great blocks of granite which in winter sweated a cold slime; treacherous footing for the draft horses with their metal shoes." Ray Ginger, *Altgeld's America: The Lincoln Ideal versus Changing Realities* (New York: Funk & Wagnalls, 1958), 24.

4. A contemporary description of the West Side ghetto corroborates

Hilda's description: "The principal streets . . . are lined with stores of every description, all of them kept by Jews and nearly all with a sign in Hebrew. . . . The streets . . . are very narrow, hardly wider than alleys, and lined on both sides with one-story cottages and garbage boxes. . . . The streets literally swarm with children, who play about the gutters. . . . in a district bounded by Sixteenth Street on the south and Polk Street on the north and the Chicago River and Halsted Street on the east and west, one can walk the streets for blocks and . . . hear nothing but the Hebrew patois of Russian Poland. In this restricted boundary, in narrow streets, ill-ventilated tenements and rickety cottages, there is a population of from 15,000 to 16,000 Russian Jews." "Our Russian Exiles," *Chicago Sunday Tribune,* 19 July 1891. A similar description is given by Charles Zeublin, "The Chicago Ghetto," in *Hull-House Maps and Papers [by] Residents of Hull-House* (1895; rpt., New York: Arno Press & The New York Times, 1970), 91–111.

5. Hilda could not have heard this song soon after she arrived in Chicago for it was copyrighted in 1896. James Fuld, *The Book of World-Famous Music,* rev. and enl. ed. (New York: Crown Publishers, 1971), 278.

6. The O'Leary house at 137 De Koven Street was between Jefferson and Clinton streets, two blocks east of Halsted Street, according to the map in *Hull-House Maps and Papers.*

7. There are no known photographs of Louis Satt or of his family. The photograph of his wife was made much later.

CHAPTER 5

1. Louis Satt may have attended Polish Congregation Beth Hamedrosh Hagodol, 307 Maxwell Street, listed in the Chicago city directory for 1891–92.

2. In 1891, when Louis Satt arrived in Chicago, the firm was listed in the city directory as Bagley & Nason (Frederick P. Bagley and Charles E. Nason) marble, W. 18th & S. Canal (p. 215). In 1892 the firm was listed as Bagley, Frederick P. & Co., marble, at the same address (p. 143).

3. The address of Louis Satt's shop after he left the Bagley firm is not known, but the Jewish Training School, which Hilda stated was next door, is listed in the city directory for 1893 as 91 Judd Street. The annual reports of the school gave its location as "Judd St., between Jefferson and Clinton . . . in the heart of the Jewish-Russian settlement." Jewish Training School, *Second Annual Report . . . 1890–91* (Chicago: S. Ettlinger, Printer, 1891), 9.

4. The school was dedicated on 19 October 1890 and opened the next day with 1,100 children accepted for admission. Jewish Training School, "Third Annual Report of the Executive Board," in *Second Annual Report,* 8, 10.

5. His forename was Gabriel, not George. Ibid.

6. "The ungraded class cared for eighty-four new comers, who are at once put into the charge of a teacher who does not understand a word of Jargon [Yiddish] and who keeps them in her class till they are sufficiently familiar with the English to keep pace with the graded class for which they are mentally fitted; fifty-seven of these were promoted this year." Jewish Training

School, *Seventh Annual Report . . . for 1895–96* (Chicago: S. Ettlinger Printing Co., [1896]), 9. The *Second Annual Report* included the statement: "Some children . . . who came to us directly from Russia, have been advanced in less than two months into the fifth or sixth grades" (p. 17). The school's negative attitude toward Yiddish was expressed in its annual report for 1895–96: "No special effort is made to abolish the Jargon, but the children naturally feel ashamed to use it, and in and about the school-house they converse only in English" (*Seventh Annual Report,* 9). The disapproval of Yiddish was common among both German Jews and social workers, including those at Hull-House, who seemed to regard it not as a language but as a debased, uncultured form of "jargon." These were the people who had the welfare of the new arrivals most at heart, and their attitude may have influenced Hilda, who spoke Yiddish fluently all her life but made no effort to teach it to her children, nor did she seem to attach any importance to it.

7. In the year that Hilda was enrolled, 1892–93, her class was listed "VII Grade—Second School Year, teacher, Mrs. Anna Torrance." Jewish Training School, *Fourth Annual Report* (Chicago: S. Ettlinger, Printer, 1893), 5, 36. The course of instruction for this grade included mathematics, English, geography, history, art, manual work, music, and gymnastics. No slates were used and the introduction to American ways was stressed. Apparently Hilda was not put into the ungraded class for children who could speak no English. The only teacher she ever mentioned was Mrs. Torrance. At ten, Hilda may have been a little old for second grade, but the assignment was fortunate for her, as she soon learned to idolize her teacher. Her naturally quick and intelligent mind thrived in Mrs. Torrance's classroom. The school was organized as Hilda described. The annual report for 1890–91 states: "Primary Grade . . . extends over four years—each class in charge of a class teacher . . ." (p. 19). When Mrs. Torrance's class completed fourth grade in the spring of 1896, it was promoted into the grammar department, where Mrs. Lena Martin took over the class. Jewish Training School, *Eighth Annual Report* (Chicago: Press of Toby Rubovits, 1897), 6. Hilda never mentioned Mrs. Martin, although she told her children that she left school in fifth grade. Perhaps Mrs. Martin made little impression.

8. The quotation from Parker was published in the *Ninth Annual Report of the Jewish Training School of Chicago for 1898–99* ([Chicago]: Fidelity Printing Co., 1898), 10. It is interesting to note that the bound copy of the annual reports in the Joseph Regenstein Library of the University of Chicago is inscribed: "For Col. F. Parker, President, with compliments, from G. Bamberger." The Jewish Training School kept records of each child applying for admission, including names of parents, nationality, how long in this country, ages of father and mother, their ages when married, number of children, and ages of oldest and youngest child. By 1897 the school had on file records for over 3,100 children (*Eighth Annual Report,* 10). Unfortunately these records have not been preserved.

9. Hilda's memory was not quite reliable on the date of the parade in honor of Columbus. New York City had pre-empted October 12, so Chicago had its parade and the dedication of the World's Columbian Exposition on

October 21, all fully described in the *Chicago Tribune* for that date, which devoted its first three pages to the details. The diagram showing the route of the parade makes it clear that the Satt children did not sit on the curb on Halsted Street in front of their home to watch the parade; the closest it came to their home was the corner of Franklin and Jackson streets, about nine blocks away. Since it is not known precisely where they lived on Halsted Street, their distance from the parade route cannot be estimated accurately. Hilda was too young at that time and had too little command of English to read the lists of dignitaries and festivities given in the *Tribune;* the parade was enough for her.

10. None of the guides and catalogs of the World's Columbian Exposition were sufficiently detailed to list the individual exhibits. Among those examined were William E. Cameron, *The World's Fair, Being a Pictorial History of the Columbian Exposition* (Chicago: Chicago Publication & Lithograph Co., 1893), and Horace H. Morgan, *The Historical World's Columbian Exposition and Chicago Guide* (St. Louis: J. H. Mason & Co., 1892), both in the library of the Chicago Historical Society. The *Sixth Annual Report* (Chicago: Hornstein Bros., Printers, 1895) for 1894–95 of the Jewish Training School proudly described ". . . the praise of prominent educators from abroad—Germany, Switzerland, France, Russia, Sweden and Austria—who repeatedly visited our School during the World's Fair, and of many others who examined our exhibit in the Educational Section of the Department of Liberal Arts. We can and must refer to the awards given us by the Executive Committee on Awards for the excellency of our work" (p. 20). The award read: "For the philanthropic and enlightened education of the poor by wise methods, securing the unfolding simultaneously of the intellectual, moral and physical powers of the child with excellent results. Mary J. Serrano, Individual Judge. Good methods of manual training and good results, especially in needle-work and wood-work. Signed: Madam Semetschkin, Individual Judge" (p. 21).

11. Louis Satt's tombstone states that he died on 4 March 1894 at age forty-five (Jewish Waldheim Cemetery, OBC Section, Gate 30, Row 1, Grave 35). Hilda wrote her fiancé in 1912: "Mother said that she sees no reason why we can't marry on the 15th [of March]. The anniversary [of father's death] is observed Thursday eve the 14th and Friday morning, so let it be Friday, March 15th. Mother counts the anniversary according to the Hebrew calendar. The anniversary of Father's death is really March 4th." Hilda Satt to William Polacheck, 2 February 1912. (All references to manuscript correspondence refer to the collection in the possession of the editor. Hereafter the writers will be designated HS and WP.) The wedding was postponed until 17 April.

CHAPTER 6

1. The directories list other intervening addresses that Hilda chose not to mention. The apartment to which the Satt family moved after Louis Satt's death may have been the one listed in the Chicago directory for 1894, the first listing of any kind for the family: "Satt, Dora, wid Louis, h. 114 Bunker," between Halsted and Desplaines streets. (Dora was apparently considered the English equivalent of Dena since it appears in the English portion of her

tombstone, although she was always called Dena by her family.) No listing appears in the 1895 or 1897–98 directories. The entry for 1896 is puzzling: "Satt, Dina, wid Louis, h. 533 N. Ashland av." Hilda never spoke of the family's moving so far west (1600 compared to Halsted at 800), and perhaps this listing is in error. The directory for 1899 lists "Satt, Dora, wid Louis, h. 181 De Koven," apparently the address with the Irish neighbors.

2. No Teghanny was listed in any of the city directories examined, but a Dennis F. Tangney, driver or teamster, was listed at 181 De Koven in 1894 and 1896. Apparently the Tangneys lived in the front house and the Satts in the rear on the alley.

3. Dena Satt's choice of occupation was not unusual: "Jewish women found various ways to earn 'the living'. . . . frequently, women were peddlers who stood in the market-place or went from house to house, baskets over their arms, selling rolls or bagels they had baked, or tea, beans, and other food-stuffs." Charlotte Baum, Paula Hyman, and Sonya Michel, *The Jewish Woman in America* (New York: Dial Press, 1976), 68.

4. Thomas Hood, "The Song of the Shirt" (ll.1–2), in Nella Braddy, ed., *The Standard Book of British and American Verse* (Garden City, N.Y.: Garden City Publishing Co., 1952), 399.

5. In 1909 an article by Hilda, "The Old Woman and the New World," was published in *The Butterfly* (3, no. 10 [October 1909]: 4–5), edited by her friend Sidney Teller. It was a perceptive and moving description of the plight of older women immigrants to the United States. She surely was writing of her mother.

The Old Woman and the New World

> Every ship that brings to our shores the much-spoken of young immigrant, who comes here to breathe the free air of political and religious freedom, who finds new educational opportunities and comfortable living conditions, whose life is still before him or her, and who leaves behind only memories of oppression and hatred, brings also the old woman whose life is left behind, and whose memories are of places that have become dear to her through association. The memory of sacred places, where love was revealed to her in all its wonderful, unselfish splendor, where hand in hand she roamed with him who became part of her being, where she felt the first exalting thrill of motherhood, and where perhaps a child may lie buried under a lowly mound of earth, comes with her, and very often makes her feel homeless, cheerless and alone. She does not come to find a new home; she tries to re-establish the old one. And right here the first bond of relationship between the old and the young is broken.
>
> The old woman enters the new world with a firm religious conviction. It is very often her only comfort, and she naturally wants to introduce it into her home. But she finds, before long,

that her children have formed their own religious opinions, and all her old cherished beliefs are cast to the winds. The religion of the young may be a more rational one, but the fact that the beliefs of the old have been bred in her for a lifetime is to be respected. So we have the desire to live the broadest life, on the part of the young, and the memory of an ancient religion, which the old wish to preserve. In short, the building of an old house, in a new country, is a sad event.

The difference of opinion in the religion very often causes the first estrangement between mother and children; it is not hard to understand that it leads to other disagreements.

The old woman seldom acquires the use of our language. This is looked upon by the young as ignorance. If the mother does learn to speak, she does not speak as clearly as her children, and that is faulty. It may be that the boy reads a story in English, and the mother may be reading Schiller, Voltaire or Tolstoi in her native tongue; still, the fact remains that the boy is reading English, and the mother cannot do it.

This idea, that the mother knows less than the child, very soon destroys respect. And before long the old woman is not only old and sad, but a lonely old woman as well. Yes, she is a childless mother with living children. . . .

Let us encourage the old woman to meet her neighbors, to create a social life which will not leave her lonely. And let us impress it upon the minds of the young that this social life is to be respected. The new world never really becomes the old woman's home, but let us help it to become a pleasant visit during the time she must stay.

Hilda Satt

6. None of the local histories of Salem, Illinois, nor biographies of William Jennings Bryan mention Mrs. Torrance, but there is no reason to doubt she was his aunt. However, her announcement of her nephew's presidential race was probably not made after his nomination in July 1896 during the school's summer vacation. Since the annual report for 1896–97 did not list Mrs. Torrance as a teacher, she probably told her class about her nephew before his nomination. Although she is listed in the city directories for 1895 and 1896, she is not listed in 1897 and may have left the city. Hilda may have included this episode to introduce the struggle for woman suffrage.

7. The reference to the Spanish-American War could not have taken place as it is described because Hilda was no longer in school in 1898 when she would have been fifteen or sixteen. If, however, she had been seven in 1892, as she wrote, she would have been thirteen in 1898. As noted above, Mrs. Torrance left the Jewish Training School in the spring of 1896. Either the episode took place somewhere else or it was a fictional detail in keeping with her lifelong opposition to war.

8. This story is out of place chronologically; it could not have happened before 1906, as the first nickelodeon was developed in Pittsburgh in November 1905. Joseph H. North, *The Early Development of the Motion Picture (1887–1909)* (New York: Arno Press, 1973), 238–39; Lewis Jacobs, *The Rise of the American Film: A Critical History* (New York: Teachers' College Press, 1967), 55.

CHAPTER 7

1. Neither the *Hull-House Bulletin* nor *Twenty Years at Hull-House* mention when the first Christmas party was held, making it difficult to date the particular party Hilda attended. For reasons to be given later, it seems most likely that this party took place in 1895.

2. "The second time that I was doing something without telling mother" apparently refers to Hilda's attending the nickelodeon described in the previous chapter.

3. A description of the continuing tradition very similar to the one Hilda described appeared in an article by Amalie Hannig, the woman who taught Hilda to cross-stitch: "An eminent author who has made a study of immigrants, especially of the Jews, said after he had listened to one of these concerts [of Christmas carols]: 'It is wonderful to see people, who in Russia would have died rather than to speak the name of Christ, here singing these songs, and their families in the audience enjoying this music.'" Hannig, "Christmas at Hull-House," reprinted in Davis and McCree, *Eighty Years at Hull-House,* 91–93.

CHAPTER 8

1. Hilda's description of the "sweating system" and of workers bringing garments home to be finished by their families is corroborated by many reports on the garment industry, 1890–1910. Florence Kelley, "The Sweating System," in *Hull-House Maps and Papers,* 27–45.

2. "I remember a little girl of four who pulled out basting threads hour after hour. . . ." Jane Addams, *Twenty Years at Hull-House* (New York: Macmillan Co., 1910, 1938), 199.

3. Elizabeth Ewen, *Immigrant Women in the Land of Dollars: Life and Culture on the Lower East Side, 1890–1925* (New York: Monthly Review Press, 1985), 123.

4. This is an accurate transcription of stanzas 2–3 of "The Flower Factory," Florence Wilkinson Evans, *The Ride Home: Poems* (Boston: Houghton Mifflin Co., 1913), 47–48, part of a group of poems titled "The City."

5. The most likely scenario is that Hilda did not return to Hull-House after the Christmas party in December 1895, and later in the winter of 1896 she decided to leave school. At that time she would have been thirteen, making it necessary to lie about her age to secure working papers. The section of the Illinois law regulating the employment of children was published in *Hull-House Maps and Papers,* 52–53. In an interview published in 1913 but given in 1912, Hilda was quoted as saying: "I went to work in a factory when I was thirteen years old, and I have been self-supporting ever since. . . . When I was about sixteen I first came to Hull-House." Elsie F. Weil, "The Hull-House Players,"

Theatre Magazine, September 1913, xix-xxii, reprinted in Davis and McCree, *Eighty Years at Hull-House,* 91.

CHAPTER 9

1. For reasons already given, it seems more likely that she had finished fourth grade and was thirteen.

2. The only knitting factory at Twelfth and State streets listed in the 1897 city directory (under "Knit Goods" in the classified section) is "Friedlander, Brady & Co., 1245 State, Gloves, mittens, etc." In the alphabetical listing the address is given as "1241 to 1249 State," which would have made it a large factory indeed.

3. Hilda's description of working conditions are corroborated by Agnes Nestor: "All the work in the sewing department is piece work, so the wages depend upon the speed of the operator. . . . At noon we have only one half hour, which means that the girls have to bring a cold lunch. . . . The girls all eat at their places. . . ." Nestor, "A Day's Work Making Gloves," *Life and Labor* 2 (May 1912): 139.

4. Agnes Nestor told of starting work at the Eisendrath Glove Factory in 1897 at the age of fourteen: "We were charged fifty cents a week for the power furnished our machines. . . . We were obliged, besides, to buy our own needles. If you broke one, you were charged for a new one to replace it. We had, also, to buy our own machine oil." Nestor, *Woman's Labor Leader: An Autobiography* (Rockford, Ill.: Bellevue Books, 1954), 29. Also: "From the wages the company deducted the cost of needles, machine parts, repairs, oil, and the power to run their machines. . . . In 1898, the stitchers and finishers began to protest the production charges and demanded that the glove manufacturers stop the deductions from their pay." Sandra Conn, "Three Talents: Robins, Nestor and Anderson of the Chicago Women's Trade Union League," *Chicago History* 9 (Winter 1980–81): 242. The happy results of union organization were reported in *Life and Labor* in 1913: "The greatest thing the union has done to increase the wages of the girls is that it has abolished paying for power. Of yore, fifty cents a week was deducted for 'power' or machine rent. . . . Then there used to be paying for oil and needles. . . ." Stella Miles Franklin, "Agnes Nestor of the Glove Workers: A Leader in the Women's Movement," *Life and Labor* 3 (December 1913): 371.

5. This was probably the Glove Workers Union, chartered by the American Federation of Labor as an international union in 1902, although seventeen locals, some of them in the Midwest, had been chartered earlier. Gary M. Fink, ed., *Labor Unions* (Westport, Conn.: Greenwood Press, 1977), 130. There is no mention of an organizing drive at Friedlander, Brady & Co. in Agnes Nestor, *Brief History of the International Glove Workers Union of America* ([Chicago: Research Department of the International Glove Workers Union of America], 1942), and there is no verification of Hilda's account of the organizing meeting, along with her dramatic speech. Her report of working conditions, however, is fully supported.

6. It may seem incredible that in four years Hilda had never seen any

part of State Street except the immediate vicinity of the factory where she had worked. One must remember, however, the strict observance of the Sabbath which her mother respected. At that time the department stores were not open on Sunday, and Hilda may have been considered too young to venture downtown by herself.

7. The waiting room was eventually replaced after Hilda's death, first by an ice-cream parlor and later by a restaurant.

CHAPTER 10

1. The newspaper may have been the *Chicago Record-Herald,* which at the time featured classified advertisements, particularly "Help Wanted." The issue for 1 November 1904, for example, offered 130 listings.

2. With no hint of its location, it was impossible to identify Hilda's new employer among the fifty-odd shirt manufacturers listed in the classified section of the 1900 city directory. Her experience in a shirtwaist factory was typical for an immigrant Jewish girl. "Among immigrant Jews in New York, Philadelphia, Boston and other large cities only the exceptional unmarried woman did not operate a sewing machine in a garment factory for part of her young adult life. . . . In America they were expected to work, for the family counted on their contributions." Alice Kessler-Harris, "Organizing the Unorganizable: Three Jewish Women and Their Union," *Labor History* 17 (Winter 1976): 6.

3. Clay was an "English author of a flood of romantic novels." William Rose Benet, ed., *The Reader's Encyclopedia* (New York: Thomas Y. Crowell Co., 1955), 218.

4. The address was 181 De Koven Street.

5. "The museum was open every Saturday evening beginning in November, 1900. . . ." Hull-House, *First Report of the Labor Museum at Hull-House* (Chicago: 1901–2), 3.

6. Mary Dayton Hill married Gerard Swope, another Hull-House resident and later president of the General Electric Company (1922–39), in August 1901. Jane Addams card file, Special Collections, University of Illinois at Chicago Library. There is no evidence that Hilda was Hill's first student.

7. "The textile shop . . . employs the entire time of Mrs. Brosnahan. . . ." *Hull-House Year Book* (May 1, 1900): 11. She may have been the "Irish woman spinning" pictured in Hull-House, *First Report of the Labor Museum,* 10.

8. Mrs. Molinari may have been the "Italian woman spinning." Hull-House, *First Report of the Labor Museum,* 4. Hilda's description of the Labor Museum is quite consistent both with that report and the descriptions written by others, for example, Marion Foster Washburne, "A Labor Museum," *Craftsman* (September 1904): 570–79, reprinted in Davis and McCree, *Eighty Years at Hull-House,* 77–82.

9. "A small blast furnace and forge and a potter's wheel. . . ." Hull-House, *First Report of the Labor Museum,* 15.

10. Amalie Hannig, Hull-House resident and sometime director of the

Music School, wrote "Christmas at Hull-House," reprinted in Davis and McCree, *Eighty Years at Hull-House,* 91–93.

11. Addams, *Twenty Years at Hull-House,* 235–46.

12. Clara Landsberg was "in charge of adult education at Hull-House. . . ." Davis and McCree, *Eighty Years at Hull-House,* 72. Among Hull-House classes (secondary) was listed "Monday, 7:30 p.m., Reading Club, Miss Landsberg." *Hull-House Bulletin* 4 (January-May 1901): 3.

13. "The essential fact of Hull-House, the dominant fact, was the presence of Miss Addams. . . . Hull-House . . . was not an institution over which Miss Addams presided, it was Miss Addams, around whom an institution insisted on clustering." Francis Hackett, "Hull-House—A Souvenir," *Survey* (1 June 1925): 275–79, reprinted in Davis and McCree, *Eighty Years at Hull-House,* 74.

CHAPTER 11

1. Hilda elided some of the places where the Satt family lived. They moved to Bunker Street after the death of Louis Satt in 1894. In 1900 they were living in the alley at the rear of 181 De Koven Street, one block north of Bunker. The family was listed at this address from 1900 until 1903; in 1904 the listing was 225 De Koven Street, as it was in 1905. Her complaints about the rooms being filled with drying laundry probably applied equally well to all the locations where they lived.

2. *Hull-House Bulletin* 6 (Midwinter 1903–4): 18.

3. His address in the 1902 Chicago city directory is "h. 456 S. Desplaines." The Langdon Apartment Building was on the corner of Desplaines and Bunker streets.

4. Kropotkin stayed at Hull-House during his lecture tour in April 1901. "It was the last trip he could make to the United States, for in 1901, not long after his departure, Czolgosz assassinated . . . President McKinley. . . . Chicago papers went so far as to suggest that the shooting of the President had been plotted at Hull-House between Kropotkin, Emma Goldman and Czolgosz. There was no truth in the story, but Kropotkin was very distressed, more for the trouble it caused his Chicago friends than for the unjust reflections upon himself. . . ." George Woodcock and Ivan Avakumovic, *The Anarchist Prince: A Biographical Study of Peter Kropotkin* (London: T. V. Boardman & Co., 1950), 287. "Prince Kropotkin had addressed the Chicago Arts and Crafts Society at Hull-House, giving a digest of his remarkable book on 'Fields, Factories and Workshops.'" Addams, *Twenty Years at Hull-House,* 403.

5. Katarina Breshkovsky came to Chicago in January 1905. Catherine Breshkovsky, *The Little Grandmother of the Russian Revolution: Reminiscences and Letters of Catherine Breshkovsky,* ed. Alice Stone Blackwell (Boston: Little, Brown and Co., 1918), 120, 123. Her visit was listed in the *Hull-House Bulletin* 7, no. 1 (1905–6): 23: "Informal Lectures and Receptions . . . Mme. Katherine [*sic*] Breshkovsky [no date]."

6. In 1905 "a small group of actors from a St. Petersburg stock company, directed by Paul Orlenev, visited New York. One member, Alla Nazimova,

[was] formerly a bit player at the Moscow Art Theater. . . ." Paul Gray, "From Russia to America: A Critical Chronology," reprinted in Erika Munk, ed., *Stanislavski and America: An Anthology from the Tulane Drama Review* (New York: Hill and Wang, 1966), 140.

7. *Tsar Feodor* is a play by Aleksei Tolstoi, Leo Tolstoy's cousin. The list of plays to be performed by "Paul Orleneff's [*sic*] Russian players" was given in the *Chicago Sunday Tribune,* 4 February 1906. The sponsorship was "Auspices Musical & Dramatic [word illegible]."

8. "Students of Contemporary Russia . . . attended a . . . reception given at Hull-House February 11th to Mr. Paul Orleneff [*sic*] and Mme. Alla Nazimoff [*sic*]." *Hull-House Bulletin* 7, no. 1 (1905–6): 22. Undoubtedly, Hilda was unaware that Emma Goldman, using the name E. G. Smith, was acting as the business manager of the company, none of whom could speak English nor understand American business practices. Alice Wexler, *Emma Goldman, an Intimate Life* (New York: Pantheon Books, 1984), 115, 120.

9. Hilda's confusion about the date of Kropotkin's visit derived probably from Jane Addams's account in *Twenty Years at Hull-House:* "Prince Kropotkin . . . was a guest of Hull-House during his stay in Chicago . . . but two years later, when the assassination of President McKinley occurred . . . this kindly scholar . . . was made the basis of an attack upon Hull-House by a daily newspaper . . ." (pp. 402–3). The assassination took place 6 September 1901, five months after Kropotkin's visit.

10. "The only cure for the acts of anarchy was free speech and an open discussion. . . ." Ibid., 178.

11. "Many younger children . . . are constantly arrested for petty thieving because they are too eager to take home food or fuel which will relieve the distress and need they so constantly heard discussed." Ibid., 251.

12. The importance Jane Addams attached to garbage collection and her career as a garbage inspector was demonstrated by the prominence she gave it in *Twenty Years at Hull-House,* beginning chapter 13, "Public Activities and Investigations," with an extended discussion of garbage and its collection: "One of the striking features of our neighborhood twenty years ago . . . was the presence of huge wooden garbage boxes fastened to the street pavement in which the undisturbed refuse accumulated day by day. . . . In sheer desperation, the following spring when the city contracts were awarded for the removal of garbage, with the backing of two well-known business men, I put in a bid for the garbage removal of the nineteenth ward. My paper was thrown out on a technicality but the incident induced the mayor to appoint me the garbage inspector of the ward" (pp. 281, 285).

13. "West of the river the great majority of the dwellings are wooden structures . . . with neither foundations nor plumbing. . . . Rear tenements and alleys form the core of the district. . . . Little idea can be given of the filthy and rotten tenements, the dingy courts and tumble-down sheds, the foul stables and dilapidated outhouses, the broken sewer-pipes, the piles of garbage fairly alive with diseased odors, and of the numbers of children. . . . In one block the writer numbered over seventy-five children in the open street."

Agnes Sinclair Holbrook, "Map Notes and Comments," in *Hull-House Maps and Papers,* 5, 12.

14. "Hull-House was the center of the typhoid fever epidemic of the past summer [1902]. . . . a careful investigation of the drainage and sewage disposal was made by Miss Howe and Miss [Maud] Gernon, who found that the number of typhoid cases was largest in those streets in which was the smallest amount of modern plumbing." *Hull-House Bulletin* 5, no. 2 (1902): 14. See also Alice Hamilton, *Exploring the Dangerous Trades: An Autobiography* (Boston: Little, Brown and Co., 1943), 99–100.

15. Dr. Hamilton does not mention her study of tuberculosis in *Exploring the Dangerous Trades,* but it was consistent with her interests.

16. See "Hull-House: A Social Settlement," appendix to *Hull-House Maps and Papers,* 219: "Originally issued as a pamphlet, Feb. 1, 1893. It is here revised to Jan. 1, 1895."

17. Addams, *Twenty Years at Hull-House,* 313–14.

18. The sum was actually $12,000. "Hull-House: A Social Settlement," 219.

19. "The Settlement, then, is an experimental effort to aid in the solution of the social and industrial problems which are engendered by the modern conditions of life in a great city." Addams, *Twenty Years at Hull-House,* 125. A letter written to Hilda described a lecture Miss Addams gave on suffrage in Milwaukee, in January 1912: "We heard Jane Addams tonight. . . . To my mind, she gave a convincing & interesting talk . . . of the many good things started by Chicago women. When these movements, such as Juvenile protection & the like, had grown so that the State took over the work, the administration of the work was considered political & these same women perforce were barred." WP to HS, 26 January 1912.

20. "Since the summer of 1893, Mr. William Kent has very generously donated to Hull-House to be administered as a public play ground the use of a piece of land on Polk Street, 312 by 110 feet, in addition to a smaller lot facing Mather street. The ground has been used in winter as well as summer, having been flooded for a number of years to form an excellent skating pond." *Hull-House Bulletin* 6 (Midwinter 1904–5): 19.

21. The theater was first listed in the *Chicago Blue Book* for 1899 at 169 S. Halsted.

22. "The English-speaking theaters had delightful old-fashioned melodrama, *Way Down East, No Child to Call Her Mother, East Lynn* [*sic*], *Uncle Tom's Cabin,* all acted just as they should be, with hero and villain, heroine and villainess, recognizable from the moment they stepped before the footlights." There was also "a Yiddish theater not far from us [at Hull-House] where we saw excellent plays, acted so well that we needed little help from interpreters in the audience to follow them." Hamilton, *Exploring the Dangerous Trades,* 79. Hilda did not mention going to Yiddish theater.

23. From Act 3 of *The White Slave,* by Bartley Campbell, in *The White Slave & Other Plays,* ed. Napier Wilt (Princeton: Princeton University Press, 1941), 227.

24. The theater was listed in the *Chicago Blue Book* as early as 1897.

25. Mrs. Campbell herself identified the play as *Expiation*, renamed for American audiences as *A Russian Tragedy:* "In 1910 I went to America again. I rang up Mr. Albee [of the Vaudeville circuit] . . . and told him that I had an effective play . . . that I would play twice a day. . . . Oh, those two performances of *Expiation!* I had to kill a man twice a day and shriek. . . ." Campbell, *My Life and Some Letters* (London: Hutchinson & Co., n.d.), 240–41. See also Margot Peters, *Mrs. Pat: The Life of Mrs. Patrick Campbell* (New York: Alfred A. Knopf, 1984), 292–96.

26. "Classes (Advanced) . . . English Poetry—Miss Monroe: (Secondary) . . . Shakespeare—Miss Landsberg." *Hull-House Bulletin* 5, no. 2 (1902): 3. "Hull-House Shakespeare Club . . . Mondays, 8 p.m. . . . under the leadership of Mr. Patterson of the University of Chicago. In December the club enjoyed two lectures . . . [including] a talk on rhythm by Miss Harriet Monroe." Ibid., 7–8. The lecture on rhythm may have been what Hilda remembered. Mr. Patterson cannot be identified further in the University of Chicago catalogs for 1902.

27. Ibid. 4 (January 1–May 1, 1901): 3–4.

28. Ibid.

29. This class must have been offered in the fall or winter of 1903–4, for Hilda's matriculation at the University of Chicago, which followed, is dated 1 April 1904. "Matric. No. 19069," University of Chicago Archives. The class, however, was not listed until the fall of 1904, when "advanced classes" included "Rhetoric . . . Mr. Chandler." *Hull-House Bulletin* 6 (Autumn 1904): 2.

30. Chandler came to the University of Chicago to teach English in the fall of 1901 and soon offered his services as a volunteer to Jane Addams. Besides his class in English composition (the course that was so important to Hilda), his prime activity was as leader of the Shakespeare Club, which he continued until 1910. He began to study law in 1903 and in 1904 gave up teaching at the university to become secretary to its president, William Rainey Harper, continuing in this position until he graduated from law school in June 1906. An incomplete manuscript entitled *Henry P. Chandler, 1880–1975: His Ancestry, Life and Work, and His Descendants* (compiled in 1977–78 by Olive Hull Chandler and Margaret C. Gibbons, with a foreword dated March 1979) was begun by Chandler and continued by his widow and daughter. As chapters were completed they were deposited in the Special Collections Department of the University of Illinois at Chicago Library. Chapters 1, 5, 7, 11, and 13 have been deposited so far but not the chapter discussing Hull-House, and attempts to obtain it have been unsuccessful.

31. "The Ghetto Market," the paper written for Mr. Chandler, was found among Hilda's papers after her death.

CHAPTER 12

1. Memorial meetings for the Haymarket martyrs were held annually, sometimes separate commemorations in English and German. See, for example, the "Memorial Address at a Meeting to Commemorate the Chicago Mar-

tyrs, Held at Liberty Hall, Nov. 12th, 1905," *The Liberator* [Lucy Parsons's publication], no. 14 (3 December 1905). As late as 1927 the Pioneer Aid and Support Association, "founded to support the wives and children who were left behind," still held "annual rites for our dead friends." [Otto Herrman], *Remember the Eleventh of November: To the Memory of Our Friends Who Were Judicially Murdered November 11, 1887* (Chicago: Pioneer Aid and Support Assn., 1927), 29; copy in the Chicago Historical Society. These facts support Hilda's report of a memorial meeting in 1903, although no documentation of the meeting has been found.

2. What Hilda called the West Side Turner Hall was probably the West Twelfth Street Turner Hall. Under "Public Halls, Blocks and Buildings" were listed two halls with similar names, the West Side Turner Hall, 770-776 W. Chicago Avenue and the West Twelfth Street Turner Hall, 253 W. Twelfth Street. *Chicago Blue Book . . . for . . . 1904,* 97, 104. The Chicago Avenue address would have been too far for the Satt sisters to walk.

3. The memorial hymn recalled by Hilda was sung to her children many times, but no one else seems to know it. It was not included in any available collection of labor or anarchist songs, and there is no trace of it in the Labadie Collection at the University of Michigan, purportedly the country's largest collection of anarchist materials. None of the people working on the commemoration of the Haymarket centennial could identify it, and even Pete Seeger had never heard of it. But there is a reference to a memorial meeting on 11 November 1897 at which was sung " 'Our Martyrs' Hymn' to the air of 'Annie Laurie', written especially for the occasion by Mrs. Shirlie Woodman . . . sung with much effect by Mrs. V. Kinsella, the audience, which had been supplied with printed copies, joining." Jay Fox, "Martyr's Day in Chicago," *Free Society,* 5 December 1897, reprinted in Dave Roediger and Franklin Rosemont, eds., *Haymarket Scrapbook* (Chicago: C. H. Kerr, 1986), 187.

4. In 1903 it would have been sixteen years since the Haymarket riot. Many people still alive had lived through the tragedy.

5. None of the many books by or about Emma Goldman mention her presence in Chicago in November 1903, but all are in agreement that she had resumed political work and public appearances by the end of 1903. Her lifelong devotion to the cause of the Haymarket martyrs was exemplified in many articles and speeches, most of all in her request that she be buried near the martyrs. There is no reason to doubt that she spoke at a memorial meeting in Chicago, as she was to do many times in her life. For example, in November 1911 she published in her journal, *Mother Earth,* an article titled "The Crime of November Eleventh": "The memory of the heroic death of Parsons, Spies, Lingg, Engel and Fischer stirs anew our admiration and love for them, filling us with a yearning for a fate equally sublime. . . ." Reprinted in Roediger and Rosemont, *Haymarket Scrapbook,* 180.

6. The best recent account is Paul Avrich, *The Haymarket Tragedy* (Princeton: Princeton University Press, 1984).

7. Caro Lloyd, *Henry Demarest Lloyd, 1847–1903: A Biography* (New York: G. P. Putnam's Sons, 1912), 1: 97–98.

CHAPTER 13

1. Miss Addams's office ". . . was an octagonal office in a one-story wing to the south. . . ." Commission on Chicago Historical and Architectural Landmarks, *Jane Addams's Hull-House and Dining Hall* (n.d.), 5.

2. "Persons who have not had the requisite amount of preparatory training, but who are twenty-one years of age, and are not seeking degrees . . . [can be] admitted . . . to courses for which, in the judgement of the Dean and instructors, they are prepared. . . . They must also submit to whatever examinations or tests particular departments or instructors attach to their courses." University of Chicago, *Circular of Information, with Courses of Instruction, 1900–1901,* 6, University of Chicago Archives.

3. Hilda's transcript in the University of Chicago Archives is dated 1 April 1904.

4. Hilda was not assigned to the introductory college course on rhetoric and English composition but to "English Composition. Required of all candidates for degrees who have completed nine Majors in the Junior Colleges, including English 1." University of Chicago, "The Colleges . . . Summer Quarter, 1903–Spring Quarter, 1904," *Circular of Information,* 3 May 1903, 62, 64–65. The classes at Hull-House must have been very substantial. The "Instructors' Reports of Courses Given during the Spring Quarter, 1904" in the University Archives lists the following courses and their grades: Elementary German, 1^b, 5 hours a week, Classroom work B, Exam grade B; English Composition $3A^b$, 5 hours a week, Classroom work C, Exam grade C; English literature, 5 hours a week, Classroom work E, Exam grade E. The "b" in class titles designated a section for women. A memo from Dan Meyer, University Archivist, states "E . . . signified 'not passed.' (The University did not have the grade of F)." Personal communication, 29 May 1985. Hilda's transcript shows no credit for the course in English literature.

5. The segregation of women into separate classes forms a little-known chapter in the history of the University of Chicago. "When the school opened in 1892, women made up 24 percent of the entering class. This figure climbed steadily until, by the end of the first decade, the freshman class was 52 percent female. 'Effeminization' of the institution was feared and forecast. . . . [After much controversy] Lexington Hall, 'the hen coop' was built on $50,000 of Mr. Rockefeller's money and opened in the spring of '03. . . . 43 percent of the men and 25 percent of the women had no separated courses while only two percent of the men and 3.5 percent of the women were segregated in all their work. . . . By 1908 the subject had been tactfully buried." Ellen Clements, "The University's First and Only Civil War," *Chicago Maroon* [student newspaper], 11 January 1977. See also Lynn D. Gordon, "Coeducation on Two Campuses: Berkeley and Chicago, 1890–1912," in *Woman's Being, Woman's Place: Female Identity and Vocation in American History,* ed. Mary Kelley (Boston: G. K. Hall, 1979), 180–88.

6. Alice Hamilton also described toting: "In Hull-House that [tote] is the convenient term for showing people over the House, and we speak of 'toters' and 'totees.'" Hamilton, *Exploring the Dangerous Trades,* 73.

7. The *Hull-House Bulletin* was not published during the summer, so no record of Hilda's first teaching assignment exists. She was not listed until the fall of 1906: "Secondary Classes: Beginner's English—Monday, 7:30 p.m. Miss Hilda Satt." *Hull-House Year Book, Sept. 1, 1906–Sept. 1, 1907,* 8.

CHAPTER 14

1. Lewis Linn McArthur was attending surgeon since 1886 at St. Luke's and Michael Reese hospitals. *The Book of Chicagoans,* ed. John W. Leonard (Chicago: A. N. Marquis & Co., 1905), s.v. "McArthur." Curiously, Jane Addams was not included.

2. "Most of us were working people who were away all day and could give only evenings to the work of the House. . . ." Hamilton, *Exploring the Dangerous Trades,* 79. "All, or nearly all of the residents were employed outside the Settlement during the day. . . . But, of course, I had duties at Hull-House when I came back. . . ." Hackett, "Hull-House—A Souvenir," 71–72.

3. The only clue to the identity of this employer was a listing in the 1905 city directory: "Satt, Hilda R bkpr, 888 Milwaukee." No known mail-order house did business at that address, and this may represent another position that Hilda chose not to mention.

4. McClurg's must indeed have been an impressive store. Its catalog listed "First floor, Art, Music, Bibles and Prayer Books, Political Economy, Rare and Out-of-Print Books, Fine Bindings, Library Department, Periodicals, Bohn's Library (complete), Agriculture, Games, Athletics, and Sports, Stationery, Playing cards, Whist sets, etc., Leather Goods . . . Bronze, Copper and Brass Articles from Foreign Markets. Second Floor, Theology, Technical Books, including Scientific and Medical, Children's and Young People's Books, School Text-Books, Pedagogical Works, Kindergarten Materials, Office Stationery, Children's Games, Low-Priced Books." A. C. McClurg & Co., *Illustrated Catalogue of Books, Standard & Holiday, 1904–1905* . . . (Chicago: A. C. McClurg & Co., 1904), 696, 180 pp., copy in Chicago Historical Society Library.

5. It is curious that Hilda claimed she first heard of Du Bois when *The Quest of the Silver Fleece* was published in 1911, for he gave an address on Lincoln's Birthday at Hull-House in 1907. *Hull-House Year Book, Sept. 1, 1906–Sept. 1, 1907,* 48. On 29 October 1911 Hilda wrote to her fiancé: "I may quarrel with my dear Mr. MacCorquodale, and be left without bread and butter. This is the story. McClurg & Co. published a new book by Du Bois, the author of *The Souls of Black Folk.* Do you know him? It is the only good piece of fiction that has been issued by our worthy press. The book called *The Quest of the Silver Fleece* is a gem, but our boys [salesmen] refuse to sell it, because it is written by a 'nigger', about 'niggers.' What I mean by refusing to sell it, is they do not recommend it. The only copies sold are those called for by customers. I told my boss that I considered this very unjust, and I am very angry about it. In the first place, it isn't business. The department is there to sell McClurg books, whether written by a nigger or a Turk. I really mean to write to McClurg if the boys continue slighting the Du Bois book. Then I must quit, for I will not work for MacCorquodale, after criticizing his methods of doing business." Happily, the

matter was resolved amicably. She wrote later: "Had a long confidential talk with Mr. MacC., and I convinced him that he was unjust to Mr. Du Bois and his book. He finished off by giving me a copy. . . ." HS to WP, 29 October and 1 November 1911.

6. The club was first mentioned in the *Hull-House Bulletin* 5, no. 1 (1902): 10: "Every Tuesday at 8 o'clock. Director, Miss [Maud] Gernon; president, Mr. J. A. Britton [both residents]; vice-president, Miss Hilda Satt; . . . editor of Club Chronicle, Mr. Louis Alter [later a featured member of the Hull-House Players]." Perhaps she was indeed asked to help organize the group. Activities of the club were described: ". . . many pleasant social events . . . a theatre party . . . informal socials . . . some very good literary programs. A three-act farce, 'The Dumb Belle,' was given on January 25th [1902] in the Hull-House Auditorium by the following cast: . . . Mr. Louis Alter, Mr. James Britton . . . and Miss Hilda Satt. The actors had been coached by Mr. James Dwyer of the Hull-House Dramatic Association . . . audience . . . large . . . seemed to enjoy both the play and the dance that followed." In the next issue of the *Bulletin,* Hilda was no longer listed as an officer. Ibid. 5, no. 2 (1902): 9. Nor was she mentioned in reports of the club's activities for 1903–5. Ibid. 6 (Midwinter 1903–4): 2, 10. In 1906, however, a benefit entertainment in the theater on 17 February was "under direction of Miss Satt." Ibid. 7 (1905–6): 4. The name of the club was not mentioned, and it is not clear whether the Ariadne Club was the sponsor. Unfortunately, no records of the club have survived, and the date of its end is not known.

7. Britton was "a Chicago physician who lived with his wife at Hull-House and worked especially with those neighborhood people who suffered from tuberculosis." Davis and McCree, *Eighty Years at Hull-House,* 72.

8. The Music School "opened in 1893. . . . Some of the pupils . . . have developed during the years into trained musicians and are supporting themselves in their chosen profession." Addams, *Twenty Years at Hull-House,* 378–80.

9. "The dramatic arts have gradually been developed at Hull-House through amateur companies. [The plays of] Shaw, Ibsen, and Galsworthy . . . are surprisingly popular, perhaps because of their sincere attempt to expose the shams and pretenses of contemporary life and to penetrate some of its perplexing social and domestic situations. Through such plays the stage may become a pioneer teacher of social righteousness." Ibid., 390–91.

CHAPTER 15

1. Addams, *Twenty Years at Hull-House,* 16–17.

2. Haldeman-Julius, *Jane Addams as I Knew Her,* 4–5.

3. Ibid., 5.

4. Ibid.

5. Lloyd Lewis, "The House that Jane Addams Built," *New York Times Magazine,* 19 May 1940, reprinted in Davis and McCree, *Eighty Years at Hull-House,* 206. See also Linn, *Jane Addams,* 158.

6. Jane Addams, *The Excellent Becomes the Permanent* (New York: Macmillan Co., 1932).

7. No documentation for this story has been found.

8. Ibid., 9. Mary Rozet Smith was "long a close friend of Jane Addams. She and her family were major financial supporters of the settlement from before 1895. . . ." Davis and McCree, *Eighty Years at Hull-House,* 72.

9. *Hull-House Bulletin* 6, no. 1 (1903–4): 20; Addams, *The Excellent Becomes the Permanent,* 29–36.

10. Louise de Koven Bowen, *Growing with a City* (New York: Macmillan, 1927), 82 et seq.

11. Ibid., 84.

12. The murals were planned by John Duncan. *Hull-House Bulletin* 6, no. 1 (1903–4): 19–20; Addams, *Twenty Years at Hull-House,* 397–99.

13. Alexander Pope, "Essay on Man," Epistle 4, l.194, in *Collected Poems,* ed. Bonamy Dobree, rev. ed. (London: J. M. Dent & Sons, [1924, 1956]), 210.

14. It would have been in keeping with Jane Addams's philosophy to permit Emma Goldman to speak, but the event has not been documented.

15. The source of this quotation has not been identified.

CHAPTER 16

1. The play was performed on 7–12 December 1903. Napier Wilt files, Special Collections, Joseph Regenstein Library, University of Chicago. It was advertised in the *Chicago Daily Tribune,* 1 December 1903.

2. "Zero Weather after Blizzard / Traffic Tied Up . . . Heavy snowfall in Chicago—record for a decade . . . hundreds of theatre patrons had to stay in downtown hotels, and some without funds remained in the Van Buren Street station [of the Illinois Central Railroad] all night." *Chicago Sunday Tribune,* 12 December 1903.

3. Chicago performances took place on 23 September–9 November 1912. Napier Wilt files. This would have been after Hilda's marriage and her move to Milwaukee. There could not have been an earlier performance, for the play was first produced in London on 19 April 1911 and in New York on 25 December 1911. Otis Skinner, *Footlights and Spotlights: Recollections of My Life on the Stage* (Indianapolis: Bobbs-Merrill Co., 1924), 19–20. On the performance in Milwaukee, see the *Milwaukee Leader,* 11 November 1912.

4. This is a misquotation of "To the Caliph I may be dirt; but to dirt I am the Caliph!" Edward Knoblock, *Kismet, and Other Plays* (London: Chapman & Hall, 1957), 109.

5. The performance of *Ghosts* was by "Visiting Players . . . Miss Mary Shaw and her company." *Hull-House Bulletin* 6, no. 2 (Autumn 1904): 22. No record has been found of a performance of *Mrs. Warren's Profession* at Hull-House, nor did Miss Shaw mention one in her article "My 'Immoral' Play: The Story of the First American Production of 'Mrs. Warren's Profession,'" *McClure's Magazine* 33 (April 1912): 684–94.

6. *Hull-House Bulletin* 6, no. 2 (Autumn 1904): 22; Joseph Home, *W. B. Yeats, 1865–1939* (New York: St. Martin's Press, 1962), 197.

7. *Hull-House Bulletin* 4 (1 January–1 May 1901): 4.

8. Addams, *Twenty Years at Hull-House,* 377–78; published in Eleanor Smith, *Hull-House Songs* (Chicago: Clayton F. Summy Co., 1914), 3–7.

9. Weil, "The Hull-House Players," xix-xxii; Laura Dainty Pelham, "The Story of the Hull-House Players," *Theatre Magazine,* September 1913, 244–62; Stuart Joel Hecht, *The Hull-House Theatre: An Analytical and Evaluative History* (Ann Arbor: University Microfilms International, 1984).

10. This was officially the Hull-House Junior Dramatic Association. Hecht, *The Hull-House Theatre,* 164 et seq.

11. The quotation is from Shakespeare's *Julius Caesar,* act 4, sc. 3: "There is my dagger, and here my naked breast. . . ." Hilda wrote to her fiancé on 3 February 1911: "The boys at H. H. gave very stirring presentations of 'Julius Caesar,' 'Wilhelm Tell,' 'The Foresters,' and even a 'Midsummer [*sic*] Night's Dream' with a boy as Titania. I wish I could take a group of boys and drill them through a play. Biblical stories, like 'Joseph and His Brethren' or 'Queen Esther,' are very good. But . . . I'd start with our friend Bill Shakespeare. It really is worth a farm . . . to have a ten year lad say: 'There is my dagger, and here my naked breast; within, a heart . . . Strike, as thou didst at Caesar.'" A later letter written to Hilda described a lecture Miss Addams gave in Milwaukee, in January 1912:

> She told one good story, which being dramatic, will interest you.
>
> Some Settlement boys wrote a patriotic play. The first act shows two Revolutionary officers in conversation. Says one: "Gee, aint it fierce that this here Revolution aint got a flag." Says the other, "Gee, it sure is fierce." Curtain.
>
> Act two shows Geo. Washington & one of the aforesaid officers. Geo. says: "Gee, aint it fierce that this here Revolution aint got a flag." The general replies: "Gee, it sure is fierce." Curtain.
>
> Act three shows Betsy Ross with a baby in her arms & Geo. Wash. He says: "Gee, aint it fierce that this here Revolution aint got a flag." She says: "It sure is, George, you hold the baby & I'll make you one."

HS to WP, 3 February 1911; WP to HS, January 1912.

12. The performance took place on 27 February 1900. Napier Wilt files. See also Catherine Sturtevant, "A Study of the Dramatic Productions of Two Decades in Chicago, 1847–1857 and 1897–1907" (Ph.D. diss., University of Chicago, 1931), 196–99.

13. Miss Bernhardt performed *L'Aiglon* in French on 21–26 January 1901 and again in October-November 1910. Napier Wilt files.

14. Miss Adams performed an English translation of *L'Aiglon* in February-March 1901. Ibid.

15. *Romeo and Juliet* was performed many times by this combination in 1904, 1906, and 1911. Ibid.

16. Mrs. Fiske performed *Becky Sharp* in February-March 1900 and October 1910. Ibid.

17. O'Neill was the most notorious of the perennial favorites on tour, performing *The Count of Monte Cristo* in Chicago in 1897, 1898, 1901, 1906, and 1908. Ibid.

18. "Between 1899 and 1908, that company presented eighty-eight different musical works at the Studebaker Theatre—twenty-eight grand operas, forty light operas, and twenty musical comedies . . . in English, at prices the average person could afford. . . ." Ronald L. Davis, *Opera in Chicago* (New York: Appleton-Century, 1966), 76–77. *Faust* was first performed by them on 3–8 April 1899 and repeated annually. Napier Wilt files. Frequent performances were also given of *Martha, The Bohemian Girl,* and *Carmen.* Ibid. All were performed so many times that listing their dates would be meaningless.

19. It is not clear when Hilda graduated to the Auditorium. Many of the singers she mentioned appeared as early as 1902: Sembrich, Gadski, Schumann-Heink, Jean de Reszke, Calvé, and Eames. Edward C. Moore, *Forty Years of Opera in Chicago* (New York: Horace Liveright, 1930), 38–39. Caruso made his debut in 1905, while Chaliapin did not appear until 1922. Ibid., 41, 259. Hilda may have come from Milwaukee to hear Chaliapin; she frequently traveled to see a performance.

20. The performances took place on 1 December 1907–May 1908. Napier Wilt files.

21. This was performed repeatedly from 1902 until 1907. Ibid.

22. This was performed intermittently in 1901, 1902, 1903, and 1909. Ibid.

23. The performances took place on 20 December 1906–10 March 1907. Ibid. See also Sturtevant, "A Study of the Dramatic Productions," 377.

24. Richard Carle, "A Lemon in the Garden of Love" [as sung in] *The Spring Chicken,* words by M. E. Rourke, music by Richard Carle (New York: M. Witmark & Sons, 1906). "Carle, Richard . . . (1871–1941) . . . high-voiced comedian. . . . He . . . starred . . . in his own adaptation of the London hit, *The Spring Chicken* (1906), stopping the show with 'A Lemon in the Garden of Love.'" Gerald Bordman, *The Oxford Companion to American Theatre* (New York: Oxford University Press, 1984), 125.

25. Lillian Russell joined Weber & Fields in 1899; the partnership ended in 1904. Felix Isman, *Weber and Fields: Their Tribulations, Triumphs, and Their Associates* (New York: Boni and Liveright, 1924), 257, 299. The backstage flood in Chicago was not mentioned either here or in biographies of Miss Russell.

26. Hilda's attitude toward clothes was expressed in a letter she wrote to Bill: "I once spoke before the Council of Jewish Women in a $3.98 dress, and had just enough in my pocket-book to keep me alive until the next payday. . . . This notion of keeping up with 'your set' is all bunk. Even shallow society women admire brains and originality. . . . The most expensive dress that I ever wore cost $18.00. And I have never been snubbed or neglected anywhere. . . . I can go to the 'sea-shore' in a $1.25 dress. . . ." HS to WP, 17 December 1911.

27. Since she did not mention an employer other than A. C. McClurg & Co., she may have left the bookstore and returned there after several years.

The chronology of her various jobs has been difficult to chart with no dates and no records on which to rely.

28. "May 13, 1906, . . . the Home threw open its doors to those who needed its loving protection and care." *History of the Marks Nathan Jewish Orphan Home, 1905–1920* (Chicago: Lawndale Press, 1920), 18. See also Meites, *History of the Jews of Chicago,* 617. It seems likely that Hilda went to work there in 1907 at the earliest.

29. By 1906 the *Hull-House Bulletin* had become the *Hull-House Year Book,* with an accompanying lack of specificity in detail of the programs offered. It is not known precisely when Hilda gave up teaching her English class, but by 1910 the class was taught by a Mr. Lucas. *Hull-House Year Book* (1910): 8.

30. "During 1906 . . . it [was] necessary for two and even three children to sleep in one bed." After many delays a new building was constructed and dedicated on 24 November 1912, after Hilda had married and moved to Milwaukee. *History of the Marks Nathan Jewish Orphan Home,* 21, 40. As late as 1910 the Home housed 162 children in only 84 beds. Ibid., 29.

31. Teller attended the Chicago School of Civics and Philanthropy in 1908–9, after he had worked at the Deborah Boys' Club, not before, as Hilda wrote. "Student Enrollment 1908-'09," *Chicago School of Civics and Philanthropy Bulletin* 1 (April 1910): 46. "Mr. Sidney Teller, of the class of 1909, who has been for the past year with the United Charities, has just been appointed Superintendent of West Park No. 2, Recreation Center." Ibid., 106. See also *Who's Who in World Jewry* (1972), s.v. "Teller, Sidney," where his work at the Boys' Club is dated 1907–8.

32. The club was "established by the Deborah Society in 1907." Meites, *History of the Jews in Chicago,* 209.

33. Miss Pines married Sidney Teller on 27 July 1916. See *Who's Who in World Jewry.*

34. A series of lectures was given annually by Jerome Raymond, of the University of Chicago Extension Division. It was given at Hull-House at least as early as 1902. "The following lectures, illustrated by stereopticon, will be given every Sunday evening at eight o'clock on 'European Capitals and their Social Significance' by Jerome H. Raymond, Ph. D., of the University Extension Department of the University of Chicago. Admission free." *Hull-House Bulletin* 5, no. 1 (1902): 1. See also Maureen Anne Fay, "Origins and Early Development of the University of Chicago Extension Division, 1892–1911." (Ph.D. diss., University of Chicago, 1976), 109–33. Hilda may have heard the lecture in 1907 or 1908.

35. In 1907 Sidney Teller began to issue a little magazine called *The Butterfly: A Little Messenger of Cooperation, Education and Inspiration.* The publisher was listed as Butterfly Association, but the extant issues give the impression of a very personal organ. (Teller's own copy of vol. 1 is in the Chicago Historical Society Library.) Publication continued through vol. 11 (January 1917), according to the *Union List of Serials.* How it was distributed is not known, but somehow it reached William Polacheck in Milwaukee, and he began to

correspond with its editor. Polacheck contributed brief essays to the magazine and became friends with Teller, whom he found more stimulating than many of his friends in Milwaukee. Since Milwaukee was only ninety miles from Chicago, visits were easy to arrange. There can be no question that Teller introduced Hilda to Bill, as Hilda wrote of Sidney: "I'll always love him for having introduced me to you." HS to WP, 17 December 1911. Bill recalled their first meeting: "I remember the first night I met you. Sidney Teller had told me about you . . . a girl . . . strong & fearless & dependable. . . . But when I saw you—it was quite late that Saturday night, I was disappointed. Your appearance was not of the stuff my dreams were made of. My dreams had an external tinge of Gibson-Fisher-Christy et al. And to say the least, you are slightly stubby & you did your hair in a top-knot like the Marchioness of Dickens. But I liked you—despite your faults. In short, I did not exactly fall in love with you on first sight." This letter was written seven months after they became engaged, three months before their marriage. WP to HS, 12 February 1912.

36. This account could not be verified.

37. The play was performed in Chicago on 22 January–11 March 1911. Napier Wilt files. The play by Jerome K. Jerome was probably not the first play they saw together. They probably met in 1908, although the manuscript telescopes the time, implying they met in 1910 or 1911. Hilda wrote Bill on 20 August 1911: "I remember the night we saw Jerome's soothing 'Passing.' We walked home through the worst part of Chicago but I felt that roses were blooming everywhere."

38. The story of Hilda's first lobster was told to her children. Lobster remained one of her favorite dishes throughout her life—the preferred treat for special occasions.

CHAPTER 17

1. Having rearranged the date of her meeting with Bill, Hilda had herself working in 1911 where she had worked in 1908. There can be no doubt that Hilda was *not* working at the club in 1911 when she decided to spend the summer in Saugatuck. Her first surviving letter to Bill instructs him, "Ring me up at McClurg's, Harrison 1920, Wholesale Book Dep't. Ask for the department, that phone is right near me." HS to WP, 15 February 1911.

2. Although Hilda attributes the idea of dramatizing *The Walking Delegate* to Jane Addams, the director of the Hull-House Players wrote in 1913 that it was her idea. "We had long desired to give an original play which would deal with local conditions, and quite unexpectedly in the spring of 1911 the opportunity came. A young Jewish girl [Hilda was twenty-nine] of the neighborhood, who was making rather ineffective attempts at play-writing, at my request dramatized Leroy Scott's stirring labor story, *The Walking Delegate*. We presented this, after many alterations and much hard work, with great success." Pelham, "The Story of the Hull-House Players," 253–54.

3. A walking delegate was defined as "an official of a labor union who sees that union rules are enforced, and that membership is kept up, and who presents grievances to employers." Sir William A. Craigie, ed., *A Dictionary of*

American English on Historical Principles (Chicago: University of Chicago Press, 1944), 4:2431.

4. The Forward Movement was formerly Epworth House, another Chicago settlement house, founded 1 March 1893 by the Rev. George W. Gray under the auspices of the Methodist Episcopal Church. It became "undenominational and independent in May, 1896." In addition to the settlement house at Monroe and Loomis streets, it maintained "Forward Movement Park, a permanent camp of 125 acres . . . furnishing vacation privileges for deaf, crippled, and blind children, cared for in groups." Robert A. Woods and Albert J. Kennedy, *Handbook of Settlements* (New York: Charities Publication Committee, 1911; rpt., New York: Arno Press, 1970), 49–50.

5. "Set on the banks of the Kalamazoo River [in western Michigan], Saugatuck is a quaint village of Victorian-style homes on tree-lined streets. . . ." *Chicago Sunday Tribune,* 22 June 1986, travel section.

6. Consider this description:

> The Forward Movement Park is situated near Saugatuck, on the eastern shore of Lake Michigan, which lies 14 miles southwest from Holland, Mich., in Allegan County.
>
> There are no railroads or boat lines running direct to Saugatuck, except the electric car lines from Grand Rapids through Holland, Mich. During July and August this line from Holland to Saugatuck runs every hour.
>
> When you buy your ticket of the Graham and Morton [ship] Line via Holland and Saugatuck, *ask for a ticket to Saugatuck,* as this will save you the expense of the electric car line from Holland to Saugatuck. . . . (*The Forward Movement of Chicago* [Chicago: 1909], 4)

> Effective on June 21, 1909 . . . To Saugatuck daily at 9 a.m. and 8 p.m. . . . Berth rates—lower, $1.00; upper, 75c. (Ibid., inside back cover, advertisement of Graham & Morton Transportation Co.)

7. This was probably Stoughton Hall, "a large rooming house for young ladies where they . . . will have the largest liberty with the most complete protection . . . located on Interlachen Hill . . . 150 feet above Lake Michigan with an outlook bounded only by the horizon. It will accommodate about sixty girls . . . in charge of a most estimable lady." Ibid., 13.

8. Hilda had written before she left Chicago: "I am going to stay in a cottage on the top of a hill, where you can touch the tops of the trees, from the window, and where you can see the lake and the river at the same time. I'll be there in two weeks." HS to WP, 11 June 1911. After her arrival she wrote, "Am very comfortably located on the top floor of a four-story house, on the top of a magnificent old hill." HS to WP, 30 June 1911.

9. "I will tell you how the roads and paths are named. The road that leads to these woods—the road to human freedom—is called Lincoln Road. A

path begins at this road, that leads to *MY* house—and the path is call[ed] Browning Path. Then there is a Tolstoi Road, Ruskin Road, Carlyle Road, Emerson Hill. And there is a wonderful path called: Lover's Lane." HS to WP, 11 July 1911.

10. "The summer outing at Forward Movement Park is for all who are trying to leave the world richer in thought, more noble in purpose, better in morals, higher in aim; more joyous, having less sorrow, less idleness, less selfishness, less meanness. Neither the idle rich nor the idle poor are invited." *The Forward Movement of Chicago,* 5.

11. "In 1909 . . . the Big Pavilion [was constructed], an immense dance hall with 5,000 colored lights in the arched ceiling that blinked on and off with the music. The wooden structure burned to the ground in less than an hour in 1960." *Chicago Sunday Tribune,* 23 June 1986, travel section.

12. "Tents same rate as rooms. . . . Board and room or tent [per week] $5.75." *The Forward Movement of Chicago,* 11, 13. Bill's letter asking her to reserve a tent has not survived, but he wrote after his return to Milwaukee about "the pleasant memories of those glorious days at Saugatuck. . . ." WP to HS, 31 July 1911.

13. Heinrich Heine, *Buch der Lieder,* ed. John Lees (Manchester: Manchester University Press, 1920), 104–5; no. 47 of "Die Heimkehr," first two lines.

14. William Butler Yeats, "The Lake Isle of Innisfree," from "The Rose (1893)," in *The Collected Poems of W. B. Yeats* (New York: Macmillan Co., 1941), 44, stanza 3, ll.1–2.

15. Bill wrote: ". . . and the dance! We did have fun that night, along the dark ways of Browning Path. . . ." WP to HS, 31 July 1911.

16. The onions became a running joke between Bill and Hilda. On his way home, he wrote from Grand Rapids (the letter was postmarked 7 A.M.) about her "eyes glistening at the prospect of THEM ONIONS." WP to HS, 31 July 1911. She wrote later: "We had onions for supper! Isn't this a romantic way of beginning?" HS to WP, 8 August 1911.

17. In a letter, Bill reminisced: "I went over the last year. . . . We went to that dance together & found our way, my arm around your waist, by lantern along Browning Path. The next day . . . the fatal walk in the rain. . . . Then the gargle was made, you led the way to Tent #1, I followed with palpitating heart." What follows is a recounting of the story of his proposal. WP to HS, 2 October 1911.

CHAPTER 18

1. Leroy Scott (1875–1929) was a one-time Hull-House resident, ". . . in newspaper work, 1897–1900; asst. headworker, Univ. Settlement, New York, 1902–03; devoted entire time to writing, New York, 1904- . . . Author: *The Walking Delegate,* 1905. . . ." *Who Was Who in America,* vol. 1: *1897–1942,* 1095.

2. "Samuel J. Parks, walking delegate for the Housesmiths, Bridgmen, and Structural Iron Workers' Union, is brought to trial to-day on the charge of extortion . . . of $2,000 to have a strike . . . settled." *New York Times,* 13 August 1903. Parks died in Sing Sing on 4 May 1904. *The Public* 7 (7 May 1904): 73.

3. "Laura Dainty Pelham (1845–1924) [was] a retired actress who came to Hull-House about 1900 to successfully direct the Hull-House Players until her death. . . ." Davis and McCree, *Eighty Years at Hull-House,* 74.

4. Pelham, "The Story of the Hull-House Players," 253–54.

5. This was an afterthought written many years later. Hilda's letters demonstrate that she did have hopes that her play might have commercial possibilities: "I am confident that if the W. D. proves a success, I'll be able to sell it. Good plays are not being thrown about. . . . I really think the play is good. I don't think it is a great play, but a strong one, dealing with a timely topic and a condition that needs reforming." HS to WP, 7 February 1912. Bill also took the play seriously, advising her: ". . . what arrangement have you made with Mr. Scott? You should see . . . some . . . good lawyer & get a legal arrangement between you, now before any news spreads about the play." WP to HS, 21 February 1912. The review in the *Chicago Sunday Tribune,* 21 April 1912, referred to Leroy Scott's proposal to "have it examined . . . for values as a commercial enterprise." Nothing further was found about a possible New York production, although Hilda wrote on 13 April 1912, "The Dramatic Publishing Co. wants to publish the dramatic version of the W. D. Isn't that rich?" There is no evidence that it was published.

6. This was the garment strike of 1910:

> . . . the first great landmark in the long struggle of the clothing workers. . . .
>
> The feature of the strike was the entirely unorganized condition of the strikers and the spontaneity and determination of their protest in spite of that fact. It has been described . . . as a simultaneous upheaval of over forty-one thousand garment workers, brought on by sixteen girls, against petty persecution, low wages, abuse and long hours; . . . the garment workers were almost without exception recently arrived immigrants, unable to speak English, and ignorant of . . . conditions of other American industries.
>
> The first spark was struck on September 22 [1910] in Shop No. 5, a pants shop of Hart, Schaffner and Marx, when several girls walked out of the shop rather than accept a cut of one-quarter cent in rates. . . .
>
> Contrary to all precedent, the walk-out in Shop 5 provoked immediate and enthusiastic response in other shops. . . . By the next day almost a thousand men and women had left the shops and long before three weeks were over, more than 40,000 were out. . . . Nothing like it had ever been known before in the history of the clothing workers. (Amalgamated Clothing Workers of America, *The Clothing Workers of Chicago, 1910–1922* [Chicago, 1922], 17, 19, 26–27)

See also Sue N. Weiler, "Walkout: The Men's Garment Workers' Strike, 1910–1911," *Chicago History* 8 (Winter 1979): 238–49, and "Chicago at the Front: A Condensed History of the Garment Workers' Strike," *Life and Labor* 1 (January

1911): 4–13. "Unorganized, helpless, starving, speaking nine different languages, with few friends, with no resources, these workers had been lost and forgotten in the great city of Chicago." Mary E. Dreier, *Margaret Dreier Robins: Her Life, Letters, and Work* (New York: Island Press Cooperative, 1950), 72.

7. "James Mullenbach of Chicago Commons served for many years as chairman of the Joint Arbitration Board of the garment workers and the clothing firm of Hart, Schaffner, and Marx." Allen F. Davis, *Spearheads for Reform: The Social Settlements and the Progressive Movement, 1890–1914* (New York: Oxford University Press, 1967), 108–9. "James Mullenbach: superintendent of municipal lodging house (1903–1909)." Woods and Kennedy, *Handbook of Settlements,* 43. To provide food for the strikers, "it was decided that there must be a commissary . . . securing for this work James Mullenbach . . . who had experience in such relief work with the miners." Dreier, *Margaret Dreier Robins,* 73.

8. "Despite difficulties and misunderstandings . . . settlement workers did support organized labor with both words and actions, and sometimes the two groups cooperated. . . . No one defended organized labor more vigorously or consistently than Jane Addams. . . . She made thousands of speeches supporting the worker's right to organize, and even . . . when anti-labor feeling was rampant, she publicly defended the worker's right to strike and to bargain collectively." Davis, *Spearheads for Reform,* 105.

9. WP to HS, 5 August 1911.

10. Hilda did not stay in Saugatuck for the month of August. On 8 August she wrote: "I am positively going to Chicago Friday morning [i.e., 11 August]." Beginning on 11 August, letters were addressed to her at her Chicago home.

11. "I have decided to re-write 'The Walking Delegate.' Mrs. Pelham and I had a long conference, and we came to the conclusion that a play of this type should present the women in a more important manner. The man, in his struggle for better living, is either pulled down or uplifted by the influence of the woman who reigns at home. And so I am about to strengthen the parts of the women already in the play, and create two or three additional ones. I may change the first act to a working man's home." HS to WP, 28 September 1911. The revised version apparently has not survived.

12. HS to WP, 30 January 1912:

> . . . I have such good news to tell you. Mrs. Pelham called me up today and told me the W. D. was very good. "I'm proud of you, Hilda; you did an excellent piece of work. I cried over the play," she said. Rehearsals begin next week. Louis Alter will play Foley, Bailey will be Tom, Keough will be Pete, Helen Silverman will be Ruth, and so on. Mrs. Pelham was very enthusiastic over the play. It thrilled me! I have had three thrills in my life. The first one occurred when Miss Addams told me I had received a scholarship at the U [University of Chicago]. I was filled with such joy, that I walked two miles without knowing it.

> The second thrill came to me when you came up to me in tent #1 . . . and said "I love you." . . .
>
> And today I was thrilled again. I am very happy! . . .

On February 4, Hilda described the play's reception:

> Mrs. Pelham . . . gave the play to Mr. Twose, the most severe critic at H.H. He . . . took it to Albany with him and this morning a telegram arrived pronouncing the play "good." Miss Addams said if Twose thinks the play "good"—it must be excellent. She is waiting, "rather impatiently," she said, to read it. But she is next. Just think, Billy darling, they're waiting for their turns at H. House. . . .
>
> Oh! I can see the vistas opening before me! I worked hard and had to resist many a temptation, but I am rewarded. . . . I am loved by the dearest man in the world. I can live my life according to my own philosophy, and what more can any human being ask for?

13. WP to Dena Miriam Satt, 18 December 1911.

14. Dena Satt replied to this letter on 21 December 1911 by dictation to Hilda, who wrote:

> My dear William:
>
> Your letter pleased me very much. As to whether I consent to your marrying Hilda, I am proud to say that I have absolute confidence in Hilda's choice. Having known her as long as I do (this is mother's joke) I am sure that she knows what she does. I freely and willingly and joyfully give you both my blessing and hope you will both be very happy. This event, as Hilda's mother, is my ultimate wish in life. I can ask for nothing more pleasing to me, than to see my children happy (literal translation). . . .
>
> I hope Hilda will prove a good wife; you see, I feel the responsibility of having trained her right. (Joke no. 2)
>
> I shall be very glad to see you. And I shall be glad to welcome you as my son. . . .

15. One of their exchanges dealt with Bill's proposal that they experiment with living on $20.00 a week. He wrote on 31 January 1912: "When I first considered the prospect of marrying you, I thot the value of an experience of living on a very small sum in a cheap location—where life is thickest & blood is reddest. I'd like to do it. . . ." Hilda replied on 27 February: "We'll show our friends that we can live on less than $20.00 per. And then we'll write a series of essays, giving the exact facts and data. A demonstration of such living would be of lasting benefit, to thousands of 'would be adventurers.'" Having given the matter serious thought, she wrote again on 11–12 March:

> I've been thinking of our plan of living for the same amount that the average worker and his family do. . . . it must be proved, beyond a criticism, possible, practical, sane, wholesome and most

> important of all, that it is not a sacrifice. Now if we live in a small house, no one can say that a small room cannot be made attractive and homelike. We can prove that doing one's own house-work is not drudgery if attacked in the right way. . . . But I do think a bath is necessary. . . . take the average family living without a bath; the woman is tired when the day is about to close, and getting a bath ready, where the water must be carried to and from the tub, is work, and so she thinks, oh, well, I'll not bathe today. She feels the same way the day after. . . . the first sign of discord between husband and wife is uncleanliness. A man loses respect for a woman who is not sweet and clean. . . . it is easy for the man to stop at the public bath house. . . . So I do think we ought to have a bath.

Bill agreed.

16. "Rose Pastor Stokes, 1879–1933 . . . proletarian Cinderella. . . . in 1905, she married James Graham Phelps Stokes, a wealthy aristocrat. . . ." Jacob R. Marcus, *The American Jewish Woman: A Documentary History* (New York: Ktav Publishing House; Cincinnati: American Jewish Archives, 1981), 538.

17. The copy of *Twenty Years of Hull-House* with Miss Addams's inscription is now with Hilda's papers in the Special Collections Department, University of Illinois at Chicago Library.

18. "I told Mother an hour ago. . . . she was in her best mood. I sat down beside her & put my arm around her & told her that I had always been a dutiful son to her & never would do anything to cause her pain—but I wanted to get married—to Hilda! It was quite a shock to her & all she could say was that she thot H. was too old, that she didn't think I would get married." WP to HS, 13 February 1912. There were other unspoken objections: Hilda had come from Poland and Carrie Polacheck's family was old German-Bohemian stock. In 1912 the antagonism between eastern and western European Jews had not disappeared. Moreover, it seems likely from Bill's accounts of his mother that she expected to choose his bride or at least to persuade him to choose someone of whom she approved.

19. Bill's paternal grandfather had emigrated from Bohemia in 1852, according to the certificate that permitted him, his wife, and children to leave Austria-Hungary, having fulfilled his military obligations to the crown. Certificate in possession of Donald Polacheck, Milwaukee.

20. Performances took place on 10, 17, 20, 27 April 1912. Enclosed in Hilda's letter of 3 April 1912 was a clipping from the *Chicago Record-Herald* of that day, written by James O'Donnell Bennett, headed "DRAMA OF THE DAY":

> Miss Satt, who is 24 [*sic*] years old and has acted on the Hull-House stage, has lived in the Hull-House neighborhood. She has been experimenting in dramatic writing for several years. . . .
>
> "The production of 'The Walking Delegate,'" said Mrs. Pelham yesterday, "will, we think, mark a turning point in our dramatic work at Hull-House. What I mean is that we begin to see our

way to the development of what Mr. Toose [Twose], one of our teachers and residents, has been pleading for ever since his return from Europe. He calls it 'Neighborhood Drama,' and what he means by that is the expression in play form of the wonderful life right at our doors. We have dramatic material all around us. Some of it is tragic; some of it comic. All of it is real and vital. The themes and the types are amazingly varied.

" 'Bring all that out,' Mr. Toose said when he got back from his studies in Munich. He thinks, and I agree with him, that there is drama enough around Halsted and Polk streets to fire the imagination and rouse the sympathies of any audience, and the question now is, can we take the first step in a work that may develop in time something approaching the freshness and grip and beauty of the compositions that the Abbey Players of Dublin have given to the world. We shall make the start in neighborhood drama; some one may appear who will infuse it with an appeal that will carry its message far beyond the boundaries of our ward. . . ."

21. A review appeared in the *Chicago Sunday Tribune* on 21 April 1912:

> "The Walking Delegate" at Hull-House. . . . the work of Miss Hilda Satt, a young playwright of the neighborhood. The piece essays with considerable conviction to portray a corrupt business agent who sells his union to a set of corrupt employers, but who is frustrated ere his end is accomplished by his handsome, honest, and upstanding rival in the organization. . . . spurious incidents or incidents written spuriously are not for them [the Hull-House Players] and their efforts at sentimentality are as counterfeit as their efforts at obvious theatrical intrigue. Both of these elements are present in Miss Satt's version of "The Walking Delegate," though it is a creditable initial experiment. Mr. Scott, the author, admits his admiration for it and proposes to have it examined by the experts near Broadway and Forty-Second Street for value as a commercial enterprise.

22. "Women are only eligible to the reflected foreign or American citizenship of their husbands. . . . they have no citizenship of their own. The Naturalization Law of 1907 (Secs. 3960 and 3961): '. . . A foreign woman acquires citizenship by marriage to an American.'" Mary Sumner Boyd, *The Woman Citizen: A General Handbook of Civics, with Special Consideration of Women's Citizenship* (New York: Frederick A. Stokes Co., 1918), 15.

23. "The final [actually, the second] performance was marked with a touch of romance, for the young author was married in the morning and came to see her play at night with all her bridal party. Miss Addams gave a reception to celebrate the event, to which players, bridal party, and residents were all bidden, and so the season closed in happiness and triumph." Pelham, "The Story of the Hull-House Players," 254.

CHAPTER 19

1. The Palm Garden was "a type of indoor beer garden . . . opened in 1896 just south of the southeast corner of Grand av. (W. Wisconsin av.) and N. 3rd st. . . . high arched ceiling festooned with lights, its pipe organ, and its stained glass windows heightening the glow of color from the rich oil paintings along the walls. The garden had its own red coated company of musicians, but nationally known orchestras often played engagements there." H. Russell Austin, *The Milwaukee Story: The Making of an American City* (Milwaukee: The Milwaukee Journal, 1946), 145. An advertisement in the *Milwaukee Leader,* 24 October 1913, announced the appearance of "Theo. Roemhildt's Orchestra from Berlin."

2. [Edith J. R. Isaacs], "The German Theatre in Milwaukee," *Theatre Arts* 28 (August 1944): 465.

3. Martini's was the original of Baumbach's in Edna Ferber's partly autobiographical novel set in Milwaukee, *Dawn O'Hara.* Austin, *The Milwaukee Story,* 146; Isaacs, "The German Theatre in Milwaukee," 465.

4. Austin, *The Milwaukee Story,* 147.

5. Ibid., 146.

6. For its repertory, see Isaacs, "The German Theatre in Milwaukee."

7. *Milwaukee Leader,* 16 January 1913.

8. Ibid., 28 March, 2 April 1914. "In 1913 the German managers, in despair at having to produce Shaw's plays after they had been reported from London as unpleasant failures, stipulated that in future the first performance should take place in Germany. Accordingly, *Pygmalion* reached the theatre in Berlin before its production by Tree at His Majesty's Theater, and after that it was Shaw's practice to give priority to foreign theaters whenever possible. . . ." R. F. Rattray, *Bernard Shaw: A Chronicle* (Luton: Leagrave Press, 1951), 137. The play was published in German translation in 1913 as *Pygmalion: Komödie in fünf Akten,* Deutsch von Siegfried Trebitsch (Berlin: S. Fischer, 1913).

9. Founded in 1900, the Settlement moved to Abraham Lincoln House in 1911. Louis J. Swichkow and Lloyd P. Gartner, *The History of the Jews of Milwaukee* (Philadelphia: Jewish Publication Society of America, 1963), 226. Bill wrote that he had gone "to the Settlement. Had my first battle for a free platform. It seems at the last board meeting, the question came up of admitting a socialist club. A nice lady told me all about it & how 'we really couldn't accept them, etc.' expecting that I would be real nice & agreeable. Well, when I had given my very decided views & arguments & quoted Jane Addams, she was gasping." WP to HS, 14 November 1911.

10. The 1903 edition of the cookbook was reissued in a facsimile edition (New York: Hugh Lauter Levin Associates, 1984) and expanded to 183 pages. Among the advertisements on unnumbered pages was one for Frank Martini, Confectionery ("Wedding cakes, ice cream . . . German tarts and other fancy cakes . . .") and one for "Chas. Polacheck & Bro. Co., gas and electric fixture manufacturers," the firm founded by Bill's father.

11. The first review signed HS appeared in the *Milwaukee Leader* on 1

November 1912 and the last on 8 April 1913. Only one article was signed "Hilda Satt," a description of the Hull-House Players who came to Milwaukee under the sponsorship of the Wisconsin Dramatic Society. Ibid., 1 February 1913. The review of their performance was unsigned. Ibid., 4 February 1913. Many of Hilda's reviews were highly critical, reflecting her conception of what the theater should be. Typical was her review of the hit musical *The Pink Lady,* which had a long run in New York: "[The play] is taken from the French. For all I care, they may have it back. . . . It contains no music and no comedy. But it has plenty of girls and a hosiery display; many handsome gowns . . . much noise and blare, suggestive actions, and a few whistleable tunes and dances. . . . They say it costs as much to launch one of these as it does to launch a battle ship. Why the need of either?" Ibid., 13 January 1913. Since her reviews continued until April, this one was not the immediate cause for her removal. Her reviews reflected the approach to the theater that she had learned at Hull-House, where its educational function was regarded as at least as important as entertainment. Vulgarity was something for which she had little tolerance. A list of her reviews is given in Appendix B.

Hilda does not mention that a play of hers was performed at Abraham Lincoln House in June 1912 (it had been presented in April 1911 at the Chicago Hebrew Institute) which preceded the idea of "neighborhood drama" of *The Walking Delegate.* "To demonstrate the value of the drama for educating the public on the problems of the day is the purpose . . . in the presentation of the play 'Case No. 29,129' . . . written by Mrs. William Polacheck, who was Miss Hilda Satt, formerly a resident of Hull-House, Chicago." (This, of course, was an error; she was never a Hull-House resident.) "The play tells the story of the tenement house evil, and how the lack of sunlight kills the babies. . . . the performance is set for June 1, at the Abraham Lincoln House." *Milwaukee Leader,* 29 May 1912.

12. "One of the most efficient political affiliations in the city's [Chicago] history [was] that of the flamboyant, showy John 'Bathhouse John' Coughlin, Democratic alderman from the wicked First Ward, and Michael 'Hinky Dink' Kenna. . . . Coughlin was a former bathhouse attendant, Kenna the owner of the Workingmen's Exchange Saloon on Clark Street; together they built an organization of saloonkeepers, gamblers, pimps, pickpockets, and brothel owners who would help them, term after term, hold their City Council seats. . . . Together they staged, annually, for more than a decade, First Ward balls at which the denizens of . . . vice districts . . . mingled with political leaders and police captains." Herman Kogan and Lloyd Wendt, *Chicago: A Pictorial History* (New York: Bonanza Books, 1958), 168–70.

13. The phonograph and records that were Hilda's engagement ring introduced her children to music. They left the family in the chaos after Bill's death, when they were given to the Old Soldiers' Home.

14. No record of this program has been found.

15. This group is still in existence. It performed in February 1986 for the Music Library Association.

16. *Milwaukee Leader,* 24 July 1912.

17. Allen F. Davis, *American Heroine: The Life and Legend of Jane Addams* (New York: Oxford University Press, 1973), 176.

18. Haldeman-Julius, *Jane Addams as I Knew Her,* 26.

19. "Nine thousand people who filled the Auditorium Monday night listened to Theodore Roosevelt, a would-be assassin's bullet in his right breast. . . . Roosevelt insisted upon making his speech. . . . He was introduced by Henry Cochems who told the audience of the . . . attempt upon the life of the candidate . . . just been made. . . . Several times he [Roosevelt] was interrupted by entreaties to quit his speech, but he refused." *Milwaukee Leader,* 16 October 1912.

20. Sachs was "known for many years at Hull-House through his skilled and unremitting efforts to reduce tuberculosis. . . ." Jane Addams, *The Second Twenty Years at Hull-House, September 1909 to September 1929* . . . (New York: Macmillan Co., 1930), 14.

21. There are pictures of the Kenyon house taken by Bill's brother Stanley.

22. The death date on Dena Satt's tombstone is 3 June 1913.

23. Addams, *Second Twenty Years at Hull-House,* 14.

CHAPTER 20

1. Charles Lessing Polacheck, born 19 January 1914, reported in the *Milwaukee Leader,* 23 January 1914. The card that accompanied the kimono sent by Miss Addams is now among Hilda's papers in the Special Collections Department, University of Illinois at Chicago Library.

2. Mercedes M. Randall, *Improper Bostonian: Emily Greene Balch, Nobel Peace Laureate, 1946* (New York: Twayne Publishers, 1964), 138–51; Addams, *Second Twenty Years at Hull-House,* 122.

3. When Wilson sent a note to the German government over the sinking of the Lusitania, which Bryan considered too strong, Bryan sent a letter of resignation, which Wilson accepted promptly. Louis W. Koenig, *Bryan: A Political Biography* (New York: G. P. Putnam's Sons, 1971), 509–49.

4. Dena Julia Polacheck, born 30 November 1916.

5. Randall, *Improper Bostonian,* 233–34.

6. There was "boycotting and condemning of people who spoke German or bore German names. . . . The Deutscher Club had become the Wisconsin Club . . . 'sauerkraut' [became] 'liberty cabbage'. . . . In June 1919 the teaching of German was to be completely discontinued in the elementary schools." Bayrd Still, *Milwaukee: The History of a City* (Madison: The State Historical Society of Wisconsin, 1948), 461–62.

7. *Dictionary of American Biography,* supp. 3 (1941–45) (New York: Charles Scribner's Sons, 1973), 740–42; Frederick Stock Papers and Horace A. Oakley Papers, Newberry Library, Chicago.

8. This is a paraphrase of lines from Antony's oration. Shakespeare, *Julius Caesar,* act 3, sc. 2: "O judgement! thou art fled to brutish beasts, And men have lost their reason."

9. Sally M. Miller, *Victor Berger and the Promise of Constructive Socialism, 1910–1920* (Westport, Conn.: Greenwood Press, 1973), 193–219.

10. This is, possibly, a paraphrase from Debs's Canton speech of 16 June 1918, submitted in evidence in his trial for espionage: "But in all the history of the world, you, the people, have never had a voice in declaring war, and . . . no war by any nation in any age has ever been declared by the people." *Eugene V. Debs Speaks,* ed. Jean Y. Tussey (New York: Pathfinder Press, 1970), 260–61.

11. Ibid., 289.

12. Demarest Lloyd Polacheck, born 13 July 1918.

13. The address was 1087 Frederick Avenue.

14. "Berger . . . referred to his adopted nephew, Carl Haessler, who was serving five years in Leavenworth Federal Penitentiary as a conscientious objector. . . ." Miller, *Victor Berger,* 211. "From June, 1919, to August, 1920, [Carl] Haessler, continued his education as an inmate of government 'institutions' at Ft. Leavenworth and Alcatraz." *Milwaukee Leader,* 23 January 1922. Haessler was a friend of the Polachecks.

15. This is a slight paraphrase of a sentence in Thoreau's essay "Civil Disobedience," in *The Writings of Henry David Thoreau* (Boston: Houghton Mifflin Co., 1906), 4:370.

16. Two of the six stanzas dated 1870, in Austin Dobson, "At Sedan," from "Vignettes in Rhyme," in *Complete Poetical Works* (London: Oxford University Press, 1923), 106–7.

17. A false rumor of armistice had spread on 7 November 1918. Austin, *The Milwaukee Story,* 182.

18. Ibid., 183.

CHAPTER 21

1. This is a paraphrase of Franklin's letter to Josiah Quincy, 11 September 1783: "I . . . rejoice with you, in the Peace God has blest us with. . . . May we never see another War! for in my opinion there never was a good War, or a bad Peace." *The Writings of Benjamin Franklin,* ed. Albert Henry Smith (New York: Macmillan Co., 1907) 9:95–96.

2. The broad support of the disarmament movement and the growth of peace societies were chronicled in the *Milwaukee Leader,* 1921–23, especially 23 June 1921 and 29 July 1922.

3. "Alla Nazimova made her debut in vaudeville . . . in a one-act play, 'War Brides'. . . . The piece proved to be a powerful sermon against war, which was excellently preached, but . . . quite tiresome. . . . [She] finally kills herself rather than bring a child into the world to carry on future wars. . . ." *New York Times,* 26 January 1915.

4. "Mrs. [Benton] Mackaye was the organizer and the first president of the Milwaukee Peace society." *Milwaukee Leader,* 19 April 1921. The date of organization has not been found, but by January 1921 the officers did not include Mrs. Mackaye. Ibid., 7 January 1921.

5. This incident could not be verified.

6. "The regular meeting of the Milwaukee Peace society will be held

. . . in the trustees' room, public museum." Ibid., 16 April 1921. For many years the public library and the museum shared the same building.

7. "Members of the Milwaukee Peace society will meet Jane Addams . . . at lunch Wednesday. . . . Miss Addams will not make an address, but will talk informally with members of the organization." Ibid., 1 November 1921. "In her talk yesterday before the Milwaukee Peace society . . . Jane Addams [spoke] about the work accomplished by the International League for Peace and Freedom. . . . The society voted to affiliate with the organization following Miss Addams' talk and will be known as the Wisconsin branch." Ibid., 3 November 1921.

8. See Jane Addams, *Peace and Bread in Time of War* (New York: King's Crown Press, 1945).

9. Hilda often quoted this statement to her children.

10. "12-Lecture Open Forum Course to be Started in Milwaukee . . . by some of the most noted lecturers and other personages of this and other countries. . . ." *Milwaukee Leader,* 11 September 1919. No reference to Hilda's being chair of the program committee has been found, although she was listed as in charge of "talks before groups, clubs, etc." Ibid., 21 September 1922. The following year she was listed as chair of the membership committee, while Bill chaired the "lecture" committee. Ibid., 28 September 1923. Perhaps this was what she had in mind.

11. Russell originally was scheduled to speak on 19 February 1924 but was forced by illness to postpone his lecture until 22 April. Ibid., 8 October 1923, 15 January, 11 February, 24 April 1924. The children were allowed to come downstairs to meet this honored guest. The reverberations of the car filled with iron junk lasted for years.

12. "Successively farm laborer, link heater, tramp, circus roustabout, chainmaker, professional pugilist, reporter on *Akron Press and Beacon Jour.,* tree surgeon, [Tully] is now engaged exclusively in writing. Tramped across U.S. 3 times. . . ." *Who Was Who in America . . . ,* vol. 2: *1943–1950* (Chicago: A. N. Marquis Co., 1950), 539–40. His career as a lecturer was not mentioned. Tully spoke on "Charlie Chaplin and Hollywood" on Tuesday, 8 December 1925. *Wisconsin Jewish Chronicle,* 4 December 1925. The buffet supper in his honor was given the previous evening. Ibid., 11 December 1925.

13. The date of Johnson's lecture in Milwaukee has not been determined, but the photograph he autographed for Hilda is dated 16 November 1927, now in the Special Collections Department, University of Illinois at Chicago Library.

14. *Wisconsin Jewish Chronicle,* 10 November 1922, 14 October 1927. Hilda was active as late as May 1928: "Mrs. Hilda Polacheck . . . is one of several officers and members of the National Council of Jewish Women to have been appointed as State Representatives by Mrs. Carrie Chapman Catt, chairman, for promoting the purpose of the National Committee on the Cause and Cure of War." Ibid., 18 May 1928.

15. Hilda's children remember this activity.

16. "The Shorewood school in cooperation with the Shorewood Parent-

Teachers' Assn. are putting on a series of afternoon concerts for children and adults. The first is a Chicago Symphony concert, Jan. 7, 3:30 p.m. Another is a piano-lecture recital by Guy Maier, Jan. 28, and the third a recital by Edna Thomas, March 8." *Milwaukee Leader,* 2 January 1924. See also *Wisconsin Jewish Chronicle,* 14 March 1924.

17. Hilda's children remember Sandburg asleep on the couch.

CHAPTER 22

1. Doris Stevens, *Jailed for Freedom* (New York: Boni and Liveright, 1920; rpt., New York: Schocken Books, 1976), 348.

2. Letter of 31 March 1776, from *Adams Family Correspondence,* ed. L. H. Butterfield (Cambridge, Mass.: Belknap Press of Harvard University Press, 1963), 1:369–70.

3. At the time, Hilda wrote: "Have been on the street all day, listening to 'No, I won't vote for the women.' 'Yes, certainly, I'm for the ladies.' It was very windy all day, and I'm sure half of Chicago's dirt is in me right now. . . . Woman's suffrage lost 2 to 1. . . . We are all blue and mad!" HS to WP, 9 April 1912. Hilda often quoted her mother's saying: "Women will never vote and there will always be a czar."

4. No record has been found of Hilda's joining the National Woman's party, but her resignation as treasurer of the Milwaukee branch was announced in the *Milwaukee Leader,* 27 June 1924.

5. Milholland was a charismatic leader of the suffragists, widely publicized for "marching in parades . . . white-robed and riding a white horse. . . ." *Notable American Women,* 1:189. But she died in March 1913 and the words of President Wilson were first burned in September 1918. Inez Haynes Irwin, *The Story of the Woman's Party* (New York: Harcourt Brace and Co., 1921), 365. Subsequent occasions on which Wilson's words were burned were reported in the *Milwaukee Leader,* 16, 17 December 1918.

6. Irwin, *Story of the Woman's Party,* 193–291; Stevens, *Jailed for Freedom,* 63–79.

7. Irwin, *Story of the Woman's Party,* 225–26; Stevens, *Jailed for Freedom,* 359.

8. Irwin, *Story of the Woman's Party,* 225; Stevens, *Jailed for Freedom,* 361.

9. Mrs. Havemeyer carried the American flag, leading a procession of 100 women to the White House where they burned President Wilson in effigy on 9 February 1919; but none of the accounts of the event, including Mrs. Havemeyer's recollections, refer to her sitting near the door of the patrol wagon with the flag streaming out. Perhaps this story was told within the National Woman's party. Irwin, *Story of the Woman's Party,* 402–3; Stevens, *Jailed for Freedom,* 315–18, 361; Louisine W. Havemeyer, "The Prison Special: Memories of a Militant," *Scribner's Magazine* 71 (June 1922): 664–66; *New York Times,* 10 February 1919.

10. "Scores of women were arrested but never brought to trial; many others were convicted and their sentences suspended or appealed. It has been possible to list . . . only those [170] women who actually served prison sen-

tences although more than five hundred women were arrested during the agitation." Stevens, *Jailed for Freedom,* 354–71.

11. Irwin, *Story of the Woman's Party,* 407.

12. Ibid.; Stevens, *Jailed for Freedom,* 355; *Milwaukee Leader,* 4 March 1919.

13. *Milwaukee Leader,* 5 February, 5, 6 March 1919. "Police Needed to Hold Crowd which Greets Prison Special . . . to the time of music furnished by the Wisconsin Veterans Drum corps, marched up Third St. to the Majestic Theater. . . ." Ibid., 6 March 1919.

14. Hilda's memory was faulty here. Her second son was an infant in March 1919 when the "Prison Special" reached Milwaukee. Her oldest son, born in 1914, must have been the culprit.

15. *New York Times,* 27 August 1920.

16. Stevens, *Jailed for Freedom,* 347.

17. This figure has not been verified.

18. To be precise: 919,799. *Encyclopedia of American Facts and Dates,* ed. Gordon Carruth, 5th ed. (New York: T. Y. Crowell, 1970), 456.

19. *Milwaukee Leader,* 23 December 1921.

20. Jessie Polacheck was born 14 September 1923.

CHAPTER 23

1. Addams, *Peace and Bread in Time of War,* vi.

2. "After World War I, because of her commitments to the Women's International League for Peace and Freedom and her declining health, Jane Addams spent less and less time at Hull-House, where the various settlement activities went on without her." Louise de Koven Bowen, "The Death of Jane Addams," in Davis and McCree, *Eighty Years at Hull-House,* 181.

3. Addams, *Peace and Bread in Time of War,* 253–54.

4. Gertrude Bussey and Margaret Tims, *Women's International League for Peace and Freedom, 1915–1965: A Record of Fifty Years' Work* (London: George Allen & Unwin, 1965), 45–52; Addams, *Second Twenty Years at Hull-House,* 173–79; *Milwaukee Leader,* 24, 29 April, 4 June 1924; *Wisconsin Jewish Chronicle,* 2, 23 May 1924.

5. "In spite of the great distances to be travelled . . . delegates were present from twenty-two national sections, the only absentees being Haiti and New Zealand. Four new sections were welcomed into membership: Belgium, Czechoslovakia, Haiti and Japan. . . . Observers also came from countries in Latin America and the Caribbean, and from Turkey and Liberia." Bussey and Tims, *Women's International League,* 45.

6. The official report of the Congress and reports by other delegates do not mention this reception, nor is it mentioned in biographies of President or Mrs. Coolidge.

7. This incident has not been verified although it seems quite believable.

CHAPTER 24

1. Bill described his view of business: "I too have my ambitions. I would like to build up a successful business on a humane social basis. I would like to

take a hand in civic affairs—not as a theorist or as a man needing a job—but as a man who has done!—& therefore will do for the city what he has done for himself." WP to HS, 4 November 1911. The results of his approach were reported: "Employees of the Polly Manufacturing Co. have organized a welfare club. . . . A committee of five was appointed to draw up a constitution and by-laws." *Milwaukee Leader,* 18 April 1921.

2. "Couple of 'Garden Homers' Learn Joy of Commuting in Blizzards. . . . It was the regular symphony concert night. . . . Frederick Stock . . . remarked, looking . . . at the half empty house, that anyone who came out in a night like that must be a music lover indeed. [On the way home] the car was snow bound. . . ." The couple finally spent the night in a car-barn. Ibid., 5 February 1924. Garden Homes was a city-financed housing development.

3. This letter was not found among Hilda's papers after her death.

4. *Wisconsin Jewish Chronicle,* 9 December 1927.

CHAPTER 25

1. Paul Kellogg, "Twice Twenty Years at Hull-House," *Survey* (15 June 1930): 265–67, reprinted in Davis and McCree, *Eighty Years at Hull-House,* 170–74; Linn, *Jane Addams,* 375–76.

2. The speaker was Dr. Alice Hamilton, who wrote that babies should be fed "nothing but milk till their teeth came. . . . I realize that those Italian women knew what a baby needed far better than my Ann Arbor professor did. I cannot feel I did any harm, however, for my teachings had no effect." Hamilton, *Exploring the Dangerous Trades,* 69.

3. There were two interim moves before Hilda left Milwaukee. Less than six months after Bill's death, the family moved from 1087 Frederick Avenue to 1047 Murray Avenue, a block away. *Wisconsin Jewish Chronicle,* 4 May 1928. That was a temporary home while Hilda built a new house on Sylvan Avenue in Whitefish Bay, where the family lived for only a few months until the business she had inherited went into bankruptcy, forcing her to move to Chicago to find work.

4. *New York Times,* 6 March 1933.

5. Linn, *Jane Addams,* 389–92; Davis, *American Heroine,* 286.

6. Linn, *Jane Addams,* 391.

7. Ibid., 392.

8. Ibid., 390.

9. Ibid., 392.

10. Joseph P. Lash, *Eleanor and Franklin* (New York: W. W. Norton, 1971), 135. This particular anecdote has not been found among Mrs. Roosevelt's writings.

11. This statement has not been located in FDR's voluminous output, verbal and written.

12. Hilda did not mention a job that preceded her stint on the Writers' Project, an assignment that gave her great satisfaction at the time. For a period, ending 15 January 1938, she selected tenants for the Jane Addams Houses, a project then under construction. She told of the incredulous delight shown by people when they were informed that they could move from dingy, dirty

tenements into clean, new apartments with plumbing. Public housing at that time was considered a blessing, not a mismanaged problem. She felt it was highly appropriate that Jane Addams's name should be attached to housing for the poor. Hilda's certificate, that she had returned "all Government property supplied to him [*sic*] while employed by the Federal Emergency Administration of Public Works . . . with no exceptions. . . . One clearance copy will be returned to the employee with his final check. Jan. 17, '38," was found with her papers.

CHAPTER 26

1. "Roosevelt's earliest executive order stipulated that at least 50 per cent of all workers on the project . . . had to be selected from the public relief rolls. . . . Having achieved certification, a motley crew applied for posts on the FWP." Monty Noam Penkower, *The Federal Writers' Project: A Study in Government Patronage of the Arts* (Urbana: University of Illinois Press, 1977), 56–57. Hilda's "Notice to report to Work on Project" was dated 11 May 1940; she was instructed to report to work as a "reporter" on Project no. 80236. The box "Certified" was marked "X." "The prevailing wage varied according to regional living costs. . . . The highest wage, from $93.50 to $103.50 a month, was paid in New York . . . $39 in Georgia and Mississippi." Ibid., 62.

2. This incident from the movie version does not appear in the book.

3. Penkower, *Federal Writers' Project,* 70–71; Jerre Mangione, *The Dream and the Deal: The Federal Writers' Project, 1935–1943* (Boston: Little, Brown and Co., 1972), 48.

4. Penkower and Mangione do not mention recertification. "The Relief Act of 1939 . . . stipulated that all persons who had been employed for eighteen months would be dropped from the roles [*sic*] for a period of thirty days resulting in three to four month lay off before reemployment." Daniel F. Ring, *Studies in Creative Partnership: Federal Aid to Public Libraries during the New Deal* (Metuchen, N.J.: Scarecrow Press, 1980), 40.

5. This is a paraphrase of "I see millions denied education, recreation, and the opportunity to better their lot and the lot of their children." Franklin Delano Roosevelt, "Second Inaugural Address, 20 January 1937," in *Franklin Delano Roosevelt, 1882–1945,* ed. Howard F. Bremer (Dobbs Ferry, N.Y.: Oceana Publications, 1971), 137.

6. "The Writers' Project," *Harper's Magazine* 184 (January 1942): 222.

7. Hallie Flanagan, *Arena* (New York: Duell, Sloan and Pearce, 1940), 342; Mangione, *Dream and the Deal,* 314.

8. Cecil Smith, *Worlds of Music* (Philadelphia: J. B. Lippincott Co., 1952), 266–67.

CHAPTER 27

1. This chapter is out of chronological order; Hilda has already described events in the early 1940s.

2. Hilda was apparently referring to the National Youth Administration, which "provided employment for persons between 16 and 25 . . . no

longer in full-time attendance at school . . . and . . . part-time employment for needy school, college and graduate students to help them continue their education." *Encyclopedia of American History,* ed. Richard B. Morris, rev. ed. (New York: Harper and Row, 1965), 351.

3. A number of these articles are preserved among the Federal Writers' Project manuscripts in the Manuscript Division of the Library of Congress, container A708, and are included in Appendix B, which lists Hilda's known writings. For example, her version of "The Devil Baby" is in the Library of Congress, but no trace has been found so far of her papers on the history of the juvenile court or the day nursery.

4. Hilda's memory was not accurate here. Her WPA work dated after Miss Addams's death.

5. Details of her lying in state and of the funeral are in Bowen, "The Death of Jane Addams," 182–83.

AFTERWORD

1. HS to WP, 31 October, 2 November 1911.

2. "Matric. No. 19069," transcript for Hilda Rifha [*sic*] Satt, University of Chicago Archives.

3. HS to WP, 5 January 1912.

4. HS to WP, 3 November 1911.

5. Davis and McCree, *Eighty Years at Hull-House,* 67.

6. *Milwaukee Leader,* 25, 29, 30 July 1922.

7. Ibid., 30 June 1921.

8. Ibid., 21 September 1922, 19 January, 2 February 1923, ("I never heard of her") 29 January 1923, ("crowd of 1,200") 31 January 1923, ("Mrs. Sanger returned") 28 September 1923, ("birth control clinic") 20, 23 November 1923.

APPENDIX B

1. HS to WP, 22 February 1911.

2. *The Sentinel* 2 (7 April 1911): 10.

3. *Milwaukee Leader,* 29 May 1912.

4. HS to WP, 13 March 1911.

5. HS to WP, 12 April 1911.

Sources Consulted

MANUSCRIPTS

The various versions of the autobiography were, of course, the primary source. Other manuscripts, found among the Federal Writers' Project papers in the Library of Congress and the Illinois State Historical Library, Springfield, are listed in Appendix B. More directly related to the autobiography were letters exchanged by Hilda and her future husband between January 1911 and their marriage in April 1912, given to me in the 1950s.

To document the accuracy of Hilda's memory, other sources were used. For her brief enrollment at the University of Chicago, the University Archives provided registration forms, course record, and grades. The unpublished autobiography in the Special Collections Department, University of Illinois at Chicago Library, of Henry Porter Chandler, the teacher who arranged for her scholarship, describes his background and character. The Napier Wilt files in the Special Collections Department, Joseph Regenstein Library, University of Chicago, supplied dates for most of the theatrical performances. The name file to the Jane Addams Papers, also in the Special Collections Department, University of Illinois at Chicago Library, was used to identify Hull-House figures.

In an unsuccessful attempt to identify the ship that brought the Satt family to America, the register of ships entering the Port of Quebec, the entry point for Montreal, for April-July 1892 was examined on microfilm through the courtesy of the Canadian Archives in the National Library of Canada. Also examined was the index to the Hamburg Staatsarchiv Auswanderungsamt I, Fach VIII, B. S. bd. 49, provided by the genealogical collection of the Church of Jesus Christ of Latter-Day Saints in Salt Lake City.

PRIMARY PRINTED SOURCES

The *Hull-House Bulletin* and *Yearbook* were searched through 1912, the year Hilda left Hull-House. *Life and Labor*, the organ of the Women's Trade Union League, provides contemporary information about the Glove Workers' Union and the garment strike of 1910. *Hull-House Maps and Papers,* originally published in 1895, yielded maps of the neighborhood and perceptive comments by Hull-House residents.

City directories chart the movements of the Satt family, giving addresses and sometimes places of employment. The annual reports of the Jewish Training School describe in vivid detail the school Hilda attended, while the

Handbook of Settlements (1911) and *The Forward Movement of Chicago* (1909) picture the place where Hilda wrote her play and became engaged.

The *Milwaukee Leader* was searched from the date of Hilda's move to Milwaukee until the outbreak of World War I, when her activities became restricted, and from the close of the war through 1928. The *Leader* was chosen over the more commercial newspapers because the Polachecks were friendly with its editors and it seemed likely their activities would be noticed in its pages. The *Wisconsin Jewish Chronicle* was searched from its first issue in 1921 through 1928. Specific events were checked in the *New York Times*, the *Chicago Tribune*, and the *Chicago Record-Herald*.

Secondary Printed Sources

A number of books about immigrant women provide a framework into which Hilda's experiences can be placed. Of special value are *The Jewish Woman in America*, by Charlotte Baum, Paula Hyman, and Sonya Michel; *Immigrant Women in the Land of Dollars: Life and Culture on the Lower East Side, 1890–1925*, by Elizabeth Ewen; and *World of Our Fathers*, by Irving Howe (New York: Simon and Schuster, 1976). Published after most of the editing had been done but confirming many of Hilda's experiences is *The World of Our Mothers: The Lives of Jewish Immigrant Women*, by Sidney Stahl Weinberg (Chapel Hill: University of North Carolina Press, 1988).

A wide variety of secondary sources were used to document specific statements in the text, ranging from Isaac Levitats's *The Jewish Community in Russia, 1844–1917* to Ray Ginger's *Altgeld's America*. Full information about them is given in the appropriate endnotes. Especially helpful were the biographies and autobiographies of Hull-House residents, from Jane Addams's *Twenty Years at Hull-House* and *Second Twenty Years at Hull-House* to Alice Hamilton's *Exploring the Dangerous Trades*. *Eighty Years at Hull-House*, edited by Allen Davis and Mary Lynn McCree, was extremely helpful in its rich account of Hull-House activities and people. Histories of the Jewish communities in Chicago and Milwaukee, particularly Hyman L. Meites's *History of the Jews of Chicago*, provided background information on the institutions Hilda mentioned.

For the chapter on the Women's International League for Peace and Freedom, a number of works were helpful. Mercedes Randall's biography of Emily Greene Balch, *Improper Bostonian*, together with Gertrude Bussey and Margaret Tims's *Women's International League for Peace and Freedom, 1915–1965: A Record of Fifty Years' Work*. On woman suffrage, two books were indispensable: Doris Stevens's *Jailed for Freedom* and Inez Haynes Irwin's *The Story of the Woman's Party*.

For the chapter on the WPA, Monty Penkower's *The Federal Writers' Project*, Jerre Mangione's *The Dream and the Deal: The Federal Writers' Project, 1935–1943*, and Hallie Flanagan's *Arena* were consulted.

Index

A Note on the Editor

Dena J. Polacheck Epstein retired from the staff of the University of Chicago Libraries in 1986 after a career as a music librarian. She served as president of the Music Library Association in 1977–1979. Her writings include *Music Publishing in Chicago before 1871: The Firm of Root & Cady, 1858–1871* (1969) and *Sinful Tunes and Spirituals: Black Folk Music to the Civil War* (Urbana: University of Illinois Press, 1977), which was awarded the Chicago Folklore Prize and the Frances Butler Simkins Award of the Southern Historical Association. In 1986 she was cited for distinguished service to music librarianship by the Music Library Association.